The Pastor as Religious Educator

Contributors

Charles R. Foster

John Lynn Carr

Robert L. Browning

Robin Maas

Joanmarie Smith

G. Temp Sparkman

William Phillips

Grant S. Shockley

Joseph Sprague

Paul Miller

John Pitney

Deborah Pitney

THE PASTOR
AS RELIGIOUS EDUCATOR

edited by
ROBERT L. BROWNING

Religious Education Press
Birmingham, Alabama

Library of Congress Cataloging-in-Publication Data
The Pastor as religious educator.

Includes bibliographies and indexes.
1. Pastoral theology. 2. Christian education.
I. Browning, Robert L.
BV4360. P37 1988 253 88-30693
ISBN 0-89135-066-7

Religious Education Press, Inc.
5316 Meadow Brook Road
Birmingham, Alabama 35242
10 9 8 7 6 5 4 3 2

Religious Education Press publishes books exclusively in religious
education and in areas closely related to religious education. It is
committed to enhancing and professionalizing religious education
through the publication of serious, significant, and scholarly works.

PUBLISHER TO THE PROFESSION

Contents

Introduction

This book is the result of the recognition of a genuine need for a major stimulus to and guide for pastoral leadership in the religious education of the people of God for their unique ministries in the world. With appreciation for those who have made significant contributions in the past to the discussion of the importance of the pastor's role as religious educator, it seemed to me and to others that a fresh interpretation of this vital concern be provided. Therefore, the expertise of some of the religious education leaders in the United States and Canada has been brought to bear on this key issue of the pastor as religious educator.

The present volume is especially addressed to pastors in the field, pastors in all the Christian churches. However, this book is also designed for professors and students in theological schools who are working to prepare future pastors to engage fruitfully in religious education. Additionally, it is hoped that this book will be very helpful to the many local church professional and lay teachers who are already developing and indeed actualizing the vision of the religious education of all Christians.

Though this book is specifically addressed to pastors and their unique religious educational opportunities, it also recognizes and celebrates the fact that religious education is a cooperative enterprise. Pastors, professional religious educators, various kinds of church workers, and laypersons are all called to incarnate and

1

communicate the vision of God's life of love, justice, and righteousness which Jesus has revealed. Recent empirical research findings
have found that pastoral leadership is crucial in effectively stimulating members of the congregation to see themselves as co-nurturers
and co-missioners. It is also true that a pastor's effectiveness in
using his or her gifts and graces in the religious education of the
whole people for their ministries depends on several factors: the
quality of the personal relationship between the pastor and a given
congregation, the ability of the pastor to engender and articulate a
vision within the faith community, and the pastor's security in
leading the people to state and to realize their self-understanding of
the church's ministry.[1]

Empirical research has also discovered that the primary quality
needed for overall pastoral effectiveness is the ability of the pastor
to assist the laity to take up their ministries. Pastors possessing this
ability are not threatened by lay leadership nor are they unduly
conflicted by resistance to their efforts to challenge laity to grow
spiritually as they participate in specific educational endeavors or
particular ministries. The research has found that pastors who are
perceived as effective are good at helping laypersons identify, sharp-
en, and focus their gifts. Moreover, such pastors participate ac-
tively in teaching and in nurturing the laity—much more so than
other pastors. If effective pastors need training in order to help
laity, then these pastors tend to be resourceful in discovering ways
to obtain this specialized training. Finally, the pertinent research
data reveal that if pastors have the commitment to share the good
news, the desire to become religiously and theologically reflective,
and are self-affirmative enough to free their creative energies they
can significantly improve the religious educational, pastoral care,
and preaching skills along the way in their careers.[2] The latter
research finding is hopeful because it attests to the potential of
pastors to change and grow professionally through well-executed
continuing education. More fundamentally, it points to the importance of the focus on the pastor as religious educator in the overall
education of future pastors.

In selecting authors and issues I have made a deliberate attempt
to project a collegial image of the pastor as educator. I have done
this in full appreciation of the many ministers and directors of
religious education and the thousands of lay leaders who have

labored joyously and effectively in the church's educational ministry. The emphasis in this book on the pastor's key role in religious education is designed to strengthen the many strong teams already in existence as well as encourage pastors to take renewed responsibility for initiating effective lay and professional teams where they do not exist.

The authors who have written for this book are committed to the belief that the pastor is a central person in stimulating the faith community to create a vision of the meaning of the universal priesthood of all believers. This fundamental vision has the power to call each person within the body of Christ to recognize the need to be educated for his or her unique ministry. The concept of the universal priesthood has been given much lip service in Protestantism and more recently in Roman Catholic and Orthodox churches. What is needed is clear vision of what this revolutionary concept means in the life of the church as well as concrete ways for this "unfinished reformation" to come to fruition.

Christian religious education is seen broadly in this book. It is in dialogue with all that the church does and is in her preaching, teaching, pastoral, prophetic, outreach, serving, and caring ministries. Especially is it seen in a broadened and deepened understanding of the sacramental and liturgical life of the church. It embraces issues of ethics and evangelism as well as nurture and conversion. It is in dialogue with basic philosophies of religious education and with the quest to find fresh alternative institutional approaches beyond the Sunday school, CCD, church school, catechetical, or parochial school patterns.

There is an effort to tackle the basic elements in a powerful and authentic education minstry but also to project practical handles, designs, and resources for both larger and smaller churches. The two case studies included are down-to-earth pictures of how pastors have actually put "the education of the whole people for ministry" at the center of their self-understanding and practice.

Charles Foster, a seasoned religious educator and longtime colleague, opens the discussion with his imaginative focus on the pastor as an agent of vision in the education of a community of faith. Pastoral educators will not be significant religious educators by learning new methods or approaches alone. They will lead the congregation to deeper commitment and clear agreements concerning specific ministries by articulating and incarnating the biblical vision of shalom. Most importantly, they are key persons in creating a shared vision of what it means to be in communion with the mystery of God's presence in the midst of everyday living. Foster tackles some disparities in the way pastors are viewed, namely, that to be scholarly and rational is not congruent with being visionary, or that pastors who help persons discover the sacred in their lives and those who are effective organizers and educators are of two different breeds. Foster challenges pastors to be religious educators of depth in a way that projects the vision as well as translates that vision into reality within the congregation. Foster pushes the meaning of vision to fresh depth and broadens the task of religious education to include the communication of the sacred story through "images, metaphors, and symbolic actions integral to the community's stories, rituals, beliefs and value systems." Foster presents specific ways pastors can translate the meaning of the vision in relation to contemporary issues. He describes particular religious educational opportunities which can help laity experience what he calls "sacramental encounters."

John Carr, a professor with many years of pastoral experience, agrees with Foster's observation concerning the profound significance of the pastor as a key educator of the faith community for ministry. He reminds us that we cannot count on the wider culture in the process of creating Christians. Rather, Carr believes that the contemporary pastor must develop a pastoral curriculum which will include preaching, sacramental life, pastoral care, formal and informal teaching, mission, and ethical behavior. He highlights the importance of the "hidden curriculum" which comes through as the church lives out its values and commitments. Carr's discussion of congruence underscores the need for pastors to be sensitive to what their individual lives and the life of the congregation already are teaching about the gospel. The words pastors use, sexist or nonsexist, for instance, "shout" to others a Christian or sub-Christian understanding of human nature and the human condition. He then calls for a core curriculm which genuinely engages the people from baptism on in preparation for and participation in the ministering community. Finally, he challenges pastors to develop a learning context which has high expectations in it and involves pastors and people in the process of making learning contracts or covenants.

Too much of religious education is perfunctory and passive. Goals for learning can and must be set if persons are to be motivated to learn and serve with joy and abandon.

My own chapter on the sacramental approach to the religious education of all members of the body of Christ for their unique ministries is designed to present specific ways for sacramental encounters to take place throughout the life span. I believe a Copernican revolution is needed, and is in the making, in respect to our understanding of the nature of sacraments, and our commitment to the education of *all* persons for ministry. The sacramental approach describes the quiet revolution in sacramental understanding and practice which is taking place ecumenically—a revolution which makes possible a widening of sacramental celebration (moving beyond the two sacraments, baptism and communion for most Protestants, to the classic seven or eight for Roman Catholicism and the Orthodox). The old battles of the past are being transcended. Moreover, the nature of religious education is being expanded to include an integration of education and liturgy around the great sacramental celebrations throughout the stages of life from birth to death.

I emphasize the tremendous religious educational opportunities which pastors and lay teams have for developing a historic but fresh design for the education of all Christians for their universal priesthood. An alternate design is presented, starting with infant baptism (as a unified initiation and primordial ordination of the child into the ministering community) and going on to eucharist, confirmation as a repeatable sacrament, marriage, ordination of clergy and the consecration of laity (the sacraments of vocation), adult baptism for those who respond to the good news from the wider community, confession or the sacrament of reconciliation, footwashing as the sacrament of servanthood, and finally the sacraments of healing and wholeness in life and death. At each of these stages the pastor can initiate powerful educational and liturgical life for the entire congregation. There is a focus on the depth dimension of a faith response on the part of each person and on the part of the total community to the holy, as experienced through the mysterion (Christ as he makes visible the love of God for all humankind).

Robin Maas, in her chapter on the pastoral educator as biblical interpreter, provides a personal witness to the importance of the love of scripture on the part of the pastor in all that he or she does. Maas's analysis of ways to get laity genuinely engaged in the study and interpretation of the scriptures sparkles with realistic and stimulating approaches to exegesis. Few pastors can read her chapter without realizing that the key to their effective interpretation of the scriptures is their own commitment of time and energy to Bible study. Such commitment or lack of it will "come through" every day in many ways. Maas deals with unintentional and intentional teaching, with specific methods of probing the meaning of the scriptures such as "sacred readings" meditation, exegesis itself, and how to employ the wide-ranging resources available to pastors and laity today. Her suggestions to pastors concerning their temptation to "set everyone straight" about the proper interpretation of the scriptures are exceedingly wise. Her generous listing of resources for pastoral and lay teams is very valuable in itself.

Joanmarie Smith's chapter on the Spiritual Education of God's People pushes deeper our understanding of God's activity in all of life. Her view of spirituality will shake most of us to the core. Spirituality is not an ethereal matter. It is seen as profoundly integral to life in all of its dimensions. It involves an awareness that to be alive is to be in God. Spirituality is not something added. Happily, Joanmarie Smith is my colleague in the religious education program at The Methodist Theological School in Ohio. She is a Roman Catholic nun with a very earthy but deeply meaning-filled way of revealing the spiritual nature of life to budding pastors within our community. In her thinking, "to be in God is to delight in the awareness of Divine Presence, to taste and see that God is good." Every aspect of a pastor-educator's work can have the character of worship, always recognizing that the ground on which we are standing is holy. Smith gives specific suggestions for spiritual education through meditation (thinking about God), discursive prayer (speaking with God), and contemplation (being in God). To her, all pastoral activities are moments of remembering, celebrating, and believing.

Temp Sparkman is a professor of religious education who served for many years as a pastor. His understanding of the pastor as a leader of a religious education team is enhanced greatly by the combination of both theory and practice that he brings. One of Sparkman's major points is that pastors can raise expectations sig-

nificantly by supporting the concept of the ordination of lay teachers to the teaching task. The pastor must be much more than a
manager or a supervisor. He or she must emphasize the mystic
which is involved in a holistic view of the office of pastor. Here,
Sparkman agrees with Foster, myself, and other authors. He presents many concrete suggestions about the dynamics of a creative
leadership team and specific approaches the pastor can take to
planning, implementing, and evaluating all the educational activities
of the total congregation. His emphasis on the potential of covenant making between the pastor and lay members of learning and
teaching groups is quite perceptive.

After reading William Phillips' chapter on "The Communications Revolution and the Religious Education of the Congregation"
it will be very difficult to perceive religious education solely in
institutional terms (Sunday school, church school, etc.). Phillips has
had wide experience as a pastor, a professor, and as a creator of a
highly engaging and responsible satellite media ministry with over
1100 lay people and clergy studying solid biblical, theological, and
ministry courses across the Province of British Columbia. His chapter calls pastors to a perception shift beyond the oral and print
patterns with which we feel comfortable. He introduces us to a
wide range of mediated experience with which the contemporary
pastor must deal whether or not he or she wishes to do so. To fail
to deal with the power of the *image* in communicating the gospel is
to imperil one's ministry. Pastoral educators can no longer be content to build a better church school or even integrate liturgy and
education as though the church is isolated from the massive explosion of messages being communicated through the media every
waking minute to pastors and people alike. Phillips helps pastors
and educational teams face the real world and come to terms with
the basic questions concerning the impact of the mediated culture
upon the faith of persons. He also projects principles and guidelines
for the use of media, the evaluation of media's impact, and the
religious significance of both media and message.

Grant Shockley's chapter makes us confront the dynamics of our
racial and ethnic diversity. We cannot approach the religious education of the people of God for their ministries without addressing
the unique contexts in which we find ourselves. The values, issues,
styles, and symbol systems of varying racial and ethnic groups

cannot be ignored if religious education is to penetrate into the consciences of individuals and into the collective consciousness of groups of persons. Social and cultural factors are often crucial in designing approaches which are both emotionally and intellectually "on target." Shockley, a religious educator with vast experience in black and other racial and ethnic settings, again helps the pastor-educator face the dynamics of change and growth in varying communities of faith. He makes a signal contribution by challenging us to deal directly with various forms of personal and corporate oppression. Moreover, he develops creative models for pastors and lay leaders to educate the faith community to deal with the difficult issues of racism, sexism, ecology, universal education, civil rights, and world peace.

The final two chapters are case studies of pastoral teams which have been quite imaginative as well as committed in their approach to the education of the whole people for their ministries of love and justice. "Whole people" means just that! Not only adults in their work, family, community, and world contexts, but youth, children, and those beyond the faith community in the "worlds" not always associated with the church.

The first case study is written by Joseph Sprague and Paul Miller, two creative and collegial pastors who have given educational ministry a high priority in their "Middle American" congregation in Marion, Ohio. The honesty with which this chapter is written, the combination of inspiring leadership and self-evaluation, the balance evident in the emphasis on adult education and the education of children and youth, the personal perceptions of each pastor concerning his self-understanding, are representative of the somewhat unusual depth and extent of the educational ministry found in this case study. Both pastors not only reveal how they and their professional and lay team members work together, they also provide a long list of specific educational designs that have, in fact, been effective. They also share a rich bank of resources that have been employed. The first case was chosen because these two pastors have put their lives "on the line" and have risked much to realize their wider understanding of ministry. Also, the church is larger, numerically, and is a positive example of how a sizable congregation can be liberating of the ministries of persons of every age and condition as it seeks to take seriously the gospel and the call to move out beyond itself.

The second case study portrays in graphic style and images a husband-wife pastoral team in two small churches in a cross-cultural context in Nome, Alaska. John and Debbie Pitney make it amply clear that no pastor can teach others without first being a learner. Their personal self-revelations concerning their team ministry with both white and Eskimo (or native) peoples in Alaska dramatically reveal their vulnerability and their need for ministries from those to whom they had gone. The recognition of their own need and their willingness to be taught comes through every story they share. The profound understanding of how God's presence and grace works through others—through their music, dance, rituals, and life stories—is a touching portrait. Their analogies concerning the sacraments of baptism, communion, ordination, and footwashing (which were discovered in their interactions with the Inuit and Yupik peoples of Alaska) provide profound illustrations of an approach to religious education that is sensitive to the sacramental encounters in which pastors and the people of God can participate with depth of meaning and joy.

In addition, the Pitneys make suggestions for pastors in other contexts. They call on all of us to learn "the language" and the values of the people with whom we are in ministry, to visit people and get inside their life situation, to let children lead, including roles in sacramental life, to "ordain" lay people for their ministries, to encourage lay persons to tell their faith stories, to establish covenant groups, to be able to laugh at ourselves, and to refuse to be alone. These and many other ideas are discussed in a way that is refreshingly honest and convincing.

The authors of these chapters have written out of their own experience and have professed their own views about the pastor as a religious educator. A remarkable consensus emerged, however, concerning the high potential for the realization of the education of the whole people for ministry where the pastor assumes his or her responsibility as a religious educator. Those who take up this responsibility become generators of a common vision, initiators of a pastoral curriculum which includes sacramental life, spiritual formation, and biblical grounding, and developers of learning-serving teams of persons who join them in living out the meaning of the universal priesthood of all believers. There is genuine confidence that when pastors and lay teaching teams are faithful to this vision of the church's educational ministry the gospel of God's love and justice may be shared and lived in greater power and integrity within the total human family.

Special gratitude goes to publisher James Michael Lee for initiating and nurturing this enterprise, to my colleagues Joanmarie Smith, Fern Giltner, and Roy Reed for their support, encouragement, and help with the manuscript. The project could not have been completed without the cooperation of the administration and staff of The Methodist Theological School of Ohio. My gratitude to President Norman Dewire and to Dean Kempton Hewitt for their generous support. My feeling of thankfulness is great for the willingness of the authors to take time from crowded schedules to write their excellent chapters. They all gave affirmative responses to my request to write out of their conviction concerning the importance of such a book. Finally, there is no way to thank certain people enough for their cooperative attitude and effort: my wife, Jackie, for her patience, loving support, and help in the editing process, and the faculty secretaries at The Methodist Theological School in Ohio, Datha Myers and Barbara Millisor, both of whom typed and corrected the manuscript with skill and grace.

ROBERT L. BROWNING
Delaware, Ohio

Notes

1. Janet Fishburn, *The Definition and Supervision of Effective Ministry.* An unpublished paper describing research undertaken as a result of a consultation sponsored by the Northeastern Jurisdiction of the United Methodist Church. 1987.
2. Ibid., pp. 9 and 10.

1

The Pastor: Agent of Vision in the Education of a Community of Faith

CHARLES R. FOSTER

INTRODUCTION

Vision has a central place in the biblical faith experience. It is evident in the recognition and acclaim given to those with the power to discern the holy in either common events and circumstances or the hidden meanings of dreams. It is also evident in the way the accounts of the encounters of an Isaiah, Mary, or Paul with the mystery of the holy have shaped the religious imaginations of the biblical faith community through the centuries. The formative power of vision on biblical faith, however, is deeper and more pervasive than the experience of a few men and women with distinctive powers to see beyond the ordinary. Walter Brueggemann has pointed out that biblical faith is formed around and given impetus by a persistent communal vision. In both Old and New Testaments this vision of the unity and harmony of creation is caught up for many today in the term *shalom.*[1]

Shalom, with its origin located in the imagery of creation harmony and its destiny evoked by such images as a promised land, a messianic banquet, and the kingdom of God, gives both identity and purpose to the people of the Bible. Memories of past events reflecting the possibilites of shalom and the anticipation of its future realization dominate the biblical narrative. Brueggemann aptly catches the spirit of this perspective in biblical faith as "living toward" the vision.[2]

In our own time vision has to do more with the capacity to distinguish what passes before the eyes than with discerning images of a destiny transcending the realities of everyday experience. It is a physiological activity setting the framework for the emphasis we place on analytical modes of discerning reality. As a post-enlightenment people, it dominates the way we make meaning out of our experience. We assume all reality is in some way observable and knowable. We believe anything unknown is only a problem to be solved or a question to be pursued to the point where we discover its answer.

A visional way of knowing, in contrast, involves the exploration of the mystery to be found in people, the world, and in the ultimate reality transcending human experience. Craig Dykstra observes that the reality of mystery accentuates skills of discernment more than those associated with the solving of problems. In this regard Dykstra describes the way of knowing Walter Brueggemann illustrates in his exposition of *shalom* as a way of doing education in the church. As a way of knowing, vision involves "a strenuous effort of moral imagination and a deep discernment" into the encounter we have with the mystery of reality known "only through a glass darkly and never exhaustively." Such knowledge is apprehended more than analyzed. It comes as gift rather than as accomplishment.[3]

Without denying the value of analytical modes of knowing, it is my conviction that the pendulum has swung too far. We have lost the power of the experience of vision in our corporate faith. We sense little of the claim of the mystery of holiness in our lives. We are suspicious of knowledge and insight if it does not come from sources that can be proven by logic or experiment as credible and reliable. We attempt to reduce the intrusion of the unknown into our lives. And yet, in the realm of mystery we encounter the deepest meanings of biblical faith in profoundly significant ways. Consequently, in the following pages I intend to explore the implications for religious education from an understanding of the pastor as agent of the vision of the community of faith.

Views of Pastoral Leadership

A survey of the literature on the ministry of the church, especially those works concerned with that special class of persons who are ordained to ministries of Word and Sacrament, reveals a disturbing disparity in the way pastors are viewed. This disparity is evident in the all too frequent perception that to be scholarly and rational is not congruent with being confessional and visionary. It is reflected in the resistance of pastors to move from literary and historical criticism of biblical literature to hermeneutical analyses of the relationship of biblical faith and contemporary life. It is most visible in the contrast between writings about the theology of ministry and writings about the functions of ministry. The former emphasizes the language of call and vocation. It is replete with images of pastors and priests as mediators of mystery. Urban Holmes observes, for example, that "once the priestly image has fallen upon an individual, it 'haunts' " him or her. When taking on this priestly image one bridges the gap between the "primordial reality of human existence" and the "consciousness of what it is to be human before the Creator." Edward Schillebeeckx speaks of ministry as "a gift of God" which is charismatic as well as ecclesial. William McElvaney notes the frequency with which writers contrast clergy as the "church *sacral* in the world" with laity as the "church *visible* in the world.[4] Each underscores the purpose of ministry as a way, in the words of Holmes, "to seek a meaningful synthesis of the tradition and the world so our lives are illumined in a *new* way by God's vision for his creation."[5] The pastor, in others words, acts as an agent of transcendence or of mystery beyond human experience and rational comprehension.

Books describing the way ministerial personnel function as counselors, teachers, administrators, and even preachers, however, concentrate upon what is rational, manageable, and even controllable. They emphasize the view of pastors as managers of ministry. They seek to help pastors guide congregations in setting goals, supervising an ever-changing roster of volunteer personnel, distributing limited resources, counseling people in crisis, and confirming people in the traditions and mores of particular communities of faith. Most suggest the importance of congregational leaders bringing together in themselves theology and the practice of ministry. This synthesis however, is rarely evident in their own writing. Even Robert Worley's recognition that "doctrines have social intent" finding "expression in concrete forms of the church and society" parallels rather than informs his provocative social analysis of church life. Holmes points out the problem in his own critique of the pastoral theologies that have not moved beyond the "psycho-theological model of Seward Hiltner coupled with verbatims from Clinical Pastoral Education." One might say the same of the management theological models of an Alvin Lindgren, Norman Shaw-chuck, James D. Anderson, Ezra Earl Jones, and Robert Worley.[6] Church life functions as both the context and focus for their work, but their operating assumptions about the work of ministry are drawn for the most part from the literature on social systems, management theory, and organizational development. Perhaps it is fortunate the literature on the pastor as religious educator has not had the popularity of the literature on the pastor as counselor or manager. Consequently it may be possible at this time to begin to develop a view of the pastor's religious educational role from education and the other social sciences, without at the same time losing sight of the source and power of the functions of ministry in the mystery of God's creative and redemptive activity.

Vision and Leadership in the Community of Faith

The leadership of a group or organization, according to Warren Bennis and Burt Nanus, provides both the vision and the ability of the group "to translate that vision into reality." A leader's vision taps "the emotional and spiritual resources" of a group by focusing on "paradigms of action" rather than on procedures for institutional maintenance.[7] Although the view of vision in Bennis and Nanus' work lacks the depth to be found in the discussions of an Urban Holmes, Walter Brueggemann, or Craig Dykstra, it appropriately discerns in the traditionally religious category of vision an important clue to effective leadership in secular as well as religious organizations.

Vision, of course, has multiple meanings. As stated earlier it is most commonly associated with the physiological processes of seeing with the eye and the psychological processes of perception. This latter perspective is evident in Dykstra's exploration of a visual way of knowing. Vision is also used to convey a mental image which serves as the "target" Bennis and Nanus identify for the work of leaders. As a mental image, vision functions as a "condition that does not presently exist and never existed before." It serves to focus the leader's and group's attention toward the future. It gives direction to the leader's decisions and actions. It focuses the commitment and energy of those who follow the leader. It bridges the present in which people find themselves and the future they are trying to create. In this sense Bennis and Nanus conclude that "vision articulates a view of a realistic, credible, attractive future for the organization." Mary Elizabeth Moore pushes this visional target beyond the accessible and knowable into the realm of transcendence. Consequently the ultimate hopes of a group or organization can also serve as a mental image of a future state or condition that underlies, informs, and reformulates the specific goals of member decisions and actions. For Moore, the mental imagery of vision reveals and projects the aspirations of a people. It leads them beyond their present experience and condition.[8]

While not ignoring the significance of vision as a mental image beckoning people toward a future target, I should like to suggest it most profoundly reflects the encounters of people with the holy. This view, according to Brueggemann, is integral to biblical faith. It is a major component in biblical perspectives on leadership. It includes several characteristics that may expand the way we describe the role and function of leaders.

The vision that has guided the faith and life of both Jews and Christians is both historical and corporate. In the biblical narratives vision is often portrayed as an intensely personal experience. We read of the dramatic encounter with the holy by Moses in the burning bush or of Isaiah in the temple or of Paul on the road to Damascus. We are impressed by their apparent unique and solitary character. But those encounters with the holy did not occur in isolation. Leonard Baillas has observed for example, that Moses, intrigued by the sight of a burning bush, turned aside from where he was walking to see it. He then experienced in the subsequent encounter, "the birthright of his ancestors Abraham, Isaac, and Jacob."[9] This event clarified both the identity and the purpose of Moses' life with that of his people. It intensified his sense of connectedness to both the heritage or story and the destiny or vision of the Israelite people. In this encounter the communal vision took a particular form.

Similarly the visions of Isaiah and Paul reinforced their own sense of participation in the mission of God's people. In this regard Thomas Groome accurately identifies the relationship of vision and story. Story encompasses the whole faith tradition of the people of God. Vision is the response of the people of God to the promise in the story. The story continues as the unfolding of the vision and the vision is renewed in the continual repetition of the story. [10] The dialectical interplay of story and vision reveal the sources of vision in events from our corporate past. At the same time the experience of vision contributes to the reappropriation of the story for our particular time and situation. The dialectic of vision and story become the content of the decisions we make about what is meaningful and faithful. The historical character of vision reminds us of the persistence of its content. The corporate character of vision reminds us of its relevance for the whole of God's people.

As a historical and corporate phenomenon, vision is central to the role of leaders at two points. In one, leaders participate in the common task of living toward or into the vision. They identify with the events that have enlivened it in the past. They bear its burdens and its hopes. They discern themselves as agents of its future. In another, leaders are expected to articulate that vision for the new time and place in which they find themselves. In other words, they too are expected to see in the story of the vision's past, possibilities for its present expression. This act of discerning the re-presentation of the community's destiny may be as dramatic as Isaiah's encounter with the mystery of holiness in the temple or it may be as ordinary as Amos' ability to see in a plumb line God's persistent quest for justice in and through the people of God. At this point we come to a second characteristic of vision.

As the gift of mystery vision empowers a people. Craig Dykstra observes that "mystery is an enduring reality that we know only through a glass darkly and never exhaustively. What we do apprehend is somehow disclosed or revealed to us." Mystery cannot be seized or deliberately explored because it transcends the limits of our finite and ordinary ways of knowing. Instead "we encounter mystery as it encounters us." It often comes from the edges of our experience intruding upon our consciousness as Moses discovered during a fateful walk in the wilderness. It may confront us directly as Saul discovered on his trip to Damascus or as Jeremiah discovered when he tried to hide from God. It may well up from the depths of our being as it did in the dreams of Jacob and Joseph. Few of us encounter mystery in such a dramatic manner. Instead mystery invades our experience in the midst of the commonplace and the routines of our lives. Our knowledge of mystery is indirect. It becomes evident in the way mystery is "reflected in the way we think and feel and act."[11]

We are like the two men returning from Jerusalem to Emmaus. We encounter a stranger whom we do not recognize. In the midst of a meal shared with the stranger we suddenly become aware of the identity of our visitor. We are filled with awe and amazement. We are thrown off balance by the surprise of our encounter. It does not fit our expectations. Yet we find ourselves empowered by our memory of the stranger's presence.

Vision, in other words, is one way we engage the content of mystery. It symbolizes the human experience allied with the intent of God's created order of relationships. We experience it as a gift, unexpected and unmerited. We may receive it with awe and humility as Isaiah and Mary did. We may resist it as Moses did. We may embrace it with the excitement of the two men from Emmaus and quickly share it with friends. Even if we greet it with sorrow and regret, it still comes as gift. We share the burden of all leaders concerning how to receive it. It is possible to ignore and set it aside. It can be reduced to manageable terms. Or it can be accepted with its consequent demands upon our time, energy, and talents.

Peter Hodgson has observed that vision works in human history as both paradigm and power. As paradigm "it offers a new shape, figure, or *Gestalt* by which the world is reconfigured, transfigured." As power "it is creative, directing, shaping, luring."[12] Hence, the Christian vision gathers up the community of faith across the ages toward an emerging future. As paradigm it is a unifying force binding people into a community patterned upon the symbols and events of the Christian story illuminating its possibilities. It pulls people into a common destiny as agents of that story for the future of God's people. It functions as the basis of the continuity of the community. As power, vision mobilizes and energizes people. It judges and chastens people. It seizes the imaginations of people, renewing, reforming, and transforming their personal and corporate lives.

A vision, in other words, is more than a picture of an alternative to our present experience. It is more than a mental image that draws us into some new future. Instead, as we encounter the power of vision, *it claims and compels us to live into it*. It functions as moral imperative. This third characteristic of vision, as Dykstra has noted, involves not only the ability to discern what "is in front of our eyes," but also "what lies within our hearts and minds." It reveals what we both "care about and can care about."[13] It becomes the force that urges us to live into the possibilities of an alternative future that spills over into the decisions and relationships of our daily lives. In this regard vision contributes a sense of urgency to our efforts.

Again its implications for leadership are obvious. As a moral imperative, vision focuses the attention of both leader and people in the specific situation and circumstances of our lives. In colloquial fashion Bennis and Nanus say that a vision grabs our attention.[14] It confronts us with possibility, a primary source of hope. Perhaps the moral urgency of vision is most evident in the many ways that Jews and Christians have been mobilized by the possibilities of freedom—from the slave camps of Egyptian brickyards and American cotton and sugar plantations, from the bondage of Babylonian exile and the yoke of Roman sovereignty, as well as from the burdens of sin, the oppression of poverty, and the grief of death. The vision of freedom has been lifted into public consciousness by the accumulating repetition of the stories of God's saving grace across the centuries, unifying and intensifying that quest wherever bondage, oppression, and injustice prevail.

The absence of a unifying vision today is most evident in the lack of moral urgency among contemporary leaders in the church and public life. Bennis and Nanus identify one source for this moral crisis in the contemporary managerial emphasis upon doing "things right" rather than doing the "right thing."[15] The former is concerned with efficiency of operation and maintenance of routines. The latter is guided by possibility and effectiveness. The former is concerned with the expedient. The latter is guided by the quest for meaning and purpose. The former perpetuates the status quo. The latter embraces the possibility of an alternative future.

This brings us to a fourth characteristic of vision. *Its content is conveyed by the images, metaphors, and symbolic actions integral to the community's stories, rituals, and belief and value systems.* Walter Brueggemann observes that the New Testament vision is "of all persons" drawn into the image of a single community "under the lordship and fellowship of Jesus." Paul Minear has demonstrated the hold and power of this bond on the New Testament church in his discussion of the many images used to describe its corporate experience. Something of the commonality, the intimacy, and the shared hope of those early Christians has continued to shape the expectations of Christians ever since. Each reformation movement in the history of the church has received its vitality, in part, from the mysterious character of the community represented in those images received from the church's past. Even today, Robert Evans has written, the quest for community is influenced by expectations caught up in the intensity and intimacy conveyed in the unifying imagery of Pentecost.[16] Martin Luther King's dream of a society in which the children of all races might sit in school together, for example, illustrates the collective power of the Christian memory of one people under the lordship of Christ. So does the hunger for intimacy to be found in many who turn to the church seeking a fellowship that might bind them into a community of compassion and nurture.

The continuing credibility of a community's vision is located in the depth of the familiarity of its members with the images, metaphors, and symbolic actions that both fill it and convey it. Urban Holmes has made this point succinctly. "We express the content of our religious experiences in the images of the religious collectivity. Buddhists do not have visions of Christ and Presbyterians do not have visions of Buddha."[17] The power of those collective images has to do with their potential to be transformed for the circumstances in which we now find ourselves. So for the slaves on a nineteenth-century cotton plantation the images of the "promised land" not only opened up the historic experience of a previously liberated people to them; it provided the specific hope for freedom from the particular form of bondage they experienced. The images of the promised land were not abstract or removed from their own experience or hope. Indeed the opposite was true. Its concreteness transformed the way they viewed their own condition.

The implications for leaders should be obvious. The language of vision is central to their work—even in the most mundane of tasks because it is evocative and transformatory. It draws upon the resources of the collective memories of a people. At the same time it gathers them into a common enterprise. It sets them apart while intensifying their identification with those they lead and serve. It confronts them, moreover, with a corporate destiny inherent in their past. The language of vision—images, metaphors, and symbolic actions—is in other words a major source for the unity, the purpose, and the vitality of community life.

The Pastor as Agent of Vision

During the past two hundred years many clergy and other religious educators have tried to lessen the hold of visionary perspectives on their sense of vocation and their work. Horace Bushnell in the nineteenth century, for example, complained of the efforts in the church to work for the conversion of children. In his famous dictum that children had the potential to grow up Christians without ever knowing they were otherwise, he claimed that salvation was a natural process and not limited to supernatural intervention. It was located in the patterns of everyday learning. Bushnell heralded a change in the way people in Protestant churches first, and later much of American Christianity, viewed the entire religious education process. The growing rationality in the church's religious education took shape around the so-called discovery methods associated with the educational philosophies of John Dewey and George Albert Coe and their efforts to introduce into education the importance of objectives in learning.

Initially "growth" and more recently "development" became the dominant metaphors for the educational process. Encounters with mystery became associated with the wonder of discovery in the learning process rather than with the intrusions of the transcendent into human experience. Comprehension took precedence over illumination in the expectations for learning. Similarly most discussions on pastoral leadership during the past one hundred years have drawn upon the experience of contemporary bureaucratic institutions and the research of social scientists into the managerial process. This pattern is evident in the appropriation of industrial models of church organization, in the fascination with efficiency in the supervision of congregational or parish life, and preeminently in the appropriation of the planning and goal-setting processes to guide congregational or parish program ministries.

These views have not dominated the studies of religious education and leadership in the church without resistance. The Protestant fundamentalist rejection of these modernizing tendencies for most of the twentieth century has contributed to the development of an extensive school-based educational system emphasizing the centrality of the supernatural in Christian education, including independent publishers of curriculum resources, teacher-training programs, para-church youth movements, as well as weekday schools and colleges. This resistance has grown into what Harvey Cox has called a "profoundly antagonistic" movement to modern theology and contemporary education. This antagonism is perhaps most evident in the critique of the teaching of evolutionary science and "secular humanism" in the public schools. But it is also found in the rejection of historical and critical approaches to Bible study, in resistance to the ordination of women, and in the privatization of religious experience.[18]

Fundamentalism, however, is not the only source of resistance to the dominant perspectives on leadership and education in the church. The existentialist critique of the sterility of contemporary institutions during the 1960s is expressed most fully in John Fry's denunciation of adult religious education as being more concerned with creating healthy groups than with communicating the content of the gospel and in J. Stanley Glen's indictment of the captivity of the church by its own quest for success in which the influence of the gospel is contradicted by the attention given to the expansion and control of church life in the congregation, denomination, and through various ecumenical larger church agencies. The result is what Glen calls a "managerial religion."[19]

In recent years sources for the resistance to the rationality of modern views of education and leadership have shifted. Harvey Cox identifies one source in the experience of marginality of the poor in Latin America and among Afro-American and other minority groups in the United States. In Latin America the institutional expression of this rejection of traditional structures of authority and power, as well as knowledge and learning is found in the base communities made up of the poor who are marginated around the premises for liberation theology.

Peter Berger and Robert Bellah, among others, identify another source of resistance in the emergence of a new pattern of consciousness infiltrating the way people view and understand contemporary life. Although the quest to understand this new phenomenon is beyond the scope of this essay, it is important to note that among the dominant characteristics of this "postmodern" mentality is the realization that mystery is reality and that vision is a primary form of apprehending the intrusion of mystery into the course of common life. This new consciousness does not reject the knowledge or tools of modern science as do many religious fundamentalists. Instead it acknowledges the ways of knowing and the ways of leading associated with the problem-solving approaches of scientific knowledge are one among many ways of knowing and learning available to contemporary people.

Although Bennis and Nanus do not explore the subliminal content of vision in their study of leadership, they correctly identify that the vision of a leader distinguishes his or her effort from the work of a "manager." Both are important to the quality of the life of any institution. The leader, however, influences, guides, and directs. The manager mediates, supervises, and regulates. The leader works with the intangible resources to be found in the mystery of the people, the situation, and beyond the realm of human imagination in the transcendent. The manager works with the tangible and immediate physical resources of a program or organization.[20] We may now begin to discern something of the role of pastoral vision in the leadership of a congregation's education.

PASTORAL LEADERSHIP AND CONGREGATIONAL RELIGIOUS EDUCATION

I should like to suggest four ways in which the vision of the pastoral leadership of a congregation or parish influences the educational ministry of a faith community.

1. In the first place the quality of congregational or parish religious education is influenced by the extent to which its pastoral *leadership serves as an agent of the promises in the Christian story.* The

consciousness and thereby the actions of a people are shaped by the story in which they participate. This is the point Urban Holmes has made when he observes that the church exists to make the experience of Jesus' life, death, and resurrection "a living reality in the present."[21] It takes on the form of that experience. Its people become the people of the cross. The vitality of this visional paradigm is to be found in the continuity of that identity through the images, metaphors, and symbolic actions to be found in the community's story. One of the most critical tasks facing the church, then, has to do with the effectiveness with which each successive generation appropriates the story of its heritage and internalizes the promises inherent in the story.

Mary Elizabeth Moore and Marianne Sawicki have called this religious education process the activity of traditioning. As Sawicki says, it is the "handing on of what has been handed down" so that religious meanings, values, and behaviors of the community's past may be "taken up anew, retold, actualized." It is a process of narrative or story. The story functions in the community both to give it a historical origin, and a future or destiny. As Sawicki continues, "Projecting God's act into the past put the community on a time line—a pilgrimage—toward a future final event." In its own symbol system, "Church time is the time between Christ's first and second coming." In the space between—the space in which we live—there is "a time and place for teaching."[22] I would suggest the time "between" is an urgent time. The continuity of the story is dependent upon the commitment of the church and its leaders to participate in the traditioning process of handing on and actualizing the intent of the story for our contemporary situation.

One of the distinctive differences between a leader and a manager has to do with the leader's commitment to rehearse the story of the community's origins and to discern in that story images for the community's destiny. The leadership of a congregation or parish and especially its pastoral leadership, has a primary investment in the conscious continuity of the story. Without the story the people of a community of faith lack the power of its unifying symbols and rituals. Perhaps a common complaint of pastors may illutrate my point. Many are frustrated by the lack of what is called the "commitment" of volunteers to the work of the church. I would suggest that this so-called lack of commitment is due more to the ignorance of people regarding the stories of faith than it is to any willful abdication of responsibility on their part. Their actions for the congregation are simply not mobilized by the power of the possibilities inherent in their relationship to the Christian story. The images and metaphors of the stories do not enliven their imaginations. The patterns of faithfulness in the story do not serve as models for their own behavior. This problem is due in great part to the inactivity of pastoral leadership in the traditioning process of telling and retelling the Christian story. This story is the substance of the pastoral leadership effort. It is not something one does only during designated times. Instead it can happen whenever one preaches, counsels, or supervises people. It should also happen as we engage people in the administrative or outreach tasks of church life as well as in formal and informal occasions for teaching.

There are two basic movements to the task of being an agent of the story. One movement is familiar. It takes place in telling and retelling the stories integral to the Christian heritage. The cycles of transmitting the stories in the lectionary or the organization of curricular resources establish formal structures for this activity. They provide, if used, a repetitive encounter with the texts of the interaction of God and the people of God in the past. With the exceptions of the larger social reinforcement of the Christmas and Easter stories in the popular media, rarely do these activities of transmitting the Christian story enliven the experience of contemporary church folk. The people of our churches do not tend to view their lives through the imagery of creation and fall, exodus and exile, crucifixion and resurrection. These images do not shape their understanding of their religious experience. Perhaps the tendency among pastors to confine their storytelling role to liturgical actions and in educational settings with children has contributed to this situation. Actually the task of storytelling permeates the whole of the pastoral work. The process is not complicated. It is not limited to classroom or nave. Instead it is often prompted by events and circumstances in the lives of people and of congregations. Such is consistent with the old formula, "That reminds me of a story." Telling the story *continually* puts into the context of the heritage of the Christian community the present experience of people.

Another movement in the task of being an agent of the community's story has to do with the processes of forming the people of a congregation into the shape of the story. Denham Grierson describes this transformatory process as taking place in the moments "when the outer expression of the congregation's life melds with its inner determining myth."[23] At this point the stories of faith are linked to the ritual and missional life of a congregation. The story is experienced in liturgical and public actions. It acquires a residue of sounds, sights, smells, relationships, memories that become associated with the enactment of the story. The most obvious of these associations are made through the liturgies and sacraments of congregational life. Just as important are those events of serving neighbor in the name of Christ. The formative interdependence of these symbolic actions and the stories of faith should lead pastors to insist upon the participation of children, youth, as well as adults in the repetitive interplay of story, liturgy, and mission.

2. A central way that pastoral leadership might influence congregational or parish religious education is to *be an advocate of the vision in the Christian story*. In this regard the pastor functions prophetically. As advocate of the vision, the pastor perceives both the meaning and the possibility of human experience through the images, metaphors, and symbolic actions of the Christian vision and enacts or embodies them for the people in the congregation or parish. The Hebrew prophets illustrated this characteristic in graphic ways. Every time Isaiah would call his children in from the street, he would remind people of the destiny to be found at the juncture of their corporate story and their current behavior. Hosea's marriage and Jeremiah's purchase of land at points of national despair confronted the nation with possibilities to be found in the mystery of God beyond their finite experience. Similar behavior was evident when St. Francis dispersed his possessions among the poor, John and Charles Wesley started preaching in the fields, Rosa Parks refused to move from her seat on the bus, Martin Luther King Jr. organized parades of protest, a friend transported a group of elderly poor on errands to help them maintain a degree of dignity and independence, and every time the people of the East Harlem Parish marched through the housing projects at sunrise on Easter morning. Similar behavior is evident in the congregations that have declared themselves to be sanctuaries for Central American refugees, opened their facilities to the homeless, or established counseling centers for the victims of the social, economic, educational, or political disruptions of our time.

To advocate the Christian vision, however, begins with the ability to "read" the values, commitments, and lifestyle of the congregation's culture in the light of the Christian story. Grierson has argued forcefully for the importance of understanding the cultural particularity of a congregation. He observes that the differences are even more striking than the similarities among congregations. Variables include their histories, circumstances, quality of leadership, local traditions, styles of life, belief systems, expectations, and corporate self-identity.[24] Among the most important of these cultural variables is the congregation's image of the future and its participation in that future. This image will be filled with substantive content drawn from the particular way the parish has understood the events and circumstances of its own history within the context of the Christian story. The parish's image of the future that emerges from the interplay of its heritage and the Christian story is often implicit and acts subconsciously in the decisions and relationships of congregational life.

The parish's self-image becomes most evident when it is called into question. This dynamic is evident in the challenge to the claim of friendliness by many former rural congregations when their new suburban neighbors began to attend their churches. It occurs whenever a parish is faced by a change in the cultural and racial heritage of people living in the neighborhood. It may happen when a pastor introduces new or at least different theological or ethical categories into the discussions of parish life and ministry. The task facing pastors and parish leaders consists of helping congregations to discern the extent to which the content and claim of their operational images of their futures are congruent with those of the Christian story. In this action parishioners may begin to locate themselves in the Christian story. They link parish memories to the symbols and metaphors that have enlivened the imaginations of Christians through the ages. They critique the adequacy of parish images over against the dominant images in the Christian vision. They expand parish images by opening up the power of the symbols in the Christian story that inform them.

This pastoral activity has a public character. It occurs when pastors lift up images of the future at work in the congregation in a sermon, a class, or during a committee discussion and explicitly link them to images in the Christian vision. Jesus' teaching illustrates this pastoral activity well. Someone in the crowd asks a question.

Jesus responds with a question to evoke the images dominating the questioner's view of reality. Then Jesus reveals a deeper and more comprehensive meaning for the image. The story of the "rich young ruler" is illustrative. "What should I do to inherit eternal life?" he asked. Jesus asked in response, "What do the law and the prophets say?" Upon hearing the young man's answer, Jesus confronts him with an alternative image of living, leaving him with a decision regarding the way he would relate to God's vision for all of humanity in the future. This action of discerning the images of the future at work in the cultural life of the congregation and naming them in the context of the Christian story helps create an environment for the advocacy of the Christian vision.

To advocate the vision, however, involves the articulation of the vision for the contemporary circumstances in which we find ourselves. It is this step in the traditioning process described by Sawicki that makes meanings associated with the origins of the Christian story relevant to our present time and place. This is the activity of participating in the Hebrew tradition of "adding to the words" of master teachers or prophets so that their words maintain their liveliness for the changes in human circumstances across time. The significance of this process is to be found in the articulation of the hope that is rooted in the story. It creates an atmosphere of expectation and possibility—even under the most distressing of conditions. King's *Letter from a Birmingham Jail*, Bonhoeffer's *Letters from Prison*, and many of the spirituals of American slaves convey the power of the persistence of hope through the imagery of the community's past. This literature is an extension of the prophetic visions of lions and lambs co-existing peacefully and of instruments of war being made into the tools of peace. The need for pastoral leaders energized by the vitality of these historic visions is no less real today.

The articulation of the vision in the story of the community of faith, however, is not limited to prophetic actions. It is also to be found in the way a congregation or parish structures its life. This point is most evident in the actions of unknown Jews and Christians at those times in their histories when the continuity of the story as the source of community identity and purpose was most threatened. It was in the exile, for instance, that the Jewish community, not only reclaimed the potential in the story of exodus for its common identity and destiny, but created a new institutional struc-

ture to safeguard the perpetuation of that story in an alien environment. The synagogue, with its emphasis upon the handing on of
the community's tradition, became a primary agency for the advocacy of the vitality of the story of the Israelites. One might make a
similar claim for the Sunday school for Protestants and the parochial school for Roman Catholics during the nineteenth century. Each
institution came into being, in part, due to the recognition among
church leaders that the prevailing patterns for handing on the story
to successive generations in a pluralistic society dominated by patterns of mobility and instability no longer worked. The fact that
this purpose was quickly domesticated to more mundane institutional matters should not hide from our view their initial advocacy
role in transmitting the Christian story.[25] Their domestication,
however, points to the needed creativity by pastors and other congregational leaders to engage in the quest for viable educational
structures for conveying and renewing the story for people in our
own time.

3. A crucial way that pastors contribute to the parish's vision
through its religious education activities is by participating in the
creation of times and places for encounters with mystery. This task is at
the heart of ministry. We recognize this responsibility for pastors in
the worship life of the congregation or parish. It is less obvious in
the way pastors approach the educational, outreach, stewardship,
and administrative work of the congregation or parish. These are
often identified as programatic functions and the pastor's role in
relation to them tends to be managerial rather than one of leadership. These congregational activities, however, may also be primary
occasions for what Andrew Greeley has called "sacred encounters."

Greeley has pointed out that the religious dimension of life, or
what we have been calling mystery, is grounded in experience.
Experience is the beginning of the religious journey. It precedes our
articulation of faith and belief into thoughts and systems of convictions. The structures and events of our lives become means for these
sacramental encounters. To engage in their creation is a part of the
public response of one with vision and of those who have accepted
the responsibility of extending the community's vision and story
into the next generation. Baillas points out that an integral response
to the sacred vision of a Jesus, Moses, Gotama, or Isaiah is to make
the meaning of the vision a part of the lives of the people. Those

enlivened by the power of the vision must awaken "the dormant spirit in the persons they touch" and bring them into contact with "the creative and re-creative forces of reality." This task mediates the numinous power of the vision to the community.[26]

The creation of experiences filled with the possibility of sacred encounters enlivens the imagination's capacity to apprehend mystery or the holy. The creation of experiences filled with images from the stories and rituals of the Christian community sets in motion the imaginative processes, first by shaping our perception of an experience; next by intensifying the meaning of that experience as it influences our recollection of it; and finally, by influencing our perceptions and shaping our responses to the events of our daily lives around those images. It is this process that contributes to the formation of a people around the shape of the images themselves.

The process sounds abstract. It is actually quite commonplace as the stories of Phyllis Tickle repeatedly illustrate. In one, for example, she recalls her five-year-old son's words to her after she had promised to replace his younger sister's much-loved blanket which had been stolen: "Don't tell her that. It won't do any good. A new one won't have her dreams in it." Some years later when this same boy was thirteen, he decided he wanted to keep and carry the palm frond from the Palm Sunday processional throughout the year rather than let his mother safeguard it. But when the time came to remove the frond from his shirt pocket to give to the women of the church to be burned Tickle writes, "He hesitated before he handed it over." When he realized she was watching, "he ducked his head" and said, "It's a lot like Rebecca's quilt...Full of dreams." To part with the palm branch or the blanket or a relationship is a death—a death which he now began to recognize as a critical step in life's journey. In this moment his mother saw in her son the emerging shape of the cross.[27]

To be able to imagine is a childlike capacity Urban Holmes has pointed out. It involves the ability to "think associatively" as this young boy did, rather than to reduce "all meaning to a logical operation imposed by society's categories of reality." This capacity helps people escape "the procrustean bed of the given culture's collective representations of experience." It is the basis for both personal and social transformation.[28]

4. Pastors serve as agents of vision in at least one other way. They

mediate the judgment integral to the vision. This role is most obvious in the encounter of prophet and king in the Old Testament. The encounter between Nathan and David is illustrative. David had overstepped the bounds of morality in the exercise of his political responsibilities. His physical lust for Bathsheba and his dispatch of her husband into the thick of battle to ensure his quick death were not unusual actions for an Oriental despot of the time. Nathan's simple story drawing David into his own recognition of the immorality of his actions, however, reveals what J. Stanley Glen has called the "offensive" character of the teaching enterprise.[29] In this case the educational activity makes visible the "procrustean layers" that distort the collective images and stories of a people.

Thomas Groome illumines this constructive activity of vision. He notes that any version of the story of a people is filled with distortion. It is incomplete because the stories have been influenced and shaped by specific historical and socio-cultural forces.[30] In the interplay of the story and vision of a people, in other words, we encounter the transformatory potential seen in the painful revelation David had of his own immorality. As Craig Dykstra in his discussion of the relationship of imagination, revelation, and the transformation of character has concluded, the images that shatter the patterns of our imagination must come from outside our own psyches. They come from the mystery that lies beyond our immediate comprehension. They come as revelation. Dykstra continues, "Revelation is not impersonal." The images of revelation reveal nothing when they "remain objects, part of an external cultural heritage. Revelation is the conversion of the imagination and takes place only when the revelatory images become ingrained in the psyche and provide the framework for all our seeing and living."[31] As such, revelation includes an encounter with mystery that establishes the context for opening ourselves to the possibility of being transformed by mystery. Nathan challenged the adequacy of the assumptions and structures of David's view of his authority and leadership and offered at the same time an alternative way of seeing and acting.

As agents of vision, pastors function in a role similiar to that of Nathan. They recognize with intense clarity the reality of the situation. They see the actions of people in social, religious, and ethical context. They are not deluded by the status, prestige, and influence of those in power—even when they are awed by or loyal to them. They are sensitive to the ethical and theological disequilibrium they experience in the actions of people and the expectations to be found in their association with the church as the body of Christ. I prefer Rollo May's description of this step in the process as doing battle with the gods that dominate the social values and ethical conduct of people. The result is a kind of rage against the distortions of the intent to be found in our historic faith story for contemporary experience.[32] Rage in this sense gives a leader the courage to stand over against the Davids of this world and "reveal" or make visible the disparity between the conduct and hopes of a people. The act of judgment to be found in Nathan's confrontation, in other words, is not a negative activity. It is the source of creativity in the community. It provides direct impetus to personal and social transformation.

CONCLUSION

One does not create a vision for a congregation's life or for its educational ministry. Instead parishes choose to participate in the Christian vision in specific ways. They experience the promises in the Christian vision out of the particularity of their own history of encounters with the mystery of God's creative and redemptive activity. Their own angle of vision is shaped by the collective memory of the interplay of the social, political, and economic realities of their common life with their experience with the Christian story. The vitality of their sense of vision is revealed in the power of the imagery in the Christian vision to influence the quality of their relationships and the character of their decisions. The power of their sense of vision is evident in the extent to which it gathers them into the shared task of living into its possibilities.

The originality of their own perceptions of the Christian vision is dependent upon their ability to discern the intent of the promises in the Christian story in fresh or new images. The congregation, at this point, participates in the continuing process of reformulating the Christian vision for its own situation. It is a re-creative process, calling for the training of the collective imagination of the congregation. Pastors, ordained to mediate the encounters of congregations with the reality of the mystery of God through Word and

Sacrament, are integral to the task of creating a visioning people. Their ministries involve the enrichment of congregational life with images of the Christian vision found in the Christian story to the point that their collective imagination is saturated with their possibilities. Their ministries include as well the identification and channeling of implications for congregational life in those images of hope. They are agents and advocates of the Christian vision. They are creators of events for the sacred encounters of people with the mystery of God. And they remind us of the judgment in the Christian vision for our unwillingness to live fully into its possibilities. Each of these tasks is central to congregational education. Each reinforces the religious education role of the pastor in the total work of the parish.

Notes

1. Walter Brueggemann, *Living Toward a Vision: Biblical Reflections on Shalom* (Philadelphia: United Church Press, 1976), pp. 15-16.

2. Ibid., pp. 33-34.

3. Craig R. Dykstra, *Vision and Character: A Christian Educator's Alternative to Kohlberg* (New York: Paulist, 1981), pp. 34-36.

4. Urban T. Holmes III, *The Priest in Community: Exploring the Ministry* (New York: Seabury, 1978), pp. 160, 163; Edward Schillebeeckx, *Ministry: Leadership in the Community of Jesus Christ* (New York: Crossroads, 1981), p. 70; William R. McElvaney, *The People of God in Ministry* (Nashville: Abingdon, 1981), pp. 38-39.

5. Holmes, *The Priest in Community*, p. 7.

6. Robert C. Worley, *A Gathering of Strangers: Understanding the Life of Your Church* (Philadelphia: Westminister, 1976), p. 95; Holmes, *The Priest in Community*, p. 7; Cf. Alvin J. Lindgren and Norman Shawchuck, *Management for Your Church: How to Realize Your Church's Potential Through a Systems Approach* (Nashville: Abingdon, 1977), Chapter 1; James D. Anderson and Ezra Earl Jones, *The Management of Ministry* (San Francisco: Harper & Row, 1978), Chapters 2,5,6.

7. Warren Bennis and Burt Nanus, *Leaders: The Strategies for Taking Charge* (New York: Harper & Row, Perennial Library, 1985), p. 92.

8. Bennis and Nanus, *Leaders*, pp. 89-90; Mary Elizabeth Moore, *Education for Continuity and Change: A New Model for Christian Religious Education* (Nashville: Abingdon, 1983), pp. 154-155.

9. Leonard J. Baillas, *Myths: Gods, Heroes, and Saviors* (Mystic, Conn.: Twenty-third Publications, 1986), p. 141.

10. Thomas H. Groome, *Christian Religious Education: Sharing Our Story and Vision* (San Francisco: Harper & Row, 1980), p. 193.

11. Dykstra, *Vision and Character*, pp. 34-36.

12. Peter Hodgson, *The Church in the New Paradigm: A Theological Exploration* (Philadelphia: Fortress, forthcoming).

13. Dykstra, *Vision and Character*, p. 50.

14. Bennis and Nanus, *Leaders*, p. 28.

15. Ibid., p. 21.

16. Brueggemann, *Living Toward a Vision*, p. 15; Robert A. Evans, "The Quest for Community," *Union Seminary Quarterly Review* 30: 2-4, pp. 189-190; Paul S. Minear, *Images of the Church in the New Testament* (Philadelphia: Westminister, 1960).

17. Urban T. Holmes, *Ministry and Imagination* (New York: Seabury, 1981), p. 77.

18. In *Religion in the Secular City: Toward a Post-Modern Theology* (New York: Touchstone Books, 1984), Harvey Cox explores both the fundamentalist and liberation theology critique of modernism.

19. John R. Fry, *A Hard Look at Adult Christian Education* (Philadelphia: Westminster, 1961), pp. 28-29; J. Stanley Glen, *Justification by Success: The Invisible Captivity of the Church* (Atlanta: Knox, 1979), pp. 22-32.

20. Bennis and Nanus, *Leaders*, pp. 21-23.

21. Holmes, *Ministry and Imagination*, p. 78.

22. Mary Elizabeth Moore, *Education for Continuity and Change: A Traditioning Model of Christian Religious Education* (Nashville: Abingdon, 1983), and Marianne Sawicki, "Historical Methods and Religious Education," paper delivered to the Association of Professors and Researchers of Religious Education, Washington, D.C. (Nov. 15, 1986), pp. 1,7.

23. Denham Grierson, *Transforming a People of God* (Melbourne, Australia: The Joint Board of Christian Education of Australia and New Zealand, 1985), p. 26.

24. Ibid., p. 17.

25. The story of the domestication of the church's education is told most completely by Jack L. Seymour, Robert T. O'Gorman, and Charles R. Foster in *The Church in the Education of the Public: Refocusing the Task of Religious Education* (Nashville: Abingdon, 1984).

26. Andrew M. Greeley, *The Religious Imagination* (New York: Sadlier, 1981), pp. 8-9; Baillas, *Myths*, p. 145.

27. Phyllis A. Tickle, *Final Sanity: Stories of Lent, Easter, and the Great Fifty Days* (Nashville: The Upper Room, 1987), pp. 26,28.

28. Holmes, *Ministry and Imagination*, p. 104.

29. J. Stanley Glen, *The Recovery of the Teaching Ministry* (Philadelphia: Westminster, 1960), p. 27ff.

30. Groome, *Christian Religious Education*, p. 194.

31. Dykstra, *Vision and Character*, pp. 79-80.

32. Rollo May, *The Courage to Create* (New York: Norton, 1975), pp. 25-35.

BIBLIOGRAPHY

Brueggemann, Walter. *Living Toward a Vision: Biblical Reflections on Shalom*. Philadelphia: United Church Press, 1976.

Farley, Edward. *Theologia: The Fragmentation and Unity of Theological Education*. Philadelphia: Fortress, 1983.

Holmes III, Urban T. *Ministry and Imagination*. New York: Seabury, 1981.

———. *The Priest in Community: Exploring the Roots of Ministry*. New York: Seabury, 1978.

Seymour, Jack L., O'Gorman, Robert T., and Foster, Charles R. *The Church in the Education of the Public: Refocusing the Task of Religious Education.* Nashville: Abingdon, 1984.

Theology Today Vol. 42, No. 2 (July, 1985). Cf. Craig Dykstra, "A Post-Liberal Christian Education?"; Edward Farley, "Can Church Education Be Theological Education"; Walter Brueggemann, "Passion and Perspective: Two Dimensions of Education in the Bible"; and Stanley Hauerwas, "The Gesture of a Truthful Story: The Church and Christian Education," pp. 153-189.

2

Needed: A Pastoral Curriculum
for the Congregation

JOHN LYNN CARR

"While my parents or their forebears assumed that the culture would help prop up the church, almost no one believes that today. Baptists, Methodists, Episcopalians, Catholics—everyone knows that something has changed. Jerry Falwell may still believe that electing a few senators, passing new laws, and restoring "Father Knows Best" to television would allow us to relax again and let the culture do our work for us, but most of us know better. It is not "our" world—if it ever was. . . .

"I believe that the day is coming, has already come, when the church must again take seriously the task of making Christians—of intentionally forming a peculiar people."[1]

I agree. With his customary clarity, William Willimon has described the situation and the challenge before us. It is equally clear to me that a revitalized church school with a new and better curriculum is not the crucial key to meeting that challenge. The key lies in pastors with a revitalized sense of their educational ministry and a new vision of what I would call "a pastoral curriculum" for the congregation.

C. Ellis Nelson[2] and John Westerhoff[3] have argued convincingly that Christians are formed in and through the total life of a church. A congregation's rites and rituals, its relationships and actions, the experiences one has in being a part of its life make up a largely unwritten and hidden curriculum which shapes or mis-shapes our

vision of the Christian life far more powerfully than anything
emanating from a church publishing house. Even the undoubted
meaning which the church school has for so many rests on the
sense of belonging it provides quite apart from the content of its
lessons.

If this is true, if the whole life of a church is the school for faith,
then the pastor becomes pivotal for what kind of a school it is. The
pastor is the *episkopos* of the congregation, ultimately responsible
for critiquing and coordinating all the aspects of its life. As long as
religious education is seen as something which goes on mainly if
not exclusively in the church school, the pastor remains at best a
cheerleader and adjunct faculty member. When we see the whole
church as educating religiously, the pastor becomes the president of
a university, the one charged with the task of making sure that the
whole ethos of the community works together for the educational
good.

Richard Niebuhr, in his *The Purpose of the Church and Its Ministry*,
asserted that "whenever there has been a clear conception of
the (pastoral) office, one of these (pastoral) functions has been
regarded as central and the other functions have been ordered so as
to serve, not indeed it, but the chief purpose that it served directly."[4] He went on to describe what he felt, thirty years ago, to be a
new emerging conception of ministry, the "pastoral director." The
pastoral director "carries on all the traditional functions of ministry—preaching, leading the worshiping community, administering
the sacraments, caring for souls, presiding over the church. But as
the preacher and priest organized these traditional functions in
special ways so does the pastoral director. His [her] first function is
that of building or 'edifying' the church; he [she] is concerned in
everything he [she] does to bring into being a people of God who as
a Church will serve the purpose of the Church in the local community and the world."[5] Rereading Niebuhr's seminal study, I am more
and more impressed with his description of the contemporary pastor's task and more and more troubled by his choice of pastoral
direction or administration as the central function informing that
task. "Building" and "edifying" call, not for pastoral administrators
to manage and maintain what's going on, but for pastoral educators
working for transformation.

But simply recognizing the centrality of the pastor's religious education task is not enough. In fact, one look at the enormity and complexity of the job in any congregation easily can lead even the most gifted among us to despair. A big part of the difficulty is the lack of a unifying vision of how to go about it. Denominations have poured millions of dollars over the years into producing carefully coordinated resources for the church school and thousands more into helping people learn to select and use them. Pastors, however, have been left largely to fend for themselves when it comes to thinking through an educational agenda and locating materials and methods for acting on it. We desperately need to develop a vision of a distinctively pastoral curriculum and to identify or create the models and material which can embody it.

THE PURPOSE AND THE PROCESS

What should such a curriculum look like? To begin with, any religious education agenda for a busy pastor serving a church in a secular culture needs a clear sense of purpose and priority. In a very real sense we are at war with "the principalities and powers, the world rulers of this present darkness,"[6] and in wartime some things become priorities, others unnecessary luxuries. Hans-Reudi Weber's fascinating examination of the early church's remarkably military way of seeing its relationship to the secular world of its day, *The Militant Ministry*,[7] offers, I believe, the purpose we need. It is to help the people of God, individually and corporately, to recognize, claim, celebrate, and live out the threefold meaning of their baptism.

In the early church, Weber writes, baptism was the initiation into the ranks of the militant church and as such conveyed the three essential marks of the true Christian life. First and foremost it meant conversion. Those who are converted recognize that the God we see in Christ is in charge of human history and that the authentic response is to give one's total life to the service of the kingdom of love. The baptized Christian was no longer a civilian (the original meaning of "pagan") but a soldier, freed from the domination of the shadowy powers which seem to rule our world and pledged to engage in a lifelong struggle with them in the service of Christ's kingdom.

Second, baptism meant incorporation, being made a member of

the body of Christ. Paul does not tell the Corinthians, "You ought to be the body of Christ and individually members of it." He says, "You are the body of Christ."[8] We do not become solitary freelance soldiers at baptism; we are made a part of the marching company of God. The Christian community in the New Testament church was not an optional aid to the Christian life. It was an integral part of the Good News, the primary sacrament making the love of God believable. Hence a central privilege which baptism bestowed was a place at the Lord's Table. Without that communion with Christ and one's fellow soldiers, engagement in the battle for the kingdom was unthinkable.

Finally, in the baptismal service of the early church converts were chrismated, which meant nothing less than that they were ordained for the ministry of Jesus Christ in the world. Baptism meant ordination to the one and only fulltime Christian ministry or service those earliest Christians knew anything about, making the love of God believable in and through one's total life.

I would submit, then, that the acid test for any pastoral curriculum is how well it enables people to see their identity and calling in life in these baptismal terms. But baptism does more than provide us with a picture of the purpose of our educational ministry; it also gives us a provocative clue as to how we can and must go about it. Baptism is, as I understand it, a dramatization of how the gospel becomes a joyful and powerful reality in a person's life. And the basic symbolism of this dramatization (regardless of the amount of water we now use) is immersion.

Consider the meaning of this immersion symbolism. The Christian faith is at its heart a spirit, a mind set, a new pervasive way of looking at and feeling about everything. As Paul writes: "From now on we look at no one from a human point of view."[9] There is no way in which people can think their way or be argued into such a point of view. It comes to them as a gift only when they are able to get inside it, to feel what it is like to hold it, in short, when they are immersed in the story from which this faith perspective springs, a community seriously struggling to embody it, and, finally, in actually trying to live out that new point of view in their daily lives.

Of course, you will remind me, baptism as most of us practice it isn't much of a dramatization of this meaning. Most of us just sprinkle. And that is just my point. Our practice of baptism is an all too accurate symbol of our educational approach to people in

present-day church life. We sprinkle them with a few bits of information and inspiration, some fragmented and superficial fellowship, and some occasional exhortations and invitations to engage in
short-term service projects. Then we wonder why very little happens! Actually something does happen. Our people are led to believe that these sprinkles are really what the gospel and the Christian life are all about, that the extravagant New Testament language
is little more than a Madison Avenue type promotional campaign.
They are effectively innoculated against the danger and the joy of
discovering their true destiny as baptized Christians.

What can a pastor do as a religious educator to turn this situation
around? What is involved in developing a pastoral curriculum
which serves this purpose and utilizes this process? I believe it
means becoming concerned and intentional about three things:
congruence, core, and context.

CONGRUENCE

By a concern for congruence I mean recognizing that one's own
ministry and the life of the parish already are communicating something about the gospel and the Christian life and becoming theologically critical and educationally creative about that. And this effort
needs to begin with one's own ministry. Take, for example, the
matter of one's use of words. The feminist movement has raised
our consciousness about sexist language, but there are other her-
esies which we need to ferret out in our speaking and writing.
What does our calling the place where we meet "the church"
convey about the nature and purpose of the church? How does
calling the pastor of a church "the minister" on the sign out front
or on the church letterhead square with an understanding of the
general ministry of all Christians? Or take the content of our
announcements, bulletins, and newsletters: What's the ratio of
maintenance to missional concerns in what we choose to highlight
and promote? What about our handling of scripture: To what
degree do we concentrate on personal and interpersonal meanings
of our texts and neglect the social and corporate implications? Do
we tend to focus on the burning bush and leave out the revolutionary task to which God was calling Moses?

Such very practical theologizing can open the way to the orches-
trating several aspects of what one already is doing to serve an

educational purpose in a powerful way. Say one wanted to focus on the primary ministry of the laity in and through their daily lives in the family, at work, and in the community.

• In pastoral calling and informal contacts one could intentionally try to steer the conversation toward how parishioners view their calling as Christians in these settings and the issues they are wrestling with in *their* ministry.

• Pastoral prayers could be planned to reflect at least a few of these concerns each week and a special effort made to make sure that one's preaching sought to bring the gospel to bear on them.

• A unison offering prayer could be introduced which speaks of the offering with the money of our total lives.

• The benediction might be made an apostolic charge, a sending into the world as servants and witnesses rather than the usual prayer for God to take care of people.

• The traditional one-shot Lay Sunday with the successful Christian businessman playing preacher might be eliminated in favor of regular reporting in or witnessing by laity in morning worship about what their faith is meaning for their lives at work or in other spheres of their ministry in the world.

• The church letterhead might be changed to read: "Minister—All the Members of this Church"; Assistant to the Ministers—Pastor Jones" and the sign out front to read: "Headquarters of First United Methodist."

This kind of strategizing can go a long way toward "immersing" a congregation in this perspective quite apart from planning a course on the subject.

But this concern for congruence cannot be the sole preserve of the pastor. In fact, the heart of the pastor's educational task is to enable the laity to engage in this same search for theological integrity and educational creativity throughout their life and work together. Do our committee meetings become experiences of Christian community? How does the church budget square with our understanding of our mission as a church? Are the usual ways we respond as a church to death and grief consistent with our faith and what we know about the needs of people at such times? How are the experiences our youth are having in their program preparing them to live as Christians in a pluralistic world?

One of the most fruitful places to start in such questioning is with the way in which the church responds to major turning points in people's lives, e.g., death, marriage, divorce, moving, retirement, birth, and so on. These are unusually teachable moments for both the people most immediately involved and for the congregation. A careful evaluation and reform of a congregation's present responses or rites at such times can have a powerful impact.

Of course, if the pastor is the only one raising these questions the results will be defensiveness and disaster. The question is how to make the search for congruence a truly shared enterprise. Thomas Groome in his *Christian Religious Education*[10] has provided us with just such a way. He outlines a "shared praxis approach" to religious education which is precisely the kind of practical and faithful process of critical reflection and cognitive decision making which a pastor can facilitate but which, even more importantly, laity can learn to use themselves. Step one in this process is getting in touch with what we are presently thinking and doing, individually and corporately, with respect to an issue. Step two is looking at the story behind our attitudes and actions and at what we see happening in the future as a result of them, both what we think will happen and what we wish would happen. Step three is stepping back and searching for a fresh vision of what the Christian story has to say about the issue. Step four is struggling to relate that vision to our own in mutual dialogue. And step five is deciding how we plan to move into the future.

In most of our meetings we tend to jump from step one (what we think about the subject) to step five (a decision) with maybe a nod to step three (what the Christian story and vision has to say) in the opening devotions. The pastor-educator's task is to convince people that working through steps two, three, and four in a disciplined way is worth doing.

CORE

Beyond a concern for congruence, however, developing a pastoral curriculum means making sure that a certain irreducible core of learning in the Christian faith and life is always available to everyone. And I would suggest that this essential core consists of a fresh encounter with the gospel and its meaning for this particular point in my pilgrimage, learning to use the means of grace, and basic training for ministry. If we do nothing else educationally, we need to insure that opportunities to experience these three things are regularly offered through the congregation.

A Fresh Encounter with the Gospel

I have two reasons for feeling that offering an in-depth opportunity for a new encounter between the gospel and where people are in their spiritual journeys is imperative. The first is a hunch that sizable numbers of our adult members are stuck in a stage or style of faith which is most appropriate to adolescence and have yet to experience either the joy or the challenge of adult faith. In adolescent faith, individuals, not yet having a sure enough grasp of their own identity or judgment to maintain an independent perspective on life, find that identity through attuning themselves to the expectations and judgments of a self-conscious community.

Adult faith comes only after people pass through a time of questioning the faith they have received and are able to own it for themselves. I am convinced that many members of our congregations have never gone through that searching phase. Moreover, confirmation and membership programs which have focused largely on telling them about what they ought to believe and orienting them to participation in the church organization have tended to discourage them from moving into it. We need to offer people the chance to step back and consider both the Christian story and their own stories side by side with the time and the trust to wrestle with what they have to say to each other. And we need to give everyone the opportunity and permission and encouragement to do this periodically. For faith has to be reowned and reenvisioned at each major turning point in our life journeys or it stagnates and dies.

Learning to Use the Means of Grace

A second priority for a core pastoral religious education curriculum is helping people learn how to use the means of grace. By "means of grace" I mean those traditional ways in which we can open ourselves to receive the gift of Christian growth: searching the scriptures, public and private worship, the sacraments, and last but not least, Christian community. The basic understandings, skills, and attitudes which go into faithful practice are not all that esoteric or hard to learn, though growing in them can take a lifetime. But we cannot assume that people are going to pick them up simply by a process of osmosis. We have to be intentional about teaching them, about bringing people to the point where they know what is involved in each of them and feel some confidence that they can in fact do it.

Nowhere is this more needed than with searching the scriptures. Our parishioners have listened to hundreds of sermons and scripture lessons. They have sat through hundreds of hours of Sunday school Bible lessons and CCD classes. Why then does the average lay person feel so guilty and inadequate with respect to making sense out of the Bible for their lives? Part of this, I'm sure, is a testimony to the utter inadequacy of completely cognitive and non-participative education they've experienced. But the fundamental reason is that pastors have not given priority to placing in their hands the exegetical and interpretive tools they need and helped them learn to work with scripture together. (See Chapter 4.)

Or to take another example, look at how laity feel about deep and meaningful Christian community. They hunger for it. They rejoice when they experience it. And they mourn its absence. However, they tend to view its occurrence as the result of some miraculous chemistry beyond their control. The tragedy is that they have not been taught that there are certain concrete things which they can do, skills they can acquire, disciplines they can undertake which can maximize the possibility of Christian community happening. Praying for and sharing with one another, burden bearing, speaking the truth in love, covenanting, celebrating are just a few of the things which can make all the difference in the world. We need to equip people with these very practical ways of deepening Christian community not just in prayer or sharing groups but in committees and task forces and boards throughout the life of the church.

Basic Training for Ministry

The third core subject with which a pastoral religious education curriculum must deal is basic training for laity's ministry in the world. I say "basic" training in recognition that preparation for lay ministry is a vast and never ending task. What lay people need at the start, I believe, are four things: a vision of what that ministry involves, a grasp of how to go about thinking through what that ministry means, some fundamental ministry skills, and most important of all, a conviction that one's learning for ministry has only begun.

At the heart of the vision is the affirmation, not that they ought to be ministers, but that they are ministers already engaged in ministry. In a little exercise I use to help people identify their "parishes," a dozen people will normally list in only five minutes the first names of anywhere from 240 to 600 persons whom their lives touch personally in an important way. I have found this kind of generally positive consciousness raising to be a very helpful prelude to the much more difficult business of seeing how we are called to be concerned about "the least of these" beyond our normal circle of life and about the principalities and powers which seem to dominate our world.

Learning a faithful and disciplined process for analyzing situations and deciding what ministry means is the next critical item. Laity may not need extensive historical, systematic, or philosophical theology; but elementary Christian ethics is essential. I am convinced that helping people learn to work with case studies is the essential method here, the eventual goal of their learning to develop and consult about their own cases with one another.

The third aspect of basic training for lay ministry has to do with equipping the laity with at least a few fundamental skills for ministry, giving them enough practice with them so that they can begin to have some sense of competence and confidence in sensitive listening and consulting, giving feedback, resolving conflict, faith sharing, and communication as well as in strategizing for change in their own lives or in the corporate life of the world.

The fourth and final element is really the acid test of whether or not this course has been successful, namely whether or not it launches people into a lifelong process of learning for lay ministry. Some sort of ministry assessment and planning of next steps in learning ought to be an integral part of the design. My experience has been that people have been so stimulated and helped by learning and working together that they do not want to give up that kind of thing.

WHO TEACHES THE CORE?

After laying all of this out, let me say here that I am not proposing that every pastor needs to personally teach all of the core of a pastoral curriculum. I am saying that every pastor is responsible for seeing that these three key subjects are taught. The kind of educational models which we need for communicating the core must be designed so that committed and gifted laity who have experienced them themselves can then lead them for others with a minimum of extra training and the support and supervision of the pastor. Developing and working with a faculty of lay colleagues is both an essential and deeply rewarding dimension of being a pastor-educator.

CONTEXT

When one considers the task of offering this core in the average parish, however, one faces still a third concern of a pastoral curriculum: the question of the setting or context in which this kind of learning can realistically be expected to go on. Our goal here is not mere information; it is transformation, empowering and equipping people to claim and live out a new life of lay ministry in a secular world. We cannot count on such life-changing learning taking place through participation in patterns of congregational life inherited from rural and small town America of the last century, patterns which assumed that persons would absorb Christianity by osmosis from a whole ecology of Christian influences in both church and culture.

This kind of learning, even at a basic level, requires a substantial amount of time and effort. It calls for a level of trust which can only be based on a clear sense of common commitment. In short, it calls for a type of learning context and contract which our traditional church educational settings (the Sunday school or CCD class, the Wednesday night program, etc.) simply do not provide. They often provide a real sense of belonging. They sometimes impart useful information and some genuine inspiration. But they cannot be expected to be situations in which persons are supported and challenged to experiment with new ways of looking at and living their lives.

What are the characteristics of educational settings or groups in which this can happen? First of all, they must be contexts in which there is *a clear common commitment to learn together and some real accountability for such a commitment*. In every other significant educational enterprise in modern life such commitment and accountability are expected. In fact, they are a measurement of the significance of the course, whether it be dedicated to slimming the waist or straightening out the psyche. The church appears to be just about the only place in our culture where we shy away from asking for the kind of involvement which everybody knows to be a necessary condition for any possibility of change and growth.

A second characteristic of the contexts we need is that *they be more than classes, workshops, or training events. They need to be full-blown experiences of Christian community*. Whatever the specific goal of the course it needs to include praying for one another, sharing with one another, and common worship as an integral part of the design. The Spirit which empowers the change and growth we are after is God's gift in and through the corporate life of Christ's body. The quality of Christian community is the key to everything else.

During the first few years after the publication of *Experiment in Practical Christianity*,[11] an attempt by my wife, Adrienne, and myself to provide a piece of the core curriculum, we were continually surprised by how new the program was to people. All of the individual elements—Bible study, sharing, prayer for one another, consulting about Christian decision making—were things going on in some way in every congregation. Then it hit us: The newness was in the mix, in the fact that people were experiencing these things in some depth together. Most church groups are only one-or two-dimensional, majoring in work, or prayer, or study, or fellowship, and thus miss out on the power of the interaction of all of them.

A third needed characteristic is *smallness—groups small enough for people realistically to come to know and care for each other*, small enough for each person to have air time. And fourth, *immersion takes time*— time in each session, intentional time between sessions, and enough sessions for living in the light of the gospel to take root in people's lives.

Finally, I believe that *any context* through which we hope people will be empowered for radically new ways of living *needs to be linked to a public rite in the liturgical life of the parish.* In most church traditions at present confirmation in late childhood or early adolescence is the last major formal public celebration of growth in the individual Christian's life. The absence of any others communicates the ridiculous message that after that the Christian life is either a plateau or an escalator. Lay persons who have gone through an important experience of growth and come to a new vision of their ministry need to have that growth and calling celebrated publicly in the fellowship. They need to be challenged to make a fresh commitment or recommitment to that vision. And they need to experience the commitment of God and their fellow members to their strengthening and support as they move ahead in their pilgrimages. One possibility would be to utilize confirmation for these purposes, making it a repeatable rite. We would then call our present use of it "First Confirmation." (See Chapter 3.)

The creation of contexts exhibiting these five characteristics is the third essential task involved in developing a pastoral curriculum. And given the fundamentalism of form which pervades even the most theologically liberal and liturgically flexible of local churches, it is the most difficult job of all.

One place to start is with persons joining or considering joining the church, offering them before they become involved a chance to take a fresh look at the gospel and the practical difference it can make for them at this stage in their lives. Old members can be cycled through such an experience as host-participants or simply on the basis of needing to renew their sense of pilgrimage. Another beginning point is offered by the traditional openness of people to doing something serious about their faith during Lent. The most powerful selling point for people is a straightforward invitation to engage in a serious process which holds the promise of giving them a whole new lease on life.

I have found that the best and least threatening startup strategy is to talk about my first effort at a pilot project, something being done on a trial basis and which will be reshaped in the light of what it means to the first brave souls who participate. The crucial thing is to make sure that a small group of people have a quality experience. They then become evangelists for the program.

MAKING THE VISION A REALITY

Nothing of what I have outlined here is drastically new. In fact, much of it comes from my own twenty years of experience in the parish and from the work of many creative pastor-educators. Important parts of this pastoral curriculum are already in use. We know that it works, it leads to changed lives and intentional Christian living.

The problem is that pastors who seek to give this priority in their ministry usually do so without much help from their seminary training or their denominational leadership. This when it is hard enough to handle the resistance of congregations who feel that many other concerns are more important! Here, therefore, are a few final thoughts about how the larger church can help make the vision a reality.

To begin with, the seminary can give special attention to congruence in its own life together. The way a seminarian comes to view the nature and importance of being a pastor educator is likely to be most powerfully influenced, not only by courses in Christian education, but also in courses in Bible and theology. I believe that such courses need to model the most effective approaches to introducing these very same subjects in the local congregation. And reflection on how and why the teaching is being done needs to be a continual part of the process.

At the national board level I can see at least two things which would be helpful. One is a "Pastoral Curriculum Planbook" which presents a carefully annotated selected list of resources organized around the pastor's educational responsibilities and teaching opportunities. A second is research and development with respect to the core of that curriculum. This means that we should locate where pieces of it are being done effectively. Then we must contract with talented and experienced pastor-educators to experiment with ways of filling in the gaps.

The bottom line, however, is whether or not the leadership of the larger church makes being a faithful pastor-educator something which is expected and recognized. On the whole, right now our leadership seems to be far more impressed with numbers added than with numbers taught, and it gives far more direct rewards for expansion than it does for depth and faithfulness. A very practical place to start in redressing that imbalance is the strong sponsorship of ongoing continuing education programs dedicated to exciting, empowering, and equipping pastors as educators.

The need for such intentionality is urgent. At stake is nothing less than the faithfulness of our witness as God's people in a world desperately in need of a gospel which makes a difference.

Notes

1. William Willimon, "Making Christians in a Secular World," *Christian Century*, October 22, 1986.
2. C. Ellis Nelson, *Where Faith Begins* (Richmond: Knox, 1971).
3. John H. Westerhoff III, *Will Our Children Have Faith?* (New York: Seabury, 1976).
4. H. Richard Niebuhr, *The Purpose of the Church and Its Ministry* (New York: Harper & Brothers, 1956), pp. 58-59.
5. Ibid., p. 82.
6. Ephesians 6:12, RSV.
7. Hans-Reudi Weber, *The Militant Ministry, People and Pastors of the Early Church and Today* (Philadelphia: Fortress, 1963).
8. 1 Corinthians 12:27, RSV.
9. 2 Corinthians 5:16, RSV.
10. Thomas H. Groome, *Christian Religious Education: Sharing Our Story and Vision* (San Francisco: Harper & Row, 1980).
11. Adrienne and John Carr, *Experiment in Practical Christianity* (Nashville: Discipleship Resources, 1985).

ANNOTATED BIBLIOGRAPHY

Alban Institute Publications
    A continual source of thoughtful essays about and material for equipping the saints for their ministries. Write 4125 Nebraska Avenue NW, Washington D.C. 20016.
Browning, Robert, and Reed, Roy, *The Sacraments in Religious Education and Liturgy*. Birmingham, Alabama: Religious Education Press, 1985.
    Immensely suggestive thinking about a crucial opportunity for pastoral educating.
Carr, Adrienne Kelly, and Carr, John Lynn, *The Experiment in Practical Christianity*, Discipleship Resources, 1985.
    An attempt to provide a central piece of the core curriculum.
The Pilgrimage Project. Nashville: The Upper Room, 1987.
    Helps people have a fresh encounter between their stories and the Christian Story.
Fowler, James, *Becoming Adult, Becoming Christian*. San Francisco: Harper & Row, 1984.

A guiding vision of the Christian maturity toward which our educational efforts need to sponsor persons and of the role of the Christian community in that process.

Groome, Thomas, *Christian Religious Education*. San Francisco: Harper & Row, 1980.

How to make the search for congruence in the congregation and in our lives a truly "shared praxis."

"Laity Exchange," Vesper Society

A monthly mailing of excellent materials on the ministry of the laity. Write Vesper Society, 311 MacArthur, San Leandro, California 94577.

Maas, Robin, *Church Bible Study Handbook*. Nashville: Abingdon, 1982.

A very thorough and practical approach to introducing laity in the local church to serious Bible study.

Palmer, Parker, *A Company of Strangers*. New York: Crossroads, 1981.

A profound yet very down to earth analysis of the church's calling to generate a vision of public life and how it can prepare a people to serve that vision.

Westerhoff III, John, and Willimon, William, *Liturgy and Learning through the Life Cycle*, New York: Seabury, 1980.

Provocative proposals for the pastoral curriculum.

Whitehead, Evelyn, and Whitehead, James, *Christian Life Patterns*. Garden City, N.Y.: Doubleday, 1979.

An agenda for equipping the congregation for ministry to one another throughout the major stages of adult development.

Wink, Walter, *Transforming Bible Study*. Nashville: Abingdon, 1980.

Provocative, practical, and prophetic introduction to Bible study which moves beyond the cognitive alone.

3

The Pastor as a Sacramentally Grounded Religious Educator: A Copernican Revolution in the Making

ROBERT L. BROWNING

Our major difficulty in religious education is our perception of what is really needed for the whole people of God to be engaged in ministry. More fundamentally, it has to do with our image of who should be educated, to what end, by whom.

While we give considerable affirmation to the concept of the universal priesthood of all believers, with its implied image of the education of all Christians for unique ministries in all areas of life, a decoding of our actual practice more often reveals quite a different set of assumptions.

All too often we find in practice a primary emphasis on the religious education of children, with declining emphasis upon youth and adults, along with minimal connection with the concept of joyous engagement in ministry within and beyond the faith community. Moreover, religious education is typically identified with institutional experiences such as the Sunday school, the church school, the CCD (Confraternity of Christian Doctrine), or the religion class in a parochial school. Persons who are not a part of these institutional forms perceive themselves *not* to be involved in or even interested in religious education. This is true even though they will say openly that they have profound need for deeper understanding of the biblical faith and more significant

opportunities to relate the Christian faith to the complex issues in
their lives. Such an institutional image often puts the primary
leadership of religious education in the hands of lay persons with
pastors only indirectly related, largely at the administrative level or
as an occasional teacher of a Bible, confirmation, or membership
class.

It must be noted that the major extant models of religious education put the pastor in differing roles in relation to the laity. In the
Sunday school model, the pastor has often had relatively low expectation for his or her involvement. Lay leaders have been primarily responsible, with the pastor providing inspirational leadership
and occasional tours as a direct teacher. In the church school
model, with its higher implied standards for teacher competence
and parental cooperation, the pastor sometimes has acted as a
teacher of teachers and an administrator or organizer of more
extensive through-the-week education programs. In the church
education model, with its recognition that the whole church teaches and learns in all of its life together, pastors often have a much
higher expectation for themselves as religious educators, but have
problems interpreting this wider concept to laity who may be
caught in long-held CCD/Sunday school or church school images.
Our assumptions about these matters affect our *expectations* about
the quality and extent of the education of the whole people of God
for ministry and about the relationship between pastors, professional religious educators, and laity in the process.

Our expectations of what it means to be a lay Christian flow out
of these assumptions. These expectations are such that most laity
either make a very imprecise and intuitive connection between the
concept of ministry and their occupation, family,and voluntary involvements or make no connection at all. Morever, both pastoral
and lay expectations about the quality and extent of the religious
education needed for lay ministry are often quite blurred, or, if
clear, are quite modest.

I should like to propose a different image of religious education
and a different set of expectations. The image is a religious education grounded in a fresh understanding of the sacramental nature
of life itself and a sacramental approach to the preparation of the
whole people of God for the universal priesthood of all believers. If
taken seriously this sacramental approach could change radically

our expectation about the times, places, goals, content, and processes of Christian religious education—and especially about *who* should be educated, by *whom*. A major change in our perception of the roles of pastors and lay persons in this process is a direct result of a major *shift* in perception involved in a sacramental model rather than a CCD/Sunday school, church school, or even a wider church education model (which has supported some of the movements in the direction of higher expectations already underway).

The Copernican revolution changed our perception of the relation of the earth to the wider universe. As we know, before Copernicus we perceived the earth to be the center of the universe with the sun, stars, and planets all moving across the earth. Of course, this was the way it seemed when we looked out upon the sun and stars. The earth was perceived to be flat. After the evidence slowly came in to confirm Copernicus' theory (that the earth was a sphere and only one of several planets rotating around the sun as the center of our solar system), we had a *perception shift*. People now are *taught* to perceive the natural world through the lens of Copernicus' theory (and up-dates of that theory).[1] The assumptions behind that theory propelled us into amazing explorations of our universe. It took huge amounts of courage to act on these new assumptions. For Columbus to sail toward the west in the belief that the world was round and that he could sail around the earth to India, without falling off, was the ultimate in risk taking. It took great faith to *act* on these assumptions. Here we see faith and reason not to be opposites. Rather, faith and reason were integrated. Or more accurately, faith included the best reason could provide in the way of a tested theory. This same risk taking has been behind all subsequent space probes, of course. Once the perception shift has become well established, it seems outrageous to perceive the world as our ordinary senses tell us it is.

If we can have a Copernican revolution in our perception of the nature of Christian religious education, many of our expectations can change radically. These changes can include movements from what we now see in practice (common sense) to what is possible when we genuinely perceive the central purpose of Christian religious education to be the preparation of *all* Christians to be *ministers* in the various spheres of life. This calls for a major shift in how we see the relation of pastors and lay persons. Pastors and laity are equally involved in preparation for and valid engagement in creative forms of ministry but with unique responsibilities and opportunities.[2] Both are perceived to be in ministry rather than the ordained pastor as the central person in pastoral work and the laity as the satellite helpers of *the* pastor.

In this view, God is the true center—not the pastor. However, the pastor has a high calling, by ordination and unique responsibility of pastoral office, to lead the whole people to find the vision God has given us through Christ. This vision is directly related to our sense of vocation as Christians. The vision is perceived and internalized as pastor and laity teach one another through Word, Table, and concrete forms of mutual ministry and mission to the world.

This shift does not call for a dismantling of existing structures of Christian religious education but a redefinition of how existing structures and groups can be related creatively to a sacramental approach. This shift will no doubt call for several fresh forms and the integration of experiences which now seem to be separate and discrete. For instance, pastors are now involved in the preparation of persons for sacramental life but may not perceive these preparations to be *religious education*. Interestingly enough, pastors are often solidly involved in counseling and, in a more limited way, in religious education of persons concerning infant or adult baptism, confirmation, communion, marriage, or issues of personal failure, illness or death and dying, but they and the whole church community often do not *see* the pastors as *religious educators* in these crucial life experiences. Morever, the people involved in these pastoral ministries often do not perceive that they have been involved in *religious education*. This may be true because their perceptions of religious education are fixated in early images of Sunday school or church school.

A *perception shift* could be quite liberating and could generate many fresh experimentations and new energy for religious education in local church, family life, work, community, and leisure contexts with pastors centrally involved.

THE COPERNICAN REVOLUTION
IN THE WAY WE SEE THE SACRAMENTS

These perception shifts cannot take place until we embrace major shifts in our understanding of the primary ways God's love and grace are at work in the universe. The way we talk about the sacraments is a clue to how we see God working among us. One of the most hopeful signs of a Copernican revolution can be seen in the revolution in our perception of the sacramental nature of life itself. An outmoded "the earth is the center of the universe" view made the church the controller of God's grace and love. The sacraments were seen as instruments of God's grace to be given to the faithful (in communion, penance, or unction) when they were in a right relationship to the church. When they were not in such a right relationship they could be and were sometimes excommunicated from God's grace, on the assumption that the church was called by God to give and hold back grace. The priest or pastor was ordained by the church and empowered to administer the sacraments and to teach the faithful the correct doctrines which supported the sacramental approach. The Protestant Reformation critiqued the sacramental system of the Roman Catholic church, moving away from the tight identification of the church as the controller of God's grace (often moving toward memorial or initiation images), but did not really leave the model completely. The perception of many pastors and laity in Protestant churches often puts the church at the center rather than God and makes the pastor, as the representative of the church, the key person with the power to administer the sacraments, with laity as the passive receivers of grace, or receivers of the memorials of God's action in Christ in the past.

The revolution in ecumenical thinking about the sacraments moves away from the church as the controller of grace or the custodian of memorials to seeing all of nature and history as revelatory of God's grace to which the various sacraments are witnesses and expressions.[3] Karl Rahner said it well when he emphasized that God's grace is bringing wholeness and salvation at the roots of human existence. In short, God's grace is built into the very fabric of life. "The world is constantly and ceaselessly possessed by grace from its innermost roots. . . . It is constantly and ceaselessly sustained and moved by God's self-bestowal."[4]

God's cosmic grace is visible in many ways but clearly in Jesus Christ, the full incarnation of it, and the church, the present ministering, caring, serving body of Christ. Therefore, the church becomes the sacrament of Christ, making visible and concrete

God's love and justice, reflecting and celebrating God's grace in the very nature of things. In this view, God's grace which is active in all of life becomes an *epiphany* in the lives of the members of the body of Christ. We become sacraments to one another, both reflectors and channels of grace to all of God's human family and to all creation. The particular sacraments point to and participate in the grace of God which *is*. Such sacraments are, therefore, very important in helping us become *aware* of and conscious of God's actions in our midst. They are crucial, living symbols of the story of God's actions through Christ and the church. The consciousness of God's presence and action in our common life from birth to death (made possible by the visible symbols of baptism, communion, confirmation, marriage, reconciliation, consecration or ordination to ministry, etc.) is crucial in respect to our daily decisions in life. Participation in sacramental life is profoundly life-affirming and social. It should not take us out of the worlds of commerce, government, politics, entertainment, family, but rather move us deeply into the issues associated with these normal activities of life.

The Copernican revolution implied in this shift is: God's grace is the central fact of existence. Christ revealed and incarnated that grace. Christ, as the primary sacrament, has called all of his followers to celebrate that grace, point to it, and be channels of it to others in every area of life. It is for this reason that the universal priesthood of all believers is crucial. All of us are to incarnate Christ's love and trust, to be sacraments, making visible the good news that "God is, and God is love," as Søren Kierkegaard said. We, as the church, do not control God's grace through the sacraments. We recognize that God's grace is centered in mystery (*mysterion* is the word used in the New Testament which was later translated as *sacramentum*). Christ himself is the mysterion of God making the love of God visible to the world and especially to those who make up his body, the church. We do not say who is in communion with God or who can come to the table. We, on the other hand, are responsible witnesses to and servants of Christ's gift of love. And, every time we celebrate through one of the sacraments, we are called to raise the consciousness of the recipients to the point of their own freely given commitment to become conscious ministers and witnesses to God's family the world over.

THE PASTOR AS RELIGIOUS EDUCATOR
THROUGH SACRAMENTAL LIFE

The Copernican revolution in sacramental thinking and practice opens up many fresh vistas for authenic, nonmanipulative religious education related closely to each of the stages of growth in the life cycle. No doubt the sacraments themselves evolved because there was clear need for a sense of the holy, for spiritual depth and meaning, at each of the major life experiences or crises—from birth to death. Because the view of sacramental life is being seen as relational and symbolic of God's presence and grace in the very fabric of life itself, wider sacramental understanding and practices have received much more acceptance within Protestantism and have been altered and related more deeply to human and faith development in Roman Catholicism and Orthodoxy. Therefore, a fresh breeze is blowing in the ecumenical church, making possible another perception shift: namely, that Protestants can begin to see the potential of the celebration of more than two sacraments (baptism and communion) and can with integrity perceive anew the possibility of correlating the seven or more historic sacraments with the stages of human and faith development and to relate religious education and liturgy to the process.

At each of the levels I shall seek to indicate what the revolution in sacramental thinking and practice has produced, and what pastors and lay teachers may be able to do in terms of the integration of religious education and liturgical life (without destroying the creative tension needed between these two aspects of ecclesial activity).[5]

The chart on the following page shows the positions on the sacraments that my colleague Roy Reed and I have taken in our recent book and how we see religious education and liturgical life related to the life cycle.

Now, let us discuss each of the sacraments and the unique opportunities for religious education that pastors who accept their responsibility for vision-making can initiate.

Infant Baptism

Every pastor has an exciting, life-renewing opportunity to interpret the essential meaning of life and the Christian vision when a

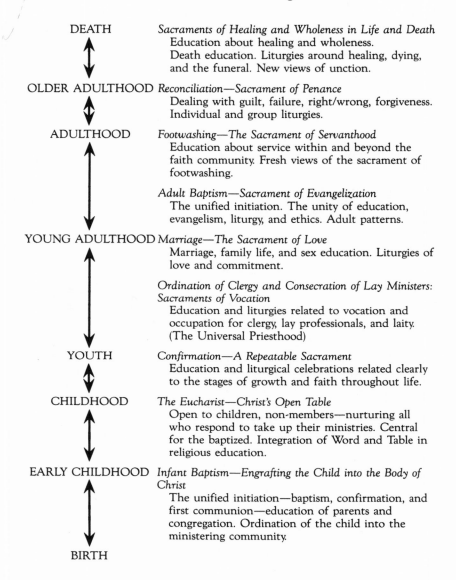

DEATH   *Sacraments of Healing and Wholeness in Life and Death*
Education about healing and wholeness.
Death education. Liturgies around healing, dying,
and the funeral. New views of unction.

OLDER ADULTHOOD   *Reconciliation—Sacrament of Penance*
Dealing with guilt, failure, right/wrong, forgiveness.
Individual and group liturgies.

ADULTHOOD   *Footwashing—The Sacrament of Servanthood*
Education about service within and beyond the
faith community. Fresh views of the sacrament of
footwashing.

Adult Baptism—Sacrament of Evangelization
The unified initiation. The unity of education,
evangelism, liturgy, and ethics. Adult patterns.

YOUNG ADULTHOOD   *Marriage—The Sacrament of Love*
Marriage, family life, and sex education. Liturgies of
love and commitment.

*Ordination of Clergy and Consecration of Lay Ministers:
Sacraments of Vocation*
Education and liturgies related to vocation and
occupation for clergy, lay professionals, and laity.
(The Universal Priesthood)

YOUTH   *Confirmation—A Repeatable Sacrament*
Education and liturgical celebrations related clearly
to the stages of growth and faith throughout life.

CHILDHOOD   *The Eucharist—Christ's Open Table*
Open to children, non-members—nurturing all
who respond to take up their ministries. Central
for the baptized. Integration of Word and Table in
religious education.

EARLY CHILDHOOD   *Infant Baptism—Engrafting the Child into the Body of
Christ*
The unified initiation—baptism, confirmation, and
first communion—education of parents and
congregation. Ordination of the child into the
ministering community.

BIRTH

child is born and parents seek baptism or, in some cases, dedication. How pastors and the faith community as a whole invite parents, the child, and others to be involved is highly revelatory of our view of the Christian faith. Increasingly pastors are seeing infant baptism as an opportunity to symbolize the love of God at the heart of all things, a love into which the child is born. Moreover, this divine love is communicated to the child through loving, trusting, faithful, honest relationships within the body of Christ, including especially the priesthood of parenthood within the family. While different views exist about the integrity of infant or adult baptism there is growing recognition of the great need of parents for counsel, education, and loving support from the congregation as they commit themselves to be ministering persons to the child. Also, the congregation is recognizing its joy and responsibility as agents of care and nurture of both the parents and the child.

So often in my discussions with pastors I have found that they and the congregation they serve have few if any clear theological agreements about baptism or what kind of preparation parents and the congregation need in order for the baptism experience to have the profound meaning inherent in it. While teaching in Canada at the Vancouver School of Theology during the summer of 1986, I was surprised to discover that eleven or twelve of the class of twenty-four pastors were engaged not only in personal counseling with parents but also in religious education of these parents regarding the nature of the sacrament of baptism. In many such seminars in the United States I have found pastors stating that they often make a visit to the parents but do not plan educational or support experiences for parents. Even more disturbing is the recognition that few have even thought of the sacrament of infant baptism as a time for religious education involving pastors, parents, and others from the congregation. A perception problem of the first order is revealed.

Try this vision of a pastoral and congregational approach to infant baptism made possible by the quiet Copernican revolution in sacramental thinking and practice.

A dominant movement in the thinking about infant baptism is in the direction of the engrafting of the child fully into the body of Christ. The Eastern Orthodox church has done this for centuries in its unified sacraments of initiation. The child is baptized with water (immersion or full washing), confirmed in the anointing with oil and the laying-on-of-hands, and participates in the eucharist through the touching of the lips of the child with the wine and

bread mixed together. This exciting celebration is central to the
liturgy of the total congregation. Now Roman Catholics and Protestants are recognizing the power and truth of the unified initiation.
The child is not baptized and then designated a "preparatory member" of the church to be brought into the fullness of life in the faith
community at confirmation (the problem of two half-sacraments, as
Karl Barth noted). Instead, the child is baptized into the loving,
faithful community and becomes a full member of the body of
Christ, and is ordained at baptism to the universal priesthood of all
believers. The child is to be *seen*, in this perception shift, as a
ministering person from baptism on. The little children shall, in
fact, lead us. Their trusting, teachable, imaginative ways will be
accepted fully in the natural ministry of the community. To be sure,
the child will need many opportunities to study, act upon, and test
the faith. Confirmation experiences, *several* not just one, will be
needed in the future, but this exploration and testing can be undertaken as a full member of the faith community.

Some possible ways for pastors and members of the congregation
to be involved with religious education of parents and the congregation along these fresh lines of thinking are as follows:

Create a supportive sponsoring group for the religious education
and preparation of the parents and the child for the sacramental
celebration. One of the most engaging ideas has come from the
Lutheran tradition. It is consistent with Luther's view that infant
baptism is the ordination of the child into the universal priesthood.
The pastor is the key to helping the parents discern the high
potential of such a supportive group of sponsoring persons from
the congregation. The idea is appropriate for churches of all sizes. It
involves the selection of an intergenerational group of two young
people, two adult friends of the couple who are peers in age, and
two adults who are the age of grandparents. These persons can
bring the gift of vision (first generation), the gift of reality (second
generation), and the gifts of memory and wisdom (third generation).
This is a pattern originally developed by John Westerhoff. The
sponsoring group meets with the parents in their home the first
week for a meal, discussions, getting to know one another and the
parents' hope for the new child. The group meets weekly for six
weeks over meals in the homes of sponsors, using imaginatively
designed resources for parent education and the education of the

sponsors and the congregation.[6] The program 1) presents studies of the nature of baptism, from a Lutheran perspective (can be supplemented by other views) and many creative ways for the sponsors to be involved in supporting the parents and the child not just at the time of the baptism but on through the years; 2) prepares and dedicates the sponsors before the congregation several weeks before the baptism; and 3) helps the whole congregation incorporate the child and the family, employing pictures, stories about the family, and the making of a giant cookie by the sponsors which is shared with the whole congregation at a postbaptismal celebration. Such an approach, with realistic adaptations, has considerable potential.

Other faith groups are designing fine resources to support pastors and people in deepening the religious education of parents, sponsors, and the congregation.

The United Church of Christ has excellent fresh resources as well. They are designed for several settings:

Courses for young parents after the baptism of their children to study how they can live with integrity in ministry with their children. Their resources are aimed at enlarging ministries "to and with families of young children and...to help local congregations look inward as well as outward regarding their present practice of observing the sacrament of baptism."[7] Several courses are available within these resources, offering pastors and people ample options.

Education of the total congregation concerning the meaning and power of baptism as a primary image for the ministry of the whole people of God. When baptism takes place, the entire service can be integrated by including baptismal scriptures, liturgical richness, imaginative preaching, and ample drama around the sacrament itself. The liturgical experience itself can be a profound emotional and mind-stretching experience for the congregation. Properly prepared, the involvement of sponsors, God-parents, and children from the congregation can be rich in relational meaning. The unified initiation employing baptism by water (with some person from the congregation bringing the water in and pouring it into the font), with confirmation representing the gift of the Holy Spirit, the laying-on-of-hands of the pastors, parents, and sponsors, and the anointing with oil with the sign of the cross on the child's forehead, the celebration of the eucharist for the child as a full member of the ministering community, and the symbolizing of the child's uniqueness through the presentation of a candle (indicating the light the child will bring to the world), and introducing the child to the congregation within the service and after the service at a celebration can in itself be very significant religious education in which the pastor has a central role. Again one of our recent graduates, serving in a rural small-town church, has found that the involvement of the congregation in the baptismal ministry and celebration in a similar but different pattern from above has been not only engaging but healing for a congregation with some hurts from the past.[8]

Give gifts to the child which can become an ongoing nurture of the child concerning the meaning and joy of his or her own baptism and the congregation's expectations for the child. These gifts can include not only a certificate of baptism but other symbols of the life of the child and the sponsoring group, such as a picture album, even a video tape of the baptismal drama, and a book for the child to be read later to the child by parents. Patricia J. Goldberg's, *A Day to Remember: My Baptism Book* (United Church Press, 1983) printed in both English and Spanish, is a fine example of such literature. The baptismal candle can also be given and lighted each year at the anniversary of the child's baptism along with a celebration in the home.

THE CELEBRATION OF THE EUCHARIST AS CHRIST'S OPEN TABLE

When we look deeply at the meaning of communion we recognize the quiet revolution in sacramental thought is producing an image of the holy meal which is in contrast to the inherited picture so common in many of our churches. The "pre-Copernican view" of communion emphasized the past, our sin and guilt which were allayed by Jesus' sacrifice of his body and blood, the cross and the atoning death of Jesus, the somber nature of the event as well as the feeling of individual unworthiness which each of us assumed to be appropriate if not necessary before coming to the table. Liturgical research has discovered the relevance of a more positive image which affirms the gift of Christ's life for the whole family of God. It emphasizes not the dead past and images of a memorial service but images of the presence of the risen Christ as the living host, the common meal as the present sharing of one another with God, and the projection of the state of inclusive love that will exist in the future where we will be surprised at who will be seated with Christ at the Messianic table. The term eucharist, which means thanksgiving, is more and more representative of this reality.[9] The image of communion which focused on the past either emphasized the grace of God given or denied in the sacrament or it emphasized the memorial to the sacrifice Christ made for our salvation. The eucharistic image does not undercut the power of Christ's sacrifice but puts it in a fresh, joyous mode of thanksgiving and present strengthening as we receive the living Christ in our lives now. We are strengthened to give ourselves to others within and beyond the faith community even as he gave himself for all humankind.

Practically, this quiet revolution means that Christ's table is open to all persons at all times—to the baptized and unbaptized, to children when they wish to come to the table of the family of those who love Christ. We are not called to exclude persons from Christ's table. Rather, we are called to help persons recognize God's presence in and through the relationships of trust and love with Christ and those at the table who are seeking to be filled with his spirit. This means pastors have a special responsibility for the education of the people of God concerning the meaning of the meal of thanksgiving. There should be no cheap grace.

Pastors, linked with other members of the faith community, educate as they bring persons into participation at the Table—through sharing the action parable which the sacrament is. By using stories and liturgies which reenact the image of the joyous banquet at which the risen Christ is the host, pastors can ground the congregation in powerful experiences of faith. Buttressed with preaching and corporate actions which proclaim and "live out" God's inclusive love and yet demanding righteousness, pastors and lay eucharistic ministers can stimulate congregational growth in understanding and practice. In addition, pastors can initiate the following:

Parent education in relation to the preparation of children to participate in and increasingly grasp the emotional impact and ideas associated with the eucharist.

Pastors, in some faith communities, have been involved in the religious education of children and parents for first communion. If children are incorporated into the body of Christ at the time of infant baptism through the unified initiation which includes first communion, or if children are welcome at the Table with their parents and others whether or not baptized, how can the pastor and the congregation help children and the parents interpret the eucharist?

Parents and teachers can be brought together to explore ways to help children prepare themselves to be active and thoughtful participants in the eucharistic celebration of the parish. Again the United Church of Christ has taken leadership in opening a discussion of the key questions. In *Children and Communion* the position is taken that "children can experience the richness of the sacrament long before they can intellectualize its meaning."[10] Here is a fine guide for pastors and congregational leaders as they plan educational and liturgical life with parents. Another good resource for pastors is *You Are Welcome*, a piece that is biblically and theologically grounded as well as related with integrity to James Fowler's understanding of faith development and Erik Erikson's views on human development.[11] A Lutheran resource, *Welcome to the Lord's Table* is based on the concept that we are lifelong catechumens and that regular participation in communion is seen as "a means of strengthening faith. It is a part of the process of confirmation, rather than its goal."[12]

Have family cluster eucharists. One of the richest and most natural celebrations of the eucharist can take place as the pastor works with several families in the family cluster pattern of religious education. In this approach children and their parents come together for community, study of the faith, worship, and mutual ministry. Meeting in different homes or at the church at an agreed upon time the families form a small church within the total congregation. Excellent resources are available. Included in this approach can be exploration of the meaning and joy of the eucharist and the celebration of the sacrament at the family dinner table. Children can be involved as liturgists and servers—a marvelously natural and warm experience of the trust and love given to the world through Christ's gift of his body and blood that we might have life abundant.[13]

Work directly with children. Pastors are increasingly including children in the planning and leadership of the congregation's eucharistic celebrations. Also pastors can talk with children in church school or eucharistic classes and can give small children the gift of a book on communion written for children themselves. John M. Barrett's *Big in God's Eyes: a Story About Children and Communion* (United Church Press, 1985) is such a book. A fine guide to help children understand the different elements of the eucharist is published by the United Methodist church entitled *Communion Book for Children* (in both English and Spanish). It is written by Diedra Kriewald and Barbara Garcia.

Seek to develop a eucharistic community that supports the notion of weekly worship which balances Word and Table for the entire congregation. This may be *the* most important educational task. Pastoral leadership is crucial in this process. However, members of the worship committee can start the study as they discuss the key questions, search significant theological works, and seek to come to agreements and policies to recommend to the other committees and boards of the congregation. Several congregations have developed their own statments about the eucharist, its openness, and its part in the total worship life of the faith community.

SEEING CONFIRMATION AS A REPEATABLE SACRAMENT

As we have stated already, confirmation was originally associated with baptism, and often eucharist, as a symbol of the presence of the Holy Spirit. It was only later that confirmation became split from baptism and eucharist as unified rites of initiation and began to have an identity as the ritual celebrating the autonomous decision of the young person to affirm or "complete" his or her baptism and the church's confirming of that fact. Such a split has distorted both baptism and confirmation and has considerable negative ramifications for the meaning of eucharist and who should be able to come to the Table and when. There are many different answers to these questions coming from various denominational studies. The following view is one which is consistent with the understanding of the Christian faith as they move through the various experiences of their lives from adolescence to young, middle, and older adulthood.

If children are initiated into the body of Christ fully in baptism, confirmation, and eucharist, they are "ordained" to ministry and are invited to participate in various facets of mutual ministry. We begin to expect children to enliven the body with their winsome openness and teachableness, their spontaneity and imagination. As they mature in self-understanding they need opportunities within an accepting community to probe the meaning of the Christian faith, to reveal their insecurities and anxieties, to test out options, and to come to honest formulations of their faith and their understanding of the unique ministries in the community of universal priesthood. This process really is lifelong if we are honest with one another. Since baptism is a one-time event, bringing persons fully into the body of Christ, what is needed in confirmation at later stages of growth or understanding is not the "completing" of baptism, or "joining the church" (a strange term for youth or adults who have participated in the faith community and who have "ministered unto" many as well as being ministered unto) but the *strengthening* and *focusing* of the faith with a renewal of one's baptism. In fact, confirmation is now being seen in the United Methodist church and in other faith communities as baptismal renewal. In the Lutheran community which has traditionally placed high value on religious education for confirmation (often three years in length) the concept is moving from confirmation to *affirmation*. In the new *Affirm* series, confirmation is seen as *ministry* and as a lifelong process.

"Viewing confirmation as a lifelong process in no way diminishes the value of the ministry you share with junior-high students in your congregation. The years of confirmation instruction are an important step in the lifelong faith development process."[14] The key issue has to do with helping youth identify more deeply with the Christian faith, its ministry and mission, in concrete ways appropriate for youth. Lutherans and others have taken this more honest position but have been less clear about the repeatable nature of confirmation which is implied in this stance.

The work of Max Thurian from the Taize community in France and the reports of the World Council of Churches' study commissions have produced a strong call for confirmation or baptismal renewal to be a repeatable sacrament which can be correlated not only with various stages of human growth but even more with the mature affirmation of the universal priesthood of all believers and the church's consecration of persons for Christian vocation.[15] Now that adults often change their occupations two, three, or four times during their lives it is even more critical for the church to have educational and liturgical occasions of redefinition and refocus of the ministry into which the individual was baptized. Such a stance is a challenge to pastoral and lay confirmation teams to rethink not only the nature of confirmation but the various occasions during life where confirmation (baptismal renewal) is needed. We shall return to this discussion when we look at the pastor's role in the sacraments of vocation.

In respect to adolescents, such a change in perspective should not water down the great importance of confirmation experiences of high quality. In fact, more than one such educational and liturgical experience seems warranted. My colleagues and I developed a three-stage religious education program for confirmation at North Broadway United Methodist Church in Columbus, Ohio, in the 1950s. A version of this program is solidly and creatively continuing at the Centenary United Methodist Church, Winston Salem, North Carolina (Disciples for seventh graders, Crusaders for ninth graders, and Pilgrims for seniors in high school with the entire youth program interrelated with confirmation education).[16] Such a religious education program is geared to the repeatable nature of confirmation and the well-established fact that youth can give away only what they understand of themselves in relation to what they understand of the faith. Since both are changing rapidly during early to late adolescence, youth need an atmosphere in which honest exploration and search can be combined with moments of decision and commitment.

There is no way that *all* religious education for confirmation can be done only by the pastor, if such a view is taken. It is the total ministering community which is being symbolized. However, pastors bring special resources to the process and have a high responsibility to take initiative in developing wider understandings and educational and liturgical expressions which meet the diverse needs of persons along life's pilgrimage.

One of the most imaginative involvements of a pastor in confirmation at the adolescent level is the work of William O. Roberts, pastor of First Church of Christ (UCC) in Middletown, Connecticut. The church has developed a very engaging program which integrates religious education and worship for the entire congregation each Sunday, calling for a two-hour commitment. Education is seen as a lifelong experience. So are worship and ministry. In addition to creative and wide-ranging education and worship experiences for children and adults, Roberts and lay leaders have designed a three-level program of initiation of adolescents into what it means to be an adult Christian in the contemporary world. The three groups are the Pre-Initiation Group (affectionately named PIGS), the Initiation Group, and the Graduates, (including all persons who have passed through these initiations). Such a program makes expectations clear, provides ample mystery about what it means to go to the next stage, and continually challenges the pastor, youth, lay teams, parents, and the entire congregation to grow together. The program is quite demanding but very realistic and lively.

The program is geared to youth from the seventh- to tenth-grade years because of tradition in the congregation, the avoidance of conflicts with school activities the last two years of high school, and the needs of adolescents and parents. The initiation groups covenant to meet twice a week, supplemented with periodic, frequent retreats. Attendance is crucial (averages at 90 percent). The pastor is key to the selection of a strong team of two adults who are responsible for the entire initiation process, relating to the initiates intensely over the two-year period, a cadre of adults who are specialists in one or more of the broad subject areas being studied—society, sexuality, spirituality, and the self (issues of theological, religious, biblical, historical, cultural, racial, and liturgical import are interrelated with the discussions in considerable depth). These adults and others are involved in the special units and in all retreats and ritual celebrations. Parents have important supporting roles and are asked to sustain the need for privacy as their youth experience different aspects of the studies, activities, and rites. There are eight rites: the Rite of Separation, the Urban Adventure, the Encounters and Silence, the Marking Ritual, the Sexuality Rite, the Ash Wednesday Service, the Wilderness Experience, and the Final Act of Initiation. The discussions immerse youth into dialogues with adults who share their personal, political, and social biases and commitments in relation to the Christian call to discipleship. Such vulnerability encourages youth to test their own views in relation to those of adults so that self-definition can take place. The interaction and content of the four units can be affirmed as quite solid theologically and educationally. The next-to-the-last ritual is indicative of the challenge that the program makes possible in the lives of youth. It is the Wilderness experience. The pastor, adult leaders, and youth take tents, sleeping bags, cooking utensils, food, and backpacks, along with the youths' first drafts of their individual statements of faith, and go away for a few days in the wilds. They climb mountains, conquer white water, create places to sleep, prepare food, and share their faith pilgrimages with one another. Experiences are planned which will test the faith and fortitude of the youth and adults to the maximum within the agreed-upon limits of safety. The statements of faith are refined and read before parents, members of the congregation, graduates, and PIGs at an incorporation banquet held the day after return. Such statements have been the result of personal and corporate struggle to refine the Christian faith in relation to a deeper understanding of the self. Youth feel the integrity of such a quest. Finally, the youth are incorporated into the adult world of responsible faith, through rituals of affirming their baptism, the laying-on-of-hands, the signing of the cross, the anointing, the commissioning for ministries in the world, the extending of the right hand of fellowship, the owning of the covenant, and the celebration of the eucharistic meal.[17]

Such a religious education program for confirmation, aimed at middle adolescents, has many strengths, is exciting, and is profoundly meaningful. However, it should not be seen as the only confirmation experience in life's pilgrimage. Several other periods of self-definition or redefinition are normal. Education and liturgical celebrations should be available during young adulthood (when young people have lived enough to be able to critique the Christian faith as a system of belief and practice and to internalize the faith in honest ways related to a sense of vocation, total philosophy of life, intimacy, and sexuality), middle adulthood (when the paradoxes of life tend to become clear and quest for a faith which deals with normal mid-life crisis is pursued), and older adulthood (where persons are seeking to simplify life and to find an inclusive, universalizing faith of deep integrity which helps them deal with the retirement years and the meaning of their own death). Such an expanded view of the stages of faith and the stages of ritualization graphically illustrates the need for confirmation or baptismal renewal as a repeatable sacrament. One of the best liturgical resources for such repeatable confirmation experiences is *Holy Baptismal and Services*

for the Renewal of Baptism, Supplemental Liturgical Resource (Westminster, 1985) , p. 80.

THE SACRAMENTS OF VOCATION: ORDINATION OF CLERGY
AND THE CONSECRATION OF LAITY FOR THE
UNIVERSAL PRIESTHOOD OF ALL BELIEVERS

Pastors have had quite clear educational and liturgical guidelines
for preparation and public celebrations of their call to ordained
ministry. The same is not true for laity. There are few clear religious
education expectations and very, very few liturgical celebrations of
the ministry of laity. This must be changed. Pastors have a unique
responsibility and opportunity to help the whole church experience
a profound perception shift. Such a revolution is possible. It calls
for pastors and lay teams to design concrete but flexible patterns of
education which will prepare lay Christians for specific forms of
ministry within and beyond the faith community. If the universal
priesthood is to become a concrete reality, it must have specific
ways for the vision to "come to earth" for youth and adults who are
seeking to make decisions about their vocations and the values they
will express in their personal, social, ethical, and occupational life.

James Fowler, in his faith development research, has affirmed
that adulthood is a much more vital time for religious education
and growth in faith than we have often perceived. Moreover, he
believes that adults need, most of all, to come to decisions about
their overall sense of Christian vocation and to relate that vision of
the meaning of their lives to their decisions about occupation,
family, voluntary service, and political life. The church is called to
become a community which nurtures each person's honest pilgrimage into what it means to become agents of love, justice, and trust—
extensions of Christ's body—in our fast-moving world. The final
three stages of faith development, in Fowler's six-phased theory, are
primarily adult. In our religious education of persons for the universal priesthood we must create an atmosphere in which young
adults can study the Christian faith as a total system of beliefs in
comparison to optional claims and competing philosophies of life
so that they can critique the Christian faith freely, rework their
earlier ideas and beliefs, and come to an internally meaningful and
consistent commitment. This stage of testing, which Fowler calls

Stage 4 (Individuative Reflective), is the period of life during which adults can most profitably engage in deeper study of biblical, theological, and ethical issues at the heart of the Christian worldview. Pastors and lay teams have a great opportunity to respond to this fundamental need to probe, to get behind the symbols of the faith, to meanings that will hold up, that bear honest questioning, in an environment that is very supportive and nurturing. If the expectations of adolescents included a clear picture of several informal and formal opportunities, designed for them when they reach young adulthood, to rethink their beliefs, their understanding of the meaning of the Bible for their lives, their specific preparation to be in ministry through their occupations, then they would *not* think of themselves as having "graduated" from religious education at the time of their confirmation. One of the celebrations associated with confirmation as a repeatable sacrament could well be the expectation that each young adult will have opportunities to prepare himself or herself for specific forms of ministry and to celebrate that decision publicly in a sacrament of vocation, namely: the consecration of the individual for her or his specific expression of the universal priesthood of all believers in the work place or in voluntary settings. Religious educators can receive considerable stimulus by following Fowler's interpretations of the central nature of vocation in the various stages of adult growth in faith. In his view, adults will need repeated opportunities to redefine themselves and their commitments so that they will be able to risk putting their Christian values into practice in more and more wide-ranging ways (Stages 5 [Consolidative Faith] and 6 [Universalizing Faith]). Sacramental celebrations of baptismal renewal can accompany such a pilgrimage and help persons refocus and refine their specific expressions of the universal priesthood as they move through life.[18] For instance, the "famous" mid-life crisis period can be anticipated by pastors and lay leaders. Mid-life support groups can be formed to assist persons in the redefinitions necessary to find deeper integration of Christian values with the changing view of the self and often changing occupation so common in our postindustrial society. Marriages of twenty years either deepen and mature in fresh ways or they can become stale and life-denying. Parenthood moves into new dimensions, calling for a looser grip on children who are themselves becoming adults. This mid-life time produces many paradoxical feelings and thoughts. Pastors can enhance the lives of the ever-enlarging number of middle adults by developing educational and liturgical experiences which make possible such reassessments and reaffirmations. The same is true for older adulthood. The anticipation of the redefinition of faith and life required for successful retirement can be a wonderful gift to maturing older adults. This incredible "army" of ministering persons can bring about a revolution of its own, reaching out across the world in mission, across cultures in community, across the generations as older persons become "grandparents" to children and young couples in need of relationships of love and trust. Such middle and older adults can be stimulated to find a fresh sense of vocation and prepare themselves for new forms of the universal priesthood.

One of the most fruitful forms of pastoral work for young, middle, and older adults is that of mentoring. Young people are in need of adults who will invite them into their occupational settings to experience what it means to be a business person, a computer programer, or factory foreman, etc., in our society. Such mentors can be recruited by the church and related to the youth of the faith community who are trying to define themselves, their own sense of vocation as Christians, and how this sense of vocation or ministry can find expression through an occupation.

Herman Niebuhr in his penetrating book, *Revitalizing American Learning*, suggests that a perception shift is needed in our view of education. We must change from seeing education as primarily schooling by public institutions to seeing education as a human learning system which includes a crucial role for churches, businesses, the family, community groups, media, colleges, and public schools. Such a shift must take place in our vocabulary as well as our perceptions. All of these learning communities should be deliberately interconnected in our minds, our vocabulary, and our ways of strategizing the education required to meet the tremendous range of human needs present and coming quickly upon us.

Our families within and beyond the church are caught in the information revolution, needing to change their ways of thinking and acting. Niebuhr believes the church will be in a crisis if it does not change its approach to education and to society. The church should not try to do all the educating within its own institution but should take initiative to link to other learning communities in the overall learning system. Niebuhr challenges the church to be the initiator of learning networks. He says, "Unless it learns its new role, it will continue to decline. The church and all institutions need to learn how to provide life planning and other kinds of guidance as we expand our agenda of explicit and intentional learning to replace the old indoctrinations. The church has the opportunity to be once again a key institution in value, role, and affective learning. It can contribute to the strengthening of family and community life through participation in local learning coalitions."[19] Such penetration of the wider learning system by the church can happen only if the Copernican revolution in thinking about the universal priesthood genuinely takes hold. We must help lay persons within these other contexts to see themselves as ministering people. This means the development of cadres of ministering persons not only in learning networks but also in serving networks which deal with poverty, racism, and just distribution of our resources. The Church of the Savior in Washington D.C. provides a model in its development of educated, committed smaller "churches" within the church, organized around specific needs in the community. Every person within the church is ordained to specific forms of ministry and commissioned to go out to the wider community as an extension of Christ's body in the world.[20]

OTHER SACRAMENTAL EXPERIENCES
WITH HIGH POTENTIAL FOR PASTORAL INITIATIVE,
EDUCATIONALLY AND LITURGICALLY

The limitation of space in this chapter mandates that the sacraments of marriage, adult baptism, penance (or reconciliation), healing and wholeness in life and death, and footwashing be discussed in a much briefer way. Such a decision does not imply that such sacramental experiences are less important. Their potential for ministries of religious education, liturgy, and pastoral care is very great indeed. Marriage and family are central realities in life and of fundamental importance within the church and society. Dealing with personal and corporate guilt, failure, and the need to receive and give forgiveness probably takes more of the pastor's time and energy than any other facet of ministry. Helping persons transcend illness of mind, body, and spirit, helping persons look their own death in the face, and to accept and absorb the death of loved ones and friends are pastoral opportunities for ministry of profound meaning. Helping persons reach out and touch the lives of others in servanthood that is authentic and renewing, symbolized by the sacrament of footwashing, is another pastoral opportunity of central importance. Again as pastors we recognize the ministries associated with these sacramental experiences but so often we do not perceive the immense opportunities for religious education of the congregation around these sacraments.

Marriage: The Sacrament of Love

Programs concerning family life, marriage, and sex education, from a Christian perspective, can be designed by pastoral and lay teams for persons throughout their life cycle: 1) for youth and others in preparation for marriage, 2) for young couples in reference to baptismal preparation, 3) for young children as they sort out their own sexual identities and their images of family and marriage, 4) for elementary children and early adolescents as they develop positive male and female images and deal with disruptions to family life in a society with increasing numbers of one-parent families and the problems and opportunities for marriage and family brought about by the giant strides in modern technology affecting reproduction, genetic interventions, and birth control—not to mention the threat of AIDS and other aberrations related to sexual experiences and relationships. Such religious education can be related to studies concerning the sacramental nature of marriage, within the wider sacramental nature of life itself. These issues are quite significant for an understanding of marriage that will relate interfaith, interracial, and nontraditional forms of commitment to sound theological, religious, and ethical norms.[21]

Adult Baptism: The Sacrament of Evangelization

The position my colleague Roy Reed and I have taken is this: We believe infant baptism is the most authentic and powerful sacramental experience for those who are born within the Christian family and that adult baptism has the most meaning for those from beyond the congregation who respond affirmatively to the good news. Adult baptism was a dramatic symbol, in the early church, of dying to the values coming from a secular culture and rising to new life in Christ. Even though both adult and infant baptism can be found in the New Testament, at different times in history when the church has sought to renew itself adult baptism with its focus on decision has been emphasized over infant baptism. Karl Barth, for instance, preferred adult baptism because he saw how the church in Europe had become conventional and lacking in commitment when it was a state church into which children were baptized and later confirmed as symbols of acceptability in society rather than as symbols of centeredness in Christ and his mission in the world.

Today, the Roman Catholic church has taken strong leadership in establishing adult baptism as the sacrament of evangelization. In the new Rite of Christian Initiation of Adults, based on the practices of initiation found in the catechumenate period in the second to fourth centuries, we see a dynamic, nonmanipulative program of training of lay visitors and sponsors to be interpreters of the faith to persons who may have deep need for commitment but have not been able to work through their beliefs in a way that is consistent enough to permit them to become conscious members of the ministering body of Christ. Excellent one- to three-year-long religious educational, liturgical, and ethically oriented resources are available and can be adapted by Protestant or Orthodox communities. Again, baptism whether infant or adult is being seen in the light of commitment to a unified initiation. This means baptism with water, confirmation with the laying-on-of-hands, and participation in the eucharist. So the new rite of adult initiation in *The Rites of the Catholic Church* (Pueblo Press, 1976), and James B. Dunning, *New Wine: New Wine Skins* (Sadlier, 1981) is an illustration of this fruitful movement. Such resources are designed for the catechumens who respond to the invitation to study the faith in depth, participate in the faith community's life of worship and service until they come to a decision to die to false securities and rise with Christ in adult baptism, usually at Easter. This celebration is followed by joyous sharing of faith stories and further preparation, during the pre-Pentecost period, to find one's unique ministry within or beyond the congregation.

Footwashing: The Sacrament of Servanthood

Most of us are aware that from any criteria regarding the definition of a sacrament the rite of footwashing, first inaugurated by

Jesus, qualifies. Yet, footwashing is seen as a sacrament by very few
Christians. There is probably no more profound and living symbol
of the core meaning of the nature of the ministry of the whole
people of God than footwashing. It does indeed make visible and
tangible the servanthood which is the essential quality of Christ's
life and teachings. Finding ways to transcend the seeming awkward-
ness and even embarrassment associated with footwashing can be a
challenge for contemporary pastors and people. Such is being undertaken with new meaning and joy. With the deeply moving liturgy
goes education for servanthood—with children and youth being
invited to participate fully along with adults. Religious education
for peace and justice with the entire church family participating can
be linked with actual service, using an action reflection approach,
culminating in the sacramental celebration of footwashing. The
latter should be planned carefully so that participants are properly
prepared and can engage in the ritual freely and with affirmation.
Some liturgies have the pastor washing the feet of lay members of
the body. I participated in such a service in Canada. It was very
meaningful. However, I wanted to wash the feet of others as well as
having my feet washed. The Church of the Brethren model provides for tables of persons washing one another's feet. Such a
sacramental act projects a strong image, calling for Christ's servanthood to be extended through the lives of all. Such extensions
of care and sacrificial living are most significant when they are tied
clearly to existing conditions of need in the human family. Again,
such a liturgical celebration can be explored sensitively by pastors
and laity with a view to making concrete the most central quality of
ministry revealed by Christ, the ministry of servanthood.[22]

The Sacrament of Confession and Reconciliation

Catholic and Orthodox pastors have been involved for centuries
in ministries, primarily liturgical, around the traditional sacrament
of penance. Today, these ministries are changing in the direction of
educational and corporate models, away from private confession
and absolution as the basic approach. Protestant pastors, from the
Reformation on, have been wary of confession, due to the distortions indentified by Luther and others. Since Vatican II Roman
Catholics have developed a new theology of penance and have

changed the name to the Sacrament of Reconciliation. Protestant pastors are inspired to reconsider the meaning of the sacrament and its potential as a ministry to those who are emotionally spent through guilt and self-hate. The new rites of the Catholic church include a) a communal celebration with the opportunity for individual confession, b) an individual confession and reconciliation, given by the priest as a representative for the church's total ministry, and c) a fresh form of communal reconciliation without individual confession. These new views of reconciliation are creating wide Protestant interest in the crucial importance of educational and liturgical designs to support an authentic form of the sacrament of reconciliation. Protestant pastors have emphasized pastoral counseling approaches but often did not deal with the deep need for confession, forgiveness, and reconciliation as expressions of the church's ministry. The door is open, ecumenically, for education of children, youth, and adults in respect to their need to face their tendencies to center life in themselves rather than in God and others. Catholic nonlegalistic resources such as *Come, Be Reconciled! Penance Celebration of Young Christians* represent creative, dialogical religious education for children and parents in primary, middle grades, and high school.[23] Support groups can be critical for adults and youth who have need for reconciliation related to personal and social disorientation resulting in chemical dependency, family strife, sexual aberrations, and interpersonal hostility. Eastern Orthodox thinkers have presented excellent educational resources which can be employed ecumenically for parents and adult leaders.[24] One of the best Protestant guides for pastors is a fine book by Clark Hyde, *To Declare God's Forgiveness: Toward a Pastoral Theology of Reconciliation* (Morehouse Barlow, 1984).

The Sacraments of Healing and Wholeness in Life and Death

As pastors, we are constantly related intimately to persons in their struggles with illness and death. Especially in the Protestant community pastors have been handicapped severely because of considerable resistance to healing ministries and our lack of liturgical security and resources in respect to healing, dying, and death. The extravagant claims for healing from television evangelists and others have made pastors especially cautious about initiating ministries of wholeness. Research findings underscore the holistic nature of health. It is clear that spiritual, physical, and emotional factors are all interrelated in causing illness or in generating health. A sacramental approach to healing employing confession and renewal, rites of laying-on-of-hands, anointing with oil, intercessary prayer, and the celebration of the eucharist can open the door of imaginative faith for those who are ill. Pastoral care and counseling can be wedded with liturgical celebrations concerning the legitimacy and necessity of authentic approaches to healing. Preparation of the congregation through study groups and surveys of congregational and community needs and attitudes can be undertaken by pastors and worship committees. Guidance for pastors seeking to prepare congregations for sound healing ministries can be found in James Wagner's *Blessed to be a Blessing* and in other resources prepared by the United Methodist Church.[25]

Death education has been conducted widely in our society, often not under the sponsorship of the church, however. Such should not be the case. Not only do pastors, lay professionals, and lay ministering persons need to visit those who are wrestling with their own impending death but they should be able to offer a sacrament of dying. Such a sacrament can be similar to extreme unction or viaticum (meaning, something for the journey) but without the legalistic and substantialistic interpretations associated with this rite. We need fresh forms of unction to be developed and used with dying persons and their families. Death education can start with children and their questions[26] and go throughout the various stages of life. Pastors can form lay educational and liturgical ministries around death and dying with great meaning for the entire congregation and for the wider community.[27]

The most overlooked ministry is a sacramental approach to the funeral itself. The funeral can be a rite of passage from this world to the life beyond death. So often pastors and church members alike have been passive, surrendering the funeral to the secular images and culture religion associated with some funeral home services. Pastors have a major educational task as they seek to reinterpret the funeral as a sacrament. James F. White has made an excellent contribution in his rationale for making the funeral a sacrament. In his various writings he urges pastors to see the funeral as a witness to God's enduring love on earth and beyond death in the establishment of new relationships within the community of saints. In death the faithful are separated from us but are passing into a wider and deeper relationship with the body of Christ. The passover theme in the eucharist is the most powerful image to project in the liturgy. The funeral celebrates the passover from the joys but limitations of this life to the life beyond and new freedom, given through Christ, the resurrected one. The visible sign is our personal commitment as participants, commitment to continue the ministry taken up by the deceased. In addition, the bread and the wine of the eucharist are powerful signs of the triumph of love and life, made visible in Christ and celebrated joyously by the body of believers. Having funerals in the church with both Word and Table can do much to reclaim the sacramental nature of the funeral.[28]

CONCLUSION

I have presented a brief picture of the Copernican revolution in sacramental thinking and practice and its potential for stimulatiing pastors and laity to reorder the way Christian religious education is undertaken. Much experimentation will be needed in order to discover the most meaningful patterns for local congregations. Protestants can get many clues from their Roman Catholic and Orthodox friends and vice versa. But, as we exchange ideas, let us keep the vision clear: the religious education of the whole people for the universal priesthood and the realization of God's realm of love and justice in the world.

Notes

1. Nicholaus Copernicus (1473-1534) is credited with the concept that the earth rotated around the sun, a concept which was refined and developed by others who followed him, such as Tycho Brake (1546-1601), Johann Kepler (1571-1630), and Galileo Galilei (1564-1642). This revolutionary shift in perception and its impact on modern theological thinking is analyzed creatively by my colleague Jeffery Hopper in his *Understanding Modern Theology: Cultural Revolutions and New World*, Vol. 1 (Philadelphia: Fortress, 1987).

2. An illustration of the strength of the "old world" view in respect to ministry can be seen in the appropriations churches make for theological schools. Funds are primarily aimed at the preparing of ordained clergy and other professionals in ministry but only tangentially to include the theological education of laity for the universal priesthood.

3. See a more complete discussion of the quiet revolution in sacramental thought and practice in Robert L. Browning and Roy A. Reed, *The Sacraments in Religious Education and Liturgy: An Ecumenical Model* (Birmingham, Ala.: Religious Education Press, 1985).

4. Karl Rahner, *Theological Investigations* Vol. XIV (London: Darton, Longman and Todd, 1976), p. 166.

5. Browning and Reed, *The Sacraments in Religious Education and Liturgy*, pp. 21-23, 119-137.

6. See Barbara J. Kunston, *Welcome to the Lord's Family* (Minneapolis: Augsburg, 1984) and George E. Handley, *We Bring This Child* (Minneapolis: Augsburg, 1983) for resources for the six sessions and for a guide for parents. Also see booklets from the United Church of Christ, Ron Cole-Turner, *Your Child's Baptism* (St. Louis: Church Leadership Resources) and *You Are a Godparent* (St. Louis: Church Leadership Resources).

7. *Birth, Baptism and Parenting* (New York: United Church Press, 1983), Plan Books. Also see Walter Brueggemann's fine study, *Belonging and Growing in the Christian Community: The First Years of Parenting* (Crawfordsville, Ind.: General Assembly Mission Board, Presbyterian Church, 1979) and the accompanying guide from the same source, *The First Years of Parenting*, produced by Shared Approaches for several cooperating denominations.

8. Valerie Stultz, *Baptism: A Claiming, Naming, Healing, Empowering Sacrament*—an unpublished paper, 1987.

9. See Geoffrey Wainwright, *Eucharist and Eschatology* (London: Epworth Press, 1971) for an excellent discussion of the biblical foundation for such an open view.

10. *Children and Communion: Suggestions for Congregational Discussions* (New York: United Church Press), p. 12.

11. Sandra R. Boler and James E. Boler, *You Are Welcome: A Children and Communion Leaders Guide* (New York: United Church Press, 1985). Biblical quotes are taken from *An Inclusive Language Lectionary*.

12. George E. Handley, *Welcome to the Lord's Table* (Minneapolis: Augsburg, 1971), p.15. Includes typical questions of both children and their parents along with family activities.

13. See Margaret Sawin's several books, especially *Hope for Families* (New York: Sadlier, 1982) for ideas to use in family cluster programs, including an approach to the celebration of the eucharist.

14. *Affirm Planning Guide* (Minneapolis: Augsburg, 1984), p. 84ff.

15. See Max Thurian, *Consecration of the Layman* (Baltimore: Helicon, 1963), p. 84ff.

16. Write Edward Ritter, Minister of Christian Education, Centenary United Methodist Church, Winston Salem, North Carolina, for more information.

17. See William O. Roberts Jr., *Initiation to Adulthood: An Ancient Rite of Passage in Contemporary Form* (New York: Pilgrim, 1982).

18. See James W. Fowler, *Becoming Adult, Becoming Christian* (San Francisco: Harper & Row, 1984).

19. Herman Niebuhr, *Revitalizing American Learning* (Belmont, Calif.: Wadsworth, 1984), pp. 104-105.

20. Based on notes from an address from Mrs. Gordon Cosby of the Church of the Savior, Washington D.C., presented at the annual meeting of the Association of Professors and Researchers in Religious Education. November 14-16, 1986, Washington, D.C.

21. See the classic study of marriage by Edward Schillebeeckx, *Marriage: Human Reality and Saving Mystery* Volumes I and II (New York: Sheed and Ward, 1965) and resources from most denominations such as, Joan and Richard Hunt, *Growing Love in Christian Marriage: The Official Marriage Manual of the United Methodist Church* (Nashville: Abingdon, 1982); and for specific approaches to marriage education in relation to the stages of ritualization and faith see Browning and Reed, *The Sacraments in Religious Education and Liturgy*, pp. 208-215.

22. See *Ritual in a New Day* (Nashville: Abingdon, 1976), pp. 24-36 for liturgical aids.

23. See Howard Hall, Maria Rabalais, and David Vavasseur, *Come, Be Reconciled!* (New York: Paulist, 1975); and Christiane Brusselmans and Brian Haggerty, *We Celebrate Reconciliation* (Morristown, N.J.: Silver Burdett, 1976).

24. Sophie Koulomzin, *Our Church and Our Children* (Crestwood, N.Y.: St. Vladimir's Seminary Press, 1975).

25. See James Wagner, *Blessed to Be a Blessing* (Nashville: The Upper Room, 1980), George Leach, *Hope for Healing* (New York: Paulist, n.d.), and Bernie S. Siegel, *Love, Medicine, and Miracles* (New York: Harper & Row, 1986).

26. See Linda Vogel, *Helping a Child Understand Death* (Philadelphia: Fortress, 1975).

27. See Robert Kastenbaum, "Death and Development Through the Life Cycle" in *New Meanings of Death*, ed. Herman Feifel (New York: McGraw-Hill, 1977), pp. 18-44, and Herbert N. Conley, *Living and Dying Gracefully* (New York: Paulist, 1979).

28. See James F. White, *Sacraments As God's Self-Giving* (Nashville: Abingdon, 1983); and *Christian Worship in Transition* (Nashville: Abingdon, 1976).

Bibliography

Browning, Robert L., and Reed, Roy A. *The Sacraments in Religious Education and Liturgy: An Ecumenical Model.* Birmingham, Alabama: Religious Education Press, 1985.

Coniaris, Anthony M. *These Are the Sacraments: The Life-Giving Mysteries of the Orthodox Church.* Minneapolis: Light and

Duffy, Regis. *Real Presence.* New York: Harper & Row, 1972.

Erikson, Erik H. *Toys and Reasons—Stages in the Ritualization of Experience.* New York: Norton, 1977.

Fowler, James W. *Stages of Faith.* San Francisco: Harper & Row, 1981.

Guzie, Tad. *The Book of Sacramental Basics.* New York: Paulist, 1981.

Holmes, Urban III. *Confirmation: The Celebration of Maturity in Christ.* New York: Seabury, 1975.

Hopper, Jeffery. *Understanding Modern Theology I: Cultural Revolutions and New Worlds.* Philadelphia: Fortress, 1987.

Hovda, Robert W. *Strong, Loving, and Wise.* Washington, D.C.: The Liturgical Conference, 1976.

Kavanagh, Aidan. *The Shape of Baptism: The Rite of Christian Initiation.* New York: Pueblo, 1978.

Miller, Donald E. *Story and Context: An Introduction to Christian Education.* Nashville: Abingdon, 1987.

Rahner, Karl. *Theological Investigations, XIV.* London: Darton, Longman & Todd, 1976.

Ramshaw, Elaine. *Ritual and Pastoral Care.* Philadelphia: Fortress, 1987. Edited by Don S. Browning.

Schillebeeckx, Edward. *Christ, the Sacrament of the Encounter With God.* New York: Sheed and Ward, 1963.

Schmemann, Alexander. *For the Life of the World.* Crestwood, New York: St. Vladimir's Seminary Press, 1973.

Segundo, Juan Luis. *The Sacraments Today.* New York: Orbis, 1974.

Thurian, Max. *Consecration of the Layman.* Baltimore: Helicon, 1963.

Wainwright, Geoffrey. *Eucharist and Eschatology.* London: Epworth, 1971.

Westerhoff, John, III and Willimon, William. *Liturgy and Learning Through the Life Cycle.* New York: Seabury, 1980.

White, James. *Sacraments as God's Self-Giving.* Nashville: Abingdon, 1983.

Worgul, G.S. *From Magic to Metaphor.* New York: Paulist, 1980.

4

The Pastor as Biblical Interpreter and Teacher

ROBIN MAAS

Then the eyes of both were opened, and they knew that they were naked....Now Adam knew Eve his wife, and she conceived and bore Cain" (Genesis 3:7a; 4:1a).

One of the first lessons learned in seminary is what the Genesis account intends when it states that Adam "knew" Eve. In this and other biblical contexts the Hebrew verb *yadah* means not simply to understand or intellectually apprehend something or someone. It means to experience the full reality of what is known as, in this case, through sexual intercourse. English speakers are accustomed to distinguishing between knowing about something in the sense of having ready access to the facts concerning it and really "knowing" it in the sense of having had immediate or first-hand experience of what is known. For the purposes of this chapter on the pastor's role as a religious educator in relation to scripture, this distinction between knowing experientially and knowing through intellectual apprehension is an essential one, for I will argue that effectiveness in this role relates directly to one's ability to "know" the Bible in both senses of the word and that one kind of knowing properly precedes the other.

LOVE YOUR BIBLE

In 1982 I published a book on Bible study for local congregations.[1] It represented several years of study on my part and a fairly

extensive range of teaching experiences with lay people. Since fin-
ishing that work a number of important changes have occurred in
my life: Among other things, I completed a doctoral dissertation
relating to the use of scripture with children[2] and was hired to
teach religious education in seminary. Now, instead of working
primarily with the laity, I work with people planning to be pastors
or professional religious educators in the church. Were I to write
the book over again from my present vantage point, there is much
that would remain the same and probably very little I would omit.
But the book would be a longer one, for I am much more aware
now of what would-be pastors and other religious educators bring
with them or *fail* to bring with them when they arrive at seminary
full of dreams and ambitions. This essay, then, is a kind of post-
script to the larger work. It reflects a recognition, on my part, that
the pastor's role as religious educator in relation to scripture—be it
as preacher or teacher—depends on much more than background
or skills. In the end, it is primarily a labor of love.

One of the first things I discovered as a new and enthusiatic
Bible study leader and teacher was how emotion-laden a symbol the
Bible really is and, consequently, how "touchy" many faithful
Christians are about it. The Bible—at least in the Protestant
churches—has become "politicized," and one is likely to be relegated to a given (positive or negative) status very quickly primarily on
the basis of the *kind of language* used to talk about scripture. In the
past, I frequently found myself teaching large classes that included
laypersons from both ends of the liberal-conservative spectrum and
was always aware of the need to "proceed with caution" on particular issues. But something rather surprising happened as I went from
one teaching experience to the other: I found that I was more or
less equally successful in relatively conservative or relatively liberal
settings. Parishioners who would probably have had a hard time
coming to terms with much of the historical-critical data I had been
exposed to in seminary could begin to explore scripture on their
own less defensively and with a more critical eye, providing they
had the aid of a few basic reference tools. Those parishioners
whose Bibles had been gathering dust on a shelf somewhere, suddenly felt a new surge of interest in this book they knew they were
supposed to want to read. And they all actually believed me when I
told them that they could learn to interpret scripture themselves
with integrity and confidence. Why?

I have thought about this a good deal over the years and am convinced that it was not simply a matter of skill or talented teaching on my part. My instructional "method," helpful as it might be, was not the deciding factor either. As I put it now to my seminary students as they prepare themselves to teach scripture: If you really *love* the Bible, they will forgive you anything! Evidently, the single biggest thing I had going for me was, first, my personal devotion to scripture and—almost as important—what others saw as a touching confidence in the religious convictions and abilities of the laity. To try to make this a little clearer and to demonstrate how these issues underlie everything else pastors do as religious educators, let me begin by sharing a bit of personal history.

Like many youngsters, I was taken every Sunday—like it or not—to Sunday school by my mother, who was sincere in her religious beliefs and practices. Most of the time I went willingly, learned my Bible verses, and was a "good little girl." I believed it all—and took it utterly for granted. But at the age of fourteen, just as I was getting ready to take on the exciting possibilities of adolescence, I was suddenly faced with a very adult responsibility for my faith and my life. My mother died of cancer, and the crisis left me to fend for myself in relation to practicing my religion. Suddenly there was no one to insist on regular religious education, church attendance, or devotional practices. I could have it all or I could leave it all. Through the gracious intervention of a loving God, I chose to have it all, and the church became my mother.

To be specific, in addition to attending church and Sunday school, I began daily devotional exercises that included substantial doses of scriptural reading from both the Old and New Testaments. I followed a set schedule of readings provided by the denomination and spent anywhere from thirty to forty-five minutes at it every morning. Inevitably, reading biblical texts led to pauses for reflection and prayer. Some of what I did I had been taught by my mother's example; but I knew that my Sunday school teachers did the same thing. It was the traditional, accepted way of being "faithful," and at the time I was unaware that what I was doing was in any way exceptional. In retrospect, I can see that out of adversity great blessing came, for I continued this practice for many years— out of devotion and out of necessity. My life had made me hungry for God. Over time, two things happened. First, I found I had the faith resources to cope reasonably well with what life was dealing out to me; second, I *knew* the Bible—knew it in the sense that my mind was furnished with biblical categories, my imagination was saturated with biblical images, and my heart was inscribed with words of promise and power. And to know the Bible in this sense is certainly to love it. When, years later, I arrived at seminary, I discovered I had a significant advantage, both academically and psychologically, for most of my classmates did not "know" the Bible in this sense, and their encounter with historical, biblical criticism was often shattering. That was thirteen years ago. The picture is not much different today. Insofar as their faith rests on a view of biblical authority that equates truth with historically verifiable fact and not on a long and strong affective relationship with the God to whom scripture testifies, seminarians remain fragile and vulnerable creatures.

KNOW YOUR BIBLE

If there is one thing the average parishoner expects of the pastor—or at least hopes for—it is a thorough knowledge of scripture. The general expectation is that a seminary education will supply this expertise. Alas! Those of us who have been seminarians know *how little* we really know. For some students, the introductory Old and New Testament surveys are as much as they get. The rest of their biblical education proceeds on the basis of consulting commentaries either for sermon preparation or teaching. The more fortunate or farseeing seminarians will have included one or two extra courses on exegesis sandwiched in with courses on homiletics, church administration, theology, ethics, religious education, and so on. There is, of course, no substitute for a thorough grounding in biblical history, theology, and exegetical technique. It is essential for sound, "efficacious" biblical preaching, and preaching, of course, is where pastors do most of their teaching. There is no escaping this. The sermon says it all—it gives the preacher away. The parishioners know (almost instantly) by the quality of biblical preaching, how much of the Bible the pastor really "knows" in *every* sense of the word.

To be specific, the sermon speaks loudly and clearly about the pastor's *personal* relationship—if we may call it that—with scripture. The way in which the pastor does—or does not—use scripture in the sermon will reveal with ruthless clarity the centrality of the Bible in his or her life and the degree of authority willingly accorded to it. By "authority" I do not refer to whether or not one believes the creation accounts in Genesis are factually correct, whether Moses did indeed write the Pentateuch, or whether there actually was a man named Jonah who survived a sojourn in the belly of a whale. This is not the bottom line. There is probably only one relatively reliable indicator of the existential authority of scripture in a person's life apart from the life itself and that is the amount of *time* one invests in it. This brings me to the first point or principle I wish to underscore: *The pastor plays a decisive role in shaping the kind of relationship parishioners will have with scripture by the kind of relationship modeled from the pulpit.* The pastor's goal should be to model a vital, personal relationship between the individual believer, the professing community, and the authoritative Word of God.

The implications of this are obvious: Pastors must look first not at preaching skills or exegetical technique but at the role scripture plays in their own devotional life. They must ask themselves, "Do I have a devotional life? Do I make time for it? Is the Bible a beloved companion, or is my contact with it strictly on a 'professional' basis? Is the Bible simply something I preach on or from? Do I ever open it for *other* than sermon preparation?" Compare the dynamics of the pastor's relationship with scripture to those of another very important, intimate human relationship: that of husband and wife. Does a spouse make time just to *be with* a beloved mate? What would be the effect on the relationship if the only time the couple spent together was when one or the other of them expected to gain material assistance with some task? Is a husband or wife a resource to be used? No. Relationships based on purely utilitarian motives are not going to be lasting or emotionally fruitful. Neither is the Word of God simply a "resource" for the pastor's professional life. It is the source of that life. The pastor must know the Bible as intimately as a marriage partner—and to know the Bible is to love it. Nothing said in a sermon will speak more powerfully than the love that impels the saying of it.

UNINTENTIONAL TEACHING:
THE AUTHORITY OF SCRIPTURE IN PREACHING

There is one lesson the laity will learn every Sunday, and they will learn it well: The role scripture plays in the sermon—whether

central or supporting—will (Sunday after Sunday) model for them
the role it should play in their own lives: central or supporting.
Many pastors would prefer that scripture play a supporting role.
They know in advance what they want to preach and are relieved
and gratified to find a biblical passage that supports their message.
This is the typical strategy used in topical preaching.

There are times when topical preaching is appropriate or even
necessary, but good topical preaching is never easy. If anything, it
requires a greater knowledge of scripture than the kind of preaching which simply seeks a straightforward exposition of a text. If
pastors customarily choose a topic or issue on which to preach and
then look for support from scripture, what are they teaching? They
are teaching that scripture is nothing more than a *resource* to be
used. The Bible becomes an instrument (or weapon) in their hands.
The pastor sets the agenda and retains control over what happens.
The pastor—not the text—determines what shall be preached.
Similarly, those who hear the pastor preach week in and week out
will feel justified in using scripture to support *their own* convictions.
A seminary education will give its graduates the edge in this endeav-
or, but it is prooftexting all the same.

Biblical, as opposed to topical, preaching teaches a different lesson. By "biblical preaching" I refer particularly to preaching which
begins with a preassigned text, as in the use of a lectionary, and
proceeds to expound the meaning of that text with special reference to the context of the local parish. In biblical preaching, the
preacher relinquishes control over the agenda which, in this case, is
set by the content of the assigned text (or texts). The relevant issues
arise out of the exposition of the text, not from the last Administrative Board or Parish Council meeting. Rather than playing the
supporting role of resource, the Bible here takes center stage and
prescribes what shall be preached. The pastor is not "consulted";
the pastor is *used*. The fact that good biblical preaching of a single
text can vary enormously should disabuse us of the notion that
fidelity to the text will somehow rob us of our chance to be "creative." Since the context in which preaching occurs changes constantly, there is ample opportunity for creativity in making the kind
of apt connections essential for personal appropriation of the gospel message. The careful spelling out of these connections done
faithfully over an extended period of time provides a particularly

effective form of religious education in biblical hermeneutics. This skill does not come naturally: Preachers are not born knowing how to do this, and they cannot take it for granted that those who listen to them preach will make these connections. We *all* must be carefully taught.

It bears repeating here that the choice of whether to do topical or biblical preaching is a fateful one. Much more hangs in the balance than mere "effectiveness." *The choice determines the essential nature of our relationship with God's word.* Will we use it or be used by it? Which kind of a relationship will we model for our parishioners?

INTENTIONAL TEACHING: THE AUTHORITY OF SCRIPTURE IN TEACHING

Bearing in mind that what pastors teach about scripture unintentionally will be the most powerful message they send as religious educators, let us consider what happens when pastors actually *intend* to teach the Bible in adult education classes.

First, let us be honest. The market is awash with Bible study materials, resources, handbooks, guides, and whatnot. Some of these materials are excellent; some are rubbish; most are simply so-so. Because most parishioners feel extremely insecure about scripture, Bible resources are big business. Religious publishing houses can count on the fact that hope springs eternal. Many pastors are convinced that finding the right method and materials will solve the problem of Bible study. Fine! Pastors should locate and use the best materials available. It needs to be remembered, however, that most of these materials assume a more or less (probably less) literate clientelle. On the other hand, a pastor who functions as a religious educator with a group of well-educated parishioners should not be surprised if they are dissatisfied with the quality of officially approved denominational curricula. Meanwhile, the under-educated layperson will continue to complain that the material is too difficult or, if the parish is financially strapped, too expensive.

The place for pastors to begin assessing their skills as teachers of scripture is in their willingness and ability to work with the "naked" text *without additional "props."* Does the prospect of sitting down with a group of teenagers with nothing in hand but the Bible

send cold chills down the pastor's spine? If so, there is some important foundational work to be done.

Second, pastors need to clarify for themselves and their constitu-
encies what the *purpose* of their Bible teaching will be. There are at
least two important yet quite different thrusts in "Bible study," each
relating to the distinction between knowing experientially versus
knowing through intellectual apprehension. On the one hand, people need to know the Bible in a personal and intimate way. They
need to learn how to give scripture a central role in their devotional
life. This means learning how to pray the scriptures and meditate
on them. On the other hand, people are also hungry to know much
more *about* the Bible in terms of its structure, content, and historical context. They need to know it in order to love it. Much confusion and disappointment can be avoided by clarifying at the outset
what the purposes of a given Bible study class will be. Many lay
people think in terms of a devotional practice when they hear the
words "Bible study." Some are rather stunned to discover that the
hard work of actual study is involved. Most laypersons would probably like to have the best of both worlds; a few are interested in
only one dimension or the other. In fact, the hard work of scripture
study *is* an act of devotion, but this attitude and the experience that
accompanies it are not easy to come by. Pastors will find their task
as religious educators much simplified by first making a clear distinction between the devotional use of scripture and a content-
oriented Bible study. Then they can more effectively and efficiently
equip themselves to deal with people in both contexts. In the end,
devotion will fuel study and study will discipline devotion. Neither
one is a substitute for the other.

SCRIPTURE AND THE LIFE OF THE SPIRIT:
TEACHING THE DEVOTIONAL USE OF SCRIPTURE

The Word of God brought the world into being; it brings us, as
Christians, into being also. The Word creates in us a new heart, it
confers a distinctive character on our communal life, it both liberates and obliges us. It is in our scriptures that we find the assurance
that we have our origin and end in God; it is here we learn that
God *wants* us and freely chooses to be in the most intimate possible
relationship with us. The "bread" of God's Word that fed Jesus in

the wilderness of Judea creates a deep and persistent hunger in us for the Author of our being. More than a need to know something *about* God, it is a thirst *for* God and a yearning to be *known by* God. Through the Word we come to want God; through the Word we discover a way to respond to God's invitation to an intimate relationship.

No charge given to the pastor as religious educator exceeds in significance the responsibility to help create and sustain in the laity a deep hunger for God. All preaching, all teaching must tend toward this end. Along with the responsibility to increase the parishioners' appetite for the Divine, comes the requirement that this hunger be fed. The Word that transforms bread and wine into the body and blood of Christ and nourishes through the sacrament of the altar is likewise spread on the table of scripture to which all Christians are invited. The problem for many pastors is identical to that of the king whose invitations to the marriage feast were ignored (Matt. 22:1-3). Parishioners often call loudly for more Bible study, but when a class is actually offered, relatively few will attend. Why should this be the case? I am more than ever convinced that this invitation to an intimate relationship with God through scripture appropriately *precedes* the more commonly issued invitation— or exhortation—on the pastor's part to learn more *about* the Bible. Put bluntly, the average layperson needs to encounter God in the efficacious Word—particularly in the person of Jesus Christ—before he or she is willing to expend much time and effort to learn *about* the Bible. It is nothing less than a hunger for God that motivates a serious investment of time and resources in the study of scripture, and the pastor is doomed to an endless cycle of failure and frustration with Bible study until and unless this very simple reality is recognized. No method or set of materials can guarantee to produce this hunger for God; the people we serve will have to see that "lean and hungry look" *in us.*

Bread for the Hungry: Sacred Reading. Where to begin, then? How does one acquire that lean and hungry look? The pastor must begin with a personal practice which, once developed, can serve as the foundation for instructing parishioners. The church's ancient answer to the question of how to create and satisfy a hunger for God is simple and direct: The more we "feed" on God's Word, the hungrier we get. Further, there is a tried and trusted method for

doing this—a method that has absolutely nothing to do with sermon preparation. It is called *Lectio Divina* and it means, quite
simply, "sacred reading." The process detailed below can be mas-
tered through steady practice and is not difficult to share with
others, as I have learned from working with seminarians.

The practice of sacred reading or "*lectio*" goes all the way back to
the origins of the monastic movement; some might push elements
of it back even further to a rootage in rabbinic Judaism. It is a very
particular, noninformational way of approaching scripture (or other
sacred texts) and is best described as a form of prayerful or meditative reading. Typically, the process was understood as a form of
"spiritual nutrition." In *lectio* we ingest the Word just as we assimilate food. The practice recognizes that, as we must eat to live, so
must we consume the bread of life to experience salvation.

To practice *lectio divina* we must begin by setting aside all our
usual "tools" for approaching scripture. Commentaries, dictionaries, wordbooks, and concordances will not help us here. Instead,
begin with a passage of scripture and start, slowly and deliberately,
to *read it aloud* to yourself in low tones. In *lectio* we read not just
with our eyes but with our mouth and our ears. We are not simply
receiving the word; we are proclaiming it. Move your lips as you
read; stop, slow down, repeat phrases that capture your attention.
Take time to reflect on the words you hear. The joint participation
of mind and body in the act of reading produces a very singular
effect: Suddenly, reading becomes much less a passive experience
and much more an active one. In the process of repeating parts of a
text over and over again, its words are inscribed on our hearts and
(even) on our lips through what one scholar refers to as "muscular
memory."[3] The audible repetition of brief biblical texts is best
thought of as a kind of mastication or "chewing" of the Word. The
Word must be chewed before it can be swallowed, digested, and
finally assimilated into our very being. Sound easy enough? It's not.

In the first place, it is difficult to find the time or place to partake
of this kind of meal. We resist spending time on such a "useless"
form of prayer or study. No immediate professional or pastoral
purpose is served by such an exercise. If we undertake it hoping to
get something out of it we will be disappointed. It is simply time set
aside in our day to open ourselves to God, to place ourselves in
God's presence, and to put ourselves at God's disposal. Everything

depends on our willingness to waste time with God, on our expectation that, indeed, it is God and not the mysterious J, E, P, or D who is addressing us with a word for *us now*—not a definitive interpretation for all time. Predictably, *lectio* leads to *meditatio*, or the act of reflection. The Word, once chewed, gets swallowed and "ruminated" on. We turn it over and over again in our minds in the effort to understand how this is a word from God for us now. And, just as predictably, *lectio* and *meditatio* lead to *oratio*, to prayer, as the true significance of this particular encounter with God begins to dawn on us. Occasionally, a person very practiced in prayer is graced with the experience of *contemplatio*. In contemplation, God seizes the initiative and acts upon the individual to produce a profound and deeply satisfying sense of union. So we discover within the disciplined framework of "wasted time" with God and the constant, rhythmic movement or exchange between reading, reflection, and prayer the foundation for a personal, intimate relationship with the God whose Word this is.

To be sustaining, *lectio* must be done with great regularity, i,e., with discipline; it is not something we can dabble in. We must find a suitably private place, set aside a particular time, and then be faithful about showing up for our appointment, whether we "feel" like doing it or not. Depend on it, to begin with you will feel self-conscious, probably even silly, muttering to yourself, "My God, my God, why hast thou forsaken me?" and the prospect of teaching others to "feed" on the Word in this sense may leave you cold. But, like food, the Word consumed in this fashion is habit forming. It *forms* us as surely as vitamins and minerals support healthy physical growth. After a while, you find yourself looking forward to this time—wasted with and for God—and I can affirm from my own experience with seminary students that the efforts you make to share this practice with persons within and beyond the faith community will bear fruit. You will be thanked for it.

Disciplining the Imagination: Christian Meditation. For centuries the church has taught that if we wish to know Jesus Christ, the surest means for approaching him is through meditation on passages from the gospels. Typically such a meditation begins with *lectio;* but the type of meditation that arises out of spiritual reading may be relatively structured or free form, relatively verbal or visual. In the practice of Christian forms of meditation over the centuries a variety of techniques have been developed for encountering Christ in the Word, but the day-to-day practice of *lectio* usually results in a very spontaneous, unstructured reflection which may or may not entail actually visualizing the passage as one might watch a scene unfold. But structured or unstructured, verbal or visual, the meditation which arises from spiritual reading should evoke a new hunger in us—the hunger for prayer.

Where should the pastor who has decided to make *lectio* a part of daily devotional life for parishioners begin? Tradition suggests beginning with one of the four gospels and working steadily through it from beginning to end. The following text has proven particularly helpful in religious education contexts for demonstrating how the process of *lectio* works. We begin with a slow and careful reading of the account of the Annunciation from Matthew's gospel (1:18-25).

> Now the birth of Jesus took place in this way. When his mother Mary had been betrothed to Joseph, before they came together she was found to be with child of the Holy Spirit; and her husband Joseph, being a just man and unwilling to put her to shame, resolved to divorce her quietly. But as he considered this, behold, an angel of the Lord appeared to him in a dream, saying, "Joseph, son of David, do not fear to take Mary your wife, for that which is conceived in her is of the Holy Spirit; she will bear a son, and you shall call his name Jesus, for he will save his people from their sins." All this took place to fulfill what the Lord had spoken by the prophet:
> "Behold, a virgin shall conceive and bear a son, and his name shall be called Emman'u-el" (which means, God with us). When Joseph woke from sleep, he did as the angel of the Lord commanded him; he took his wife, but knew her not until she had borne a son; and he called his name Jesus.

Reading through the passage, problems present themselves immediately. Compared to Luke's graceful and relatively elaborate description of the Annunciation, Matthew's account seems brief, straightforward, and not particularly evocative. Furthermore, the material is so familiar, we are likely to dismiss it as too "tired" or uninspiring to be fruitful for a meditation. There may be few if any lines or words in the passage that strike us sufficiently for us to want to repeat or "chew on." Yet it would be a mistake to dismiss it and rummage through the book for something more helpful.

In the first place, the fact that it is Joseph and not Mary who is the center of attention here should give us pause. What changes about the Annunciation when we are invited to see it through Joseph's eyes? We might begin by trying to imagine the deep disappointment and dismay Joseph almost certainly would have felt when he discovered that his young fiancee had dishonored him and herself by becoming pregnant. What must he do? Could another woman ever take her place? What would become of this young girl whose future—like his own dreams—was now shattered? And then, having finally reached a pragmatic decision that seemed like the lesser of two evils—divorce—what new turmoil would Joseph have endured to discover that God had other plans for him and for her? Given that he was not to be spared the humiliation of taking a bride whose virtue appeared compromised, just how reassuring would the angel's words—"that which is conceived in her is of the Holy Spirit; she will bear a son . . . he will save his people from their sins"—have been? Perhaps not very! Was Joseph consulted beforehand? Did anyone ask *him* if he was willing to protect and provide for this peasant girl and her apparently illegitimate offspring? Was it fair that Mary's prior and totally unilateral decision— her faith-filled "yes"—should govern *his* future? What choice was he left but to say "yes" to her "yes"? Was the angel's message so clearly a cause for rejoicing, or might it not have left Joseph filled with perplexity and pain? Was this great privilege in actual fact an invitation to self-sacrifice?

These considerations or reflections constitute a "disciplining" of the imagination. They force us to extend ourselves beyond the confines of our own ego, our own agenda and needs. We know that placing ourselves in another person's shoes, so to speak, enlarges our heart and enables us to see and experience things as we might never otherwise do. The exercise of scriptural meditation changes us by changing our perspective and, as a consequence, we begin to experience emotions and insights that would otherwise be inaccessible to us. Joseph's pain and perplexity, his personal self-sacrifice, now have the power to touch us deeply.

Repentence and Prayer. The new student of *lectio* needs to be helped to see that the biblical text is speaking directly to him or her and that to experience all the promise and possibility offered in the

Word of God, a personal response is required. Here the teaching pastor is uniquely qualified to help shape an authentic response.

The true fruits of a disciplined exercise of the imagination in meditation are repentance and prayer. If the process is allowed to come to fruition we must be willing to be vulnerable before the Word. Where before we were examining it, now we must submit to being examined by it. Our capacity for receiving new truth from *lectio* in general and meditation in particular is linked to our readiness for self-examination and repentance.

It is often at this point—when the emotions become engaged—that we feel moved to address the Lord directly in prayer: Why, Lord? Who was this man who bore the responsibility for raising you? Why was he willing to lay aside his own ambitions of honor and offspring on the basis of a promise that somehow this unknown child—you—would save his people from their sins? Given his unselfish service to the cause of salvation, how is it we know next to nothing about him? Why is so much made of Mary's "yes" when without Joseph's "yes" she could have been put to death or, at best, left utterly destitute? Would I have said "yes" to someone else's—even my best beloved's—"yes" if it meant giving up my own cherished plans for the future? What if it meant swallowing my pride, becoming the object of gossip or, worse yet, the *pity* of my peers? Lord, have I put people I love in that position? Has someone else had to say "yes" to my own, unilaterally delivered "yes" to God? What did it mean for my family or spouse to support me in my call to minister? Have I understood what it cost in terms of dreams deferred?

New truth. New light on our lives, the choices we make, and their impact on those we love; new insight into the ways in which our ministries may depend on the patience, forbearance, and self-sacrifice of others. A reason for repentance. How can we *not* feel moved to make some resolution, take some action in response to this new truth? Is a grand gesture called for, or is all that is required of us some small gift of love, patience, and gratitude for those who had to say "yes" to our "yes." Are we willing, like Joseph, to have a hidden ministry and to remain essentially unknown?

Our reading, meditation, and prayer are not complete until we have faced up to the ethical consequences of "knowing" the Word of God and being known by it. An encounter such as this requires something of us—a new awareness of the difference between assents which are costly and those which come cheap.

STUDYING THE SCRIPTURE

An actual encounter with Christ in the Word moves the individual to repentance, and—whether we like it or not—a humbled, hungry heart is the necessary prerequisite for effective study. Only a humble heart is "teachable." Typically, it is the converted who long to *study* scripture. To affirm this is not to deny that the insights that come from study cannot convert. They do, and when this happens, study becomes just one more act of devotion.

The discipline of study—worthwhile in itself—should ultimately provide a sound superstructure for devotion. It protects pastor and parishioner both from a self-satisfied subjectivity; it opens the mind (often a painful form of surgery) so that more of the truth that makes us free may enter it. It is hard, slow, and not always rewarding work, but those who have become hungry for God will undertake it.

The laity look to their pastors to help them learn more about the Bible; and they are deeply disappointed when the clergy cannot "find the time" to do this on a regular basis. When this happens, the unspoken message sent by the pastor is quite clear: Bible study is not all that important; if the laity want it, they must provide it for themselves. The more determined members of the parish will often attempt to lead their own Bible study groups and classes—sometimes with good effect but more than not with disappointing and frustrating results. In many churches, church school teachers are left to themselves to select materials from catalogues and then to teach them with no other assistance than what a teacher's guide can provide. Few laypersons have either the confidence or the skills needed to function as teachers of scripture, but many would gladly do so if these two vital elements could be supplied.

Most of my church-based teaching has been an attempt to provide these missing elements. Given the reality of the average pastor's job description, it is probably wishful thinking to expect clergy to be available on a regular basis to lead Bible study. Besides, there is a danger here in perpetuating the idea that the laity are essentially incapable of doing responsible religious education on their own.

The issue for the pastor is to decide how best to deploy the time available for instruction in the Bible: *What kind of religious education will serve to equip the laity to carry on effectively in the pastor's absence?* If my own experience can be seen as a reliable guide, then the pastor must not think in terms of teaching only content; the primary task is to teach parishioners *how to study.* Since the scope of this chapter will not permit a thorough discussion of a method for doing this—I refer the interested reader to my earlier work mentioned above[4]—I will confine myself here to discussing a few foundational guidelines and principles found through experience to be fruitful and trustworthy.

1. *The method of study employed will determine the nature of our relationship to scripture.* Just as preaching reveals with stunning clarity the role of scripture in the pastor's own life, so the method of Bible study employed in the parish religious education program will determine whether scripture will play a central or supporting role in the life of the laity. Biblical preaching keeps the role of scripture central by allowing the biblical text to set the agenda—to "have the first word." The time-trusted way of ensuring that this occurs is through an exegetical approach to preaching. The same holds true for Bible study. If the laity are to be taught in such a way that the Bible has the "first word," then the method of study employed should be essentially exegetical. Anyone with seminary training knows what "exegesis" means, but explaining it effectively to the laity requires some skill.

Exegesis is best explained as process of leading or guiding meaning out of a text. It is a bit like unpacking your late great aunt's old steamer trunk stuffed full of interesting—and some not so interesting—things. In the unpacking process, a kind of sifting and sorting occurs; some items are immediately revealing or useful, others are puzzling or apparently inconsequential and must be temporarily set aside. If it is a large trunk, the unpacking will take some time, but the process can be very illuminating. Each new item tells us something more about the person who chose to save it, but we would be well advised not to leap to any hasty conclusions until the sorting and sifting process has been completed. Even then questions may remain to haunt us.

The process of unpacking the trunk may not tell us everything we want to know about our great aunt, but the process itself is rewarding; it puts us in touch with her. Furthermore, it places us in a position of having taken the initiative to go "looking for her," so to speak. Although our aunt may be long gone, we have been *active* in seeking her out; we have not had to wait for someone else to come along and explain everything there was to know about her to us. The process of looking for her has itself been somehow exhilarating, and whenever we have been able to deduce something about her from the evidence—to make a discovery on our own—she has seemed that much more real and vital to us.

A few simple guidelines on how to approach a text exegetically can have an absolutely transformative effect on the experience of Bible study of many parishioners because it places them in an active—rather than a passive—role in relation to the entire process. Given the opportunity, laity can make exciting and satisfying discoveries about the biblical message, and pastors can be certain that the discoveries individual laypersons or groups make on their own *by virtue of a personal investment of time and labor* will be remembered long after any lesson taught by the clergy and will carry significant authority.

2. *Concentrate on a few basic skills and resources.* The point of exegesis is, first, to determine as precisely as possible *what the text says* and only then to draw conclusions about *what the text means.* The sorting and sifting by means of which these tasks are accomplished consists in the exercise of a few basic, but essential skills. These exegetical skills allow one to examine the text's vocabulary and grammatical structure, its literary form, historical context, and theological themes. Careful, critical reading of the text, the ability to compare and contrast different translations, and insight in making important connections between information cited in reference tools are all helpful in discovering what the text says and means. The good news is that basic exegetical skills can be taught with surprisingly effective results to people possessing varying levels of educational background. Moreover, only a few standard reference tools (e.g., a concordance, Bible dictionary, theological wordbook) need be purchased in order to exercise these skills. It is not necessary—or even desirable—for individual laypersons to purchase a full set of commentaries since, typically, this type of resource does the exegetical exploration for us and thus keeps our relationship to scripture essentially passive in nature. Teaching pastors should rid

themselves once and for all of the illusion that what they need to find are the *right kind of materials*; their primary need is to find students with converted, humble hearts. Under these conditions, pastors will mine gold almost anywhere they dig, whereas the best materials available are no guarantee of success.

3. *Have confidence in the laity.* The laity are hungry for knowledge. Many if not most are bright, capable people, and a few will have had more schooling than the pastor has. Even so, the laity often try to sell themselves short—"You know so much; I know so little. . . . We can't possibly have a proper Bible study without professional leadership." If pastors invest their time and attention in their parishioners, they will respond accordingly. Church classrooms and library should be well stocked with multiple copies of basic reference tools and a variety of English language versions of the Bible. Pastors need to encourage the laity to stretch their minds as they wrestle with the text, praise them when they take risks and share questions and insights, and find opportunities to let them use what they've learned in other contexts. The pastor who expects commitment to the study of scripture from parishioners must model that same commitment.

4. *Teach those who will teach.* Instruction in exegetical skills should be made available to anyone in the parish who wishes it. Nonetheless, the pastor has a special responsibility to teach those who have been called to engage in religious education on a volunteer basis. Historically, the clergy have paid little attention to religious education programs in the local church aside from complaining about the low quality of materials and instruction. Considering how formative an experience—for better or worse—church school has been and continues to be, this attitude is shortsighted and reprehensible.

Clergy who serve more than one parish face special problems in relation to supporting volunteer religious educators. However, whether or not pastors are in a position to teach a class themselves or occasionally participate and observe, it is essential that they find ways to minister to the spiritual needs of lay teachers and catechists. I do not speak here of countless "training" sessions; these almost always focus on specific age-related skills and resources. Rather, pastors should be concerned that the people the community relies on to transmit the faith through the teaching of scripture be nurtured *by scripture* on a regular basis. Who sees to it that these faithful ones who are called on week after week to give of themselves have opportunities to be spiritually challenged *at their own level of development?* It is unrealistic to expect that the "teacher's guide" supplied by the curriculum writers will do the trick; its function is simply to help the teacher in presenting the material clearly and effectively. My own experience has taught me that if volunteer religious educators are given an opportunity to explore the biblical material together as a group of adults committed to a common mission, enthusiasm for teaching the Bible to others will be sustained.

5. *Resist the urge to purge people quickly of their biblical literalism.* Heaven help the new pastor who arrives fresh on the job, ready to "enlighten" the laity about what is really to be believed in scripture! What the newcomer to the parish needs to do is to sit down and *listen* to what the parishioners are saying about their faith. The new pastor needs to find out first of all whether—and how—the Bible functions as part of the furniture of the parishioners' minds. What *kind of a relationship* (or lack thereof) already exists between the parish and the Word? The content of that relationship rather than the claims made about the Bible should be the focus of the pastor's attention. A degree of detachment from the vexing issue of biblical literalism and the task that lies ahead can be found if the new pastor is willing to become familiar with the findings of faith development theory and research. Great harm can be done by trying to disabuse people of their apparent "crudities" of interpretation before the necessary conditions for personal growth are present—or before the pastor can claim to something better to offer the faithful believer. And be clear—it must indeed be "better" in the sense that it leads to a purification of and increase in faith.

Again, it is best to let lay people discover for themselves that biblical authority need not always rest in its congruence with "fact" as this is defined by scientists or historians. Over time, the systematic encounter with biblical texts using an exegetical study method will gradually test and ultimately *modify* the claims that they—and the pastor—make for the Bible. Personally, I have found that nothing has helped me more as a religious educator facing sensitive authority issues than a rudimentary understanding of the history of biblical interpretation. The first misconception to go when one begins to learn something about this history is that it was somehow much easier in pre-Enlightenment times to take all that the Bible says at face value. It was *never* easy to swallow the claims that scripture makes on the believer, including those we absolutely must take literally! The issue of biblical literalism is an old issue—as old as the church itself. What is new is the idea that biblical authority should be determined solely on the basis of *factual* accuracy. The modern heresy is one which narrows or equates "truth" with what is empirically verifiable.

There have always been theologians who have employed various demythologizing strategies in interpreting scripture. They have done this in an attempt both to make the Bible accessible to the people and, at the same time, to *preserve* its authority where it would otherwise be rejected. Even a relatively cursory study of the history of biblical interpretation reveals that methods of interpretation change from one period to another and that no age is free from the limitations of cultural conditioning in its encounter with the Bible.

I have always found it helpful to think in terms of two kinds of biblical authority: formal and actual. Claims about the formal authority of scripture will always be more or less contentious, and I, for one, am tired of trying to convince people that they should or should not dispense with certain labels ("infallible," "inerrant," etc.). Instead, I try to focus on what I call "actual" authority, and by this I mean looking at measures of the centrality of scripture's role in the life of an individual or a parish. How much *time* are we willing to invest in praying with or studying scripture? What kind of *changes in character or lifestyle* can we point to as a consequence of our encounter with scripture? To what extent has the individual or collective *imagination* been formed by the images and worldview of scripture? Can pastors point to changes in *corporate worship and witness* that give evidence of the centrality of scripture in our lives? How has the Bible affected the way in which parishes invest their *financial resources*? In the end, these kinds of existential measures mean much more than the labels we use to define either scripture—or ourselves, for that matter.

6. *Finally, always clarify what is at stake theologically.* No matter how interesting or engaging the exegetical process itself may be, the point of the exercise is to discover what *God* is saying to the church

in a given text. Obvious as it may seem, this essential ingredient is often missing in Bible studies of any description, and that means that instead of receiving "bread," hungry people have been given only "stones." It is the Word of and from God that satisfies. Further, the pastor's ability to identify and focus on the theological issues in a passage is the single greatest protection available against unnecessary and unfruitful sparring over authority issues. As an example of what I mean here, let me refer to my earlier work which describes how one might take this approach when working with a Bible story usually relegated to children's classes:

The book of Jonah is one of those Bible narratives, along with the stories of creation, the prophet Daniel, or the virgin birth, typically used to separate the "sheep from the goats." Conservatives usually accept these accounts as historically accurate, while liberals are inclined to consider them pious fictions. The pastor who ventures to teach Jonah, or any one of these controversial texts, is moving into territory dotted with emotional landmines. All too often the discussion will be derailed by questions such as, "Was Jonah actually swallowed by a whale?" "Could a human being really survive for three days and nights under those conditions?" "Can God do *anything*?"

In fact, only the last of these three questions can properly be termed "theological" in nature; the first question is historical—*did it occur?*— while the second is scientific— *could* it occur? The issue as to whether there are any limits on what God can do is an appropriate question to ask in studying the book of Jonah, but it will be considerably more fruitful and personally significant if it is asked in relation to what God accomplishes in the conversion of the Ninevites—a particularly vicious and ruthless population— through a reluctant and vindictive Hebrew prophet. This, too, was a "miracle."

When attention is focused on the "great fish," as it inevitably will be, the pastor needs to stress the *function* the whale plays in relation to God's purposes and Jonah's response to God. Is the whale there to punish or to deliver? How does Jonah's response to being "swallowed" give us a clue to that function? Is the narrator interested primarily in the miraculous delivery or in Jonah's determination to flee God?

The pastor needs to recognize that questions about meanings and relationships are, ultimately, "theological" questions. As such, they can be dealt with without constant reference to the possibility—or lack thereof—of empirical verification. Furthermore, no arguments advanced on either side of the issue are likely to convince those who hold to the opposite view. Positions assumed as to the "truth" of biblical material almost always rest on something deeper and dearer than human logic. In most parish groups or classes there are likely to be laypersons who differ on the historicity of these accounts. Be that as it may, they will all find something personally challenging in the story of a God who requires us to minister to those whom we despise and who dispenses mercy when we call for revenge. It will not be hard, then, for them to understand why Jonah ran away.[5]

A PERSONAL POSTSCRIPT

When I accepted the editor's invitation to write this chapter, I anticipated it would not be particularly difficult since it dealt with a familiar subject. I was wrong, this has not been an easy essay to write. The difficulty lay not in the need to plow some new ground by stressing an experiential way of "knowing" the Bible; rather, it was difficult because I felt, while writing, that if I were to be truthful, I would have to write some things the reader would prefer not to read.

Like many pastors, I would like to believe that a good seminary education, excellent resources, and dedication on our part is sufficient to supply what is wanting in us as interpreters of scripture. Alas, this is only partially true. The essential ingredient of a personal passion for scripture is not something that can be acquired by passing a course. The passing of time and a gain in experience convinces me that without a prior willingnesss on our part to *be known*—to be both ruthlessly and lovingly examined by a Word that is sharper than any two-edged sword—pastors and the people they serve cannot be cured of what ails them.

In their quest for knowledge, the original ancestors of the human race discovered things about themselves they would have gladly not "known." They discovered their own nakedness before God and each other. Even so, as we come to know scripture—and therefore to love it—we will discover things about ourselves and others that

we would rather not "know." We too will discover our own nakedness before God and each other.

Notes

1. Robin Maas, *Church Bible Study Handbook* (Nashville: Abingdon, 1982).
2. Robin Maas, "New Foundations for Biblical Education with Children: A
Challenge to Goldman," PhD dissertation, The Catholic University of America,
(Ann Arbor: University Microfilms, 1985).
3. Jean Leclercq, *The Love of Learning and the Desire for God: A Study of Monastic
Culture*, trans. Catherine Misrahi (New York: Fordham University Press, 1961,
1974).
4. Maas, *Handbook*.
5. Ibid., pp. 177-178.

Bibliography

I. FOR THE DEVOTIONAL USE OF SCRIPTURE

Francis de Sales. *Introduction to the Devout Life*. Trans. by John K. Ryan. New York:
Harper & Row, 1966.
Harper, Steve. *Devotional Life in the Wesleyan Tradition*. Nashville: Upper Room,
1983. See chapter 3, pp. 28-35.
Leclercq, Jean. *The Love of Learning and the Desire for God*. Trans. by Catherine
Misrahi. New York: Fordham University Press, 1974. See pp. 18-22, 87-109.
Mulholland, Robert. *Shaped by the Word*. Nashville: Upper Room, 1985.
Muto, Susan Annette. *Approaching the Sacred: An Introduction to Spiritual Reading*.
Denville, New Jersey: Dimension, 1976.
————. *The Journey Homeward on the Road to Spritual Reading*. Denville, New
Jersey: Dimension, 1977.
————. *Pathways of Spiritual Living*. Garden City, New York: Doubleday Image,
1984. See pp. 63-92.
————. *Renewed at Each Awakening: The Formative Power of Sacred Words*. Denville,
New Jersey: Dimension, 1979.
Wesley, John. "Advice on Spiritual Reading," from the Preface to Wesley's Abridge-
ment of Thomas a Kempis' Treatise of the *Imitation of Christ*, in Frank Whaling,
ed. *John and Charles Wesley*. New York/Mahwah: Paulist Press, 1981. See pp.
88-89.

II. BASIC RESOURCES FOR THE EXEGETICAL STUDY OF SCRIPTURE

Achtemeier, Paul J., ed. *Harper's Bible Dictionary*. San Francisco: Harper & Row,
1985.
Bailey, Lloyd R., ed. *The Word of God: A Guide to English Versions of the Bible*.
Atlanta: Knox, 1982.
Bauer, J. B., ed. *Encyclopedia of Biblical Theology: The Complete Sacramentum Verbi*.
New York: Crossroads, 1981.

Cruden, Alexander. *Concordance to the Old and New Testaments*. Editions by several publishers available in hard and soft covers. Be sure to use a complete rather than an abridged version.

Cully, Iris V., and Cully, Kendig Brubaker. *A Guide to Biblical Resources*. Wilton, Connecticut: Morehouse-Barlow, 1981.

Gehman, Henry S. ed. *The New Westminster Dictionary of the Bible*. Philadelphia: Westminster, 1970.

Hayes, John H., and Holladay, Carl R. *Biblical Exegesis: A Beginner's Handbook*. Atlanta: Knox, 1982.

Maas, Robin. *Church Bible Study Handbook*. Nashville: Abingdon, 1982.

May, Herbert G. *Oxford Bible Atlas*, 2nd ed. New York: Oxford University Press, 1974.

Richardson, Alan. *A Theological Wordbook of the Bible*. New York: Macmillan, 1950.

Strong, James. *Strong's Exhaustive Concordance*. Editions by several publishers available in hard and soft covers.

Throckmorton, Burton H., Jr. *Gospel Parallels*. New York: Nelson, 1967.

Young, Robert. *Analytical Concordance to the Bible, revised*. Grand Rapids, Michigan: Eerdmans, 1955.

III. EXEGETICAL APPROACHES TO BIBLE STUDY

Brueggemann, Walter. *The Creative Word: The Canon as a Model for Biblical Education*. Philadelphia: Fortress, 1982.

Robinson, Wayne Bradley. *The Transforming Power of the Bible*. New York: Pilgrim, 1984.

Wink, Walter. *Transforming Bible Study*. Nashville: Abingdon, 1980.

Yoder, Perry. *From Word to Life: A Guide to the Art of Bible Study*. Scottdale, Pennsylvania: Herald, 1982.

IV. HISTORICAL, CULTURAL, AND THEOLOGICAL FACTORS IN THE INTERPRETATION OF SCRIPTURE

Barr, James. *The Scope and Authority of the Bible*. Philadelphia: Westminster, 1980.

Grant, Robert M., with Tracy, David. *A Short History of the Interpretation of the Bible*, 2nd ed. Revised and enlarged. Philadelphia: Fortress, 1984.

Greenspahn, Frederick E. *Scripture in the Jewish and Christian Traditions: Authority, Interpretation, Relevance*. Nashville: Abingdon, 1982.

Hagen, Kenneth, et. al. *The Bible in the Churches: How Different Christians Interpret the Scriptures*. New York: Paulist, 1985.

Kung, Hans, and Moltmann, Jürgen, eds. *Conflicting Ways of Interpreting the Bible*. New York: Concilium, Seabury, 1980.

Rogers, Jack B., and McKim, Donald K. *The Authority and Interpretation of the Bible*. San Francisco: Harper & Row, 1979.

Smart, James D. *The Cultural Subversion of the Biblical Faith*. Philadelphia: Westminster, 1977.

5

The Spiritual Education
of God's People: Pastoral
Burden or Opportunity?

JOANMARIE SMITH

If and when pastors get the opportunity to reflect on the image in their title "shepherd," it must seem as if a cruel joke is being played on them. The shepherd is pictured as having long days in grass-filled pastures, leisurely guarding and guiding animals. Could that picture be further removed from the too often frenetic pace and always well-peopled environment in which today's pastors ply their calling? Having neither the shepherds' time and space nor their comparatively low-level responsibility, pastors in this era might be expected to view the call to intensify their own spirituality and promote the spiritual development of their congregations as one more task among others which will strain their resources toward burnout.

But that view would be unfortunate because more than any other task in the pastor's job description, the spiritual education of God's people offers the most fertile opportunity for pastors to shape their lives in a more humane way while promoting a sensitivity to and relish for the Divine Presence among the people in their parishes. The difference in viewpoints turns on the way one conceives of spirituality, God's presence in creation, and spiritual leadership.

In this chapter I will speak of spirituality as encompassing all of life, God as saturating existence, and leadership as an informing activity. I intend to demonstrate that the spiritual education of God's people is not a burden but a unique opportunity for personal and congregational growth. Therefore, I shall focus on the vision of spirituality, the vision the pastor as religious educator brings to his or her ministry, and how that vision can take root in specific ways.

SPIRITUALITY AS LIFE

The opposite of spirit is not matter; it is death. Our spirituality is not a dimension of our life; it is our life.

Our Western images have been so influenced by our Greek heritage that we sometimes forget our more fundamental heritage which is Jewish. In Hebrew, *ruah, neshamah,* or spirit is the life-breath. If you have ever been to Israel you may have noticed that people there still refer to souls rather than people. So, for example, a taxi driver might refer to so many souls living in a housing development you were passing. Apparently, the identification of soul with the whole person, of spirit with life itself, is still operative among the Jews.

Our tendency is to think of spirituality as some privatized culti-vation of the soul and to think of the soul as some part of a person as in "I have a body and *soul.*" A more accurate statement would be "I *am* my body and more; soul is the be-ing, the live-ing, the is-ing of my I."

Let me give you an example of what is meant here. Gabriel Marcel, the French philosopher, was an ambulance driver during World War I. Part of his job was to report the death of soldiers to their families. He realized after he had done this a few times, that the terrible grief he witnessed was not related to any descriptions which he had in his dispatches. They were not grieving over the loss of the person's height or weight, or education, or even his name. What they agonized over was the loss of the be-ing, the is-ing, the existence of their son, or husband, or brother.[1] What they missed was the loved one's soul.

Spiritual formation addresses the shape this life, our entire life should take. Foundationally the questions to be addressed are: Whence this life? Thence this life? Why this life? The answers ground the spirituality found in any religious tradition. Almost all traditions answer "from God, to God, and for God." But the life, death, and resurrection of Jesus the Christ characterizes this God in a particular way and puts a stunning spin on the answer to an additional question, Where is God?

GOD'S PRESENCE IN CREATION

God is transcendent of course but immanence has always been a central note of that transcendence. The Hebrew scriptures report the radical nature of God's indwelling.

We have already remarked that *ruah, neshamah,* or spirit is the life-breath. But here we note that it is not just any breath or life; it is the breath of God; that is, it is the Godhead which trembles over the water in the opening verses in Genesis (1:2b). It is God's breath, life, spirit that animates, ensouls *ha adam* the earth creature who becomes *ish* and *ishah,* man and woman (Genesis 2:8). The Psalmist reminds us "that when God sends out this spirit (God's breath), we are created and the face of the earth is renewed" (Ps. 104:30). And the Psalmist also reminds us that when God withdraws this breath, we die; we return to dust (Ps. 104:29). The same theme is in Job. "The Spirit of God has made me and the breath of the Almighty gives me life" (Job 33:4). "If God should take back this spirit, if God should withdraw God's breath, all flesh would perish together and humans would return to dust" (Job 34:14). God is present to us as the life that is our life.

The Christian tradition continues to treasure that insight, and if anything, to expand the notion of God's presence. Thomas Aquinas, addressing the question of God's presence to creation, used the analogy of sunlight in lighted air. Just as the sun is present as the light of lighted air, so is God (who is Be-ing, Esse in Thomistic theology) present as the be-ing or is-ing of everything that is.[2] But be-ing is that which is most fundamental about anything that is, as Marcel recongized. Therefore we can conclude that God is the ultimate reality of anything that is real—even as the sun is light of anything that is lighted. What Thomas described metaphysically, Augustine had described mystically centuries before when he wrote "God is more me than I am myself,"[3] reiterating in turn what Genesis had revealed: Our life is *ruah,* God's life.

The doctrine of the Incarnation forestalls the temptation to view

God's indwelling dualistically. Any attempt to separate is-ing from that which is, or life from that which is alive is subverted in the doctrine which proclaims a God that is disclosed in flesh, stuff, in the elements of our world. If the Incarnation, realized in Jesus the Christ, is a clue to the rest of reality rather than an exception, then the entire universe is the theater of God's manifestation, is theophanic.

In the light of the convictions that spirituality encompasses all of life and that all of reality is saturated with Deity, I do not propose adding programs of spiritual formation over and above the tasks and programs that already define the pastor's work. The spiritual education of God's people may not always call for classes that address the standard items in the spiritual disciplines: prayer, fasting, Bible study, meditation, and so on. Although, obviously, such programs may be involved and can be either led or encouraged by the pastor as a natural outgrowth of a deep commitment to the spiritual development of the congregation (see resources at the end of the chapter). More fundamentally, it calls for a basic stance toward this spirit/life. The pastor can educate toward this stance by excercising an informing leadership.

PASTORAL LEADERSHIP AS INFORMING

Somewhere along the line the term *informing* came to mean the giving of information. That is not how I am using it here, nor is it the original meaning. To inform meant to give form, life, or soul to something or someone. To animate. God informs the void in Genesis. God's breath is the animating principle. God inspires creation into existence. That would seem to be the ultimate leadership: to cause to come into being. God creates by hovering and breathing, by being present to and inspiring.

I am not using "inspiring" in its most demanding sense. I am using it as almost interchangeable with breathing because I am claiming that there is a perspective that one can bring to one's schedule *as it is* which will have an educational effect. Simply by breathing as it were (but breathing out of the convictions that spirituality is an all-encompassing mode of being alive and that God is radically present in this time and in this place), spiritual formation can happen in a congregation.

There is more than one way for pastors to exercise an informing leadership. There is the animation, inspiration one gives in one's life and there is the inspiration given through one's life.

INFORMING AN INFORMING LEADERSHIP

For centuries the monastic, contemplative vocation was considered a specific calling for a few persons. The Reformation, among other revolutions in insight, returned to the gospel view that solitary prayer is everyone's sweet yoke and light burden.

When we look at Jesus' life in the gospels, we note that only one class on prayer is recorded. On the other hand, the schedule of his public life is shot through with periods of solitary prayer, beginning with the prayer retreat which preceded that last period of his life. We know that he took part in the liturgical prayer life of any lay Jewish male of his time as did the disciples. The disciples' request for a prayer class then must not have stemmed from this shared prayer experience of which they were well aware, it must have been inspired by the paradox in his schedule. Such a busy man, so much to do, so little time to do it, so many prescribed prayers and rituals—and yet he regularly leaves them, leaves the work, and prays alone. What must *this* prayer be?

If God is the life of our life, if God surrounds us like the light of lighted air, if God is more us than we are ourselves, attending to that Divine Presence within and without us would appear to be as necessary and organic as eating and sleeping or perhaps, more in keeping with the emphasis in this chapter, as necessary and organic as breathing. Occasional difficulties in eating and sleeping may only inconvenience us, but their persistence signals disturbing problems. Difficulties in breathing are almost always life-threatening emergencies. Moreover, we expect to, and most often do, look forward to eating and sleeping. We know that we cannot put off the need to eat and sleep too long, no matter what unanticipated interruptions and crises warrant postponement. We must have nourishment and rest to survive, not to mention thrive.

If attending to the Divine Being is similiar to these activities, why does it not seem more organic? Why does so much effort seem to be involved? Why are our intentions to pray and meditate, for example, so easily subverted by the first good excuse to put off our resolution. Why is silence with the Deity so often a straining experience. I offer as one possible reason that we have not been taught to expect to be delighted by God.

Recall how very young children are taught to relish eating. The parents taste the child's food, smack their lips, and tempt the child to the delicious experience they offer. The psalmist tempts us similarly: "Taste and see that God is good . . ." (Ps. 34:8). When Henri Nouwen, a well-known writer on spirituality, was asked the usual question, "How did you find time for prayer?" his answer indicated that he had succumbed to the psalmist's invitation. "Once practiced methodically, finding time for solitary prayer and contemplation is not the problem, the time is eagerly anticipated. And, instead of postponement, the question becomes how much time is too much time spent in solitary prayer."[4]

In my classes on spirituality I exhort the participants to put the burden of our experiencing God as delightful on God. Revelation is God's responsibility not ours. We just have to be there. Yet there are ways that we can be there, can attend the Divine Presence that work with our natural inclinations and not against them. To paraphrase a central tenet of Thomism, "God leads us by desire."[5]

Which suggests another reason that we find it so hard to find time to stop and be God-aware with regularity; namely, we have such a narrow view of prayer. When we consider all the different kinds of food our planet provides to nourish us, we should expect at least as many varieties of prayer which can nourish our appreciation of the Divine Presence.

Anthony de Mello tells the story of a fellow Jesuit who was told by a Hindu guru, "Concentrate on your breathing." His friend followed the guru's instructions, aware that our breath is the source and index of our being alive, of our God-ing. De Mello concludes his story by assuring us that his friend "discovered in this exercise a depth and satisfaction and spiritual nourishment that he hadn't found in many, many hours he had devoted to prayer over a period of many years."[6]

Not that this prayer form would be everyone's cup of tea. But that is my point, one need not be trapped into thinking that any particular form is *de rigeur*. Prayer is whatever nurtures *our* God-awareness. Different kinds of prayer may appeal on different days or different periods of one's life as a pastor or in the lives of members of the faith community.

SPIRITUAL GROWTH THROUGH PRAYER

The following approaches to spiritual depth first of all are essential for pastors as persons in their own prayer life. Second, these approaches and the methods suggested can be taught to members of the congregation either through modeling or through natural extensions of the pastor's teaching ministry.

Prayer is usually divided into three broad types: meditation (thinking about God), discursive prayer (speaking with God), and contemplation (be-ing in God). Actually, we will see that these prayer types frequently break in upon each other.

Meditation: It is interesting to note that the history of language relates medical and meditate to the same Latin root, meaning *to see.* That being the case, it should not surprise us that healing, wholeness, and holy are similarly related. The beginnings of our language reflect a perspective that we now have to work at achieving.

In meditative prayer we take something, a reading, a person, a piece of music, a piece of nature for reflective study, perhaps as one would study the writings, features, or belongings of a loved one.

It goes without saying that the scriptures are a favorite subject of meditation. Studying the gospels, people have found it fruitful to place themselves in the scene or story by becoming a character in the scene, either one mentioned by scripture or one created for the meditation. Gauge the time of year and time of day. Feel the atmosphere. Note the colors. Hear the sounds around you. See the persons involved as vividly as possible. Then, enter the story.

Sample: Prayerfully read the story of Zaccheus (Luke 19:1-10). Imagine the time of year, of day, and so on (see above). Now place yourself in the scene. Who are you? Why are you there? What do you know about Jesus? What are people around you saying about him? As the crowd indicates his arrival, what are your feelings? What is your attitude toward Zaccheus as you see him scamper up a tree? How do you feel as Jesus speaks to him? Are you among those who have supper with them? In the house you see Jesus looking at you in a questioning way as he has just looked at Zaccheus. You respond to this look. What do you say? What does Jesus say in return?

There is an infinite number of variations on this scene that would constitute a meditation on the story. I offer this version merely as an example of a way to come to a fresh study of scripture[7] and to point out how readily we slip into discursive prayer (speaking to Jesus).

The effort and energy required by such a sustained engagement with the scripture may be more than we can manage on any particular day. Locking ourselves into a particular prayer form, even, or especially, one we have found fruitful, can be the occasion of our putting off our deliberate and solitary prayer sessions. If we are too weary to consider going into a gospel in the way I have described and we do not have other less-demanding ways of praying, ways that are more congenial to our mood at the time, we will soon feel that we have no time.

Perhaps the most effortless way to meditate is simply to let our mind wander. This "exercise" may seem downright lazy, but Charles Peirce, an American philosopher, suggests that such meanderings constitute a "Neglected Argument for the Reality of God."[8] It is his contention that we will invariable "bump" into the Reality that is God. Such bumping is inevitable if the universe is saturated with Deity. "Where can we 'meander,' and you are not there?" (Ps. 139:7)

Of course, implied in the suggestion that we can meditate on nothing in particular is also the suggestion that we can meditate on anything in particular and it can be prayer. Having intentionally placed ourselves in the context of God's omnipresence, meditation on any person, situation, or event can become the way of reading a fifth gospel.

Discursive prayer: We are undoubtedly most familiar with this prayer form. Hymns, prayers of petition, liturgical prayer whether of the Hours or of the Eucharist and other sacraments, involve verbalizing our God-awareness. Perhaps, because it is so familiar, the form can sometimes seem empty, tedious, and least likely to promote our appetite to taste God. Let me offer two strategies that can vitalize discursive prayer for pastors in their own spiritual growth or for use in the spiritual development of the laity.

Preparation: Actually it is a misnomer to speak of preparing for prayer. If the essence of prayer is the turning of our minds and hearts to God, the very intention to do so becomes prayer. But my point is that we cannot spend too much time ordering our bodies and environments. I sometimes offer as a rule of thumb that we should spend as much time "preparing" for prayer as we do praying.

The most time-honored way of preparing our bodys/psyches is through relaxation exercises. Placing ourselves in a comfortable position in the first place, then attending to the different parts of our bodies, consciously relaxing each part will dispose us to engage God more deliberately and delightfully. Deep breathing exercises contribute to this disposition.

Memorization: A second suggestion I offer is to memorize some prayers. There is something of a prejudice against memorized prayer forms; they smack of formulas. I rather think of them in terms of my experience of Gospel Choirs. The choir members almost never have the music in front of them. They sing everything from memory. Or, as we so insightfully say, they know the hymns by heart. To know something by heart is to be shaped by it. One can pour oneself into the discourse without distraction. One can pray until one is prayed as the Zen Buddhists might phrase it and as the singers in a Gospel Choir can testify.

Memorized prayers and hymns become like mantras which can carry us into the heart of God-awareness. The expression "I love you" provides an analogy. Too often used in the most banal and thoughtless way, in a certain electric context the phrase can raise a relationship to a new level of intensity and commitment. Similarly, the expression "I'm sorry" can be an unthinking convention offered upon stepping in front of a person. But "I'm so sorry" can also appropriately convey one's profound sympathy in the presence of another's tragedy. So too, a familiar prayer, recited by heart can capture the fullness of that heart in an exchange with the Deity.

As in meditative prayer, God need not be the direct object of our study, so God need not be the direct object of our discourse either. The psalmists have taught us that engaging the mountains, the inhabitants of the seas, other people—even talking to ourselves— can be authentic prayer. The distinguishing note seems to lie in the context in which this takes place. An abiding recognition that in God we live and move and have our being is the context for prayer.

Contemplation: Meditative and discursive prayer are frequently punctuated by contemplative moments. The experience would be similar to studying a photograph or a letter of a loved one and periodically giving oneself over to the wordless joy of loving and being loved by that person. Or it might be comparable to engaging in an intense conversation with a beloved person, perhaps on a topic far removed from the mutual love which is shared, and being overwhelmed and silenced during the conversation by sheer delight in the other.

Contemplation is the simple be-ing in God. The operative word is simple. Contemplative prayer is uncluttered by words or images. This prayer is the most delightful form of engagement with, to, and in God as it is the most delightful form of engagement in any relationship. But, as in any relationship, it is pure gift. We can predispose ourselves for the gift however by practicing a contemplative attitude. Giving ourselves over to the experience of beauty, allowing ourselves to be overcome as we watch sunsets or seas, studying paintings or poetry, or listening to music are good ways for predisposing ourselves.

In a sense, everything that I have been describing as prayer is more accurately described as disposing ourselves for prayer. All prayer is a gift as Paul reminds us. "We do not know how to pray" (Romans 8:26). Our contribution is to Be There—not straining, just being present and presuming that prayer is a gift that God is delighted to give.

Then grounded and rooted in the conviction that the universe is theophanic we can go about our business.

AN INFORMING PASTORAL LEADERSHIP AT WORK

My thesis is that the spiritual formation of a congregation is not one more task among others that falls on the pastor's shoulders; rather it is a perspective on all tasks and one which can go a long way toward making a pastor's life more humanely organized. The crux of this perspective is that every work of the pastor should have the character of worship, classically described as remembering, celebrating, and believing. That is to say, that every meeting at which the pastor presides, every class that is taught, every visitation made, and obviously every worship service conducted should evidence these moments of remembering, celebrating, and believing.

Always the ground on which we stand is holy, always in God, as we teach and visit and have our meetings.

REMINDING AND RE-MEMBERING
AS PASTORS AND PEOPLE

There is long tradition in Christianity of regularly reminding ourselves that our God is Emmanuel—God with us. For years in the convent, whenever a clock struck the hour, a sister would announce to whomever was present, "Let us remember the presence of God." To which the reply was, "And adore the Divine Majesty." At six o'clock in the morning, at noon, and again at six in the evening churches rang the bells in a special pattern called the Angelus. In Catholic neighborhoods up through the late sixties, it was not uncommon to see lay people stop in the streets and recite the Angelus prayer which reminds us of the Incarnation "made known by the message of an angel," Christ's passion and death, and the glory of his resurrection. Ordained clergy and most members of religious orders in the Catholic church were required to read, recite, or chant the Divine Office each day. Beginning before dawn and continuing until just before retiring for the day, the schedule was/is an extended way of "Remembering the Presence of God and Adoring the Divine Majesty." The obligation is no longer so stringently imposed on clergy and professed members of religious orders. Interestingly, many Protestants have picked up the practice now called the Liturgy of the Hours.

If the church bells have been silenced in the interest of quieter neighborhoods and later sleeping hours, if our clocks rarely chime, we are in need of other reminders of whose world this is. If the sun and seasons no longer mark our day, we must find the ways our days are marked and use those as reminders. These days seem to be blocked out in tasks. Certainly a pastor's time is. All of which may be a roundabout way of calling for such reminders as we begin a meeting, a class, or a visitation or, in other words, an opening prayer.

While this is not a revolutionary idea and in fact many pastors do just that, what I think is called for is an opening prayer in the context in which I have just presented it—a reminder that before all else we are called to adoration, worship. That notion is sometimes lost in a prayer for the successful outcome of the task at hand.

Having set the context, pastors would do well to solicit others to prepare future opening prayers, reinforcing the realization that worship is not the private domain of the ordained. In this way, pastors working in a sensitive way with lay leaders, can slowly transform prayer times from perfunctory exercises to experiences of personal and corporate renewal and depth.

But it is not enough to remind ourselves of the presence of God as we attempt to put a worship cast on our meetings, classes, and visitations. We must also re-member. The opposite of remembering is not forgetting, it is dis-membering. After we remind ourselves of the Real Presence, but before we do anything else, I think we must re-member. We must recognize that the people attending are not coming *to* church, their coming together *is* church. But before a group can become a community the members must see each other, hear each other aside from the embodied positions taken at a meeting, or the questions and responses of a classmate. Therefore, time spent on seeing and hearing one another in a completely nonthreatening atmosphere contributes to the worshipful character of the event.

So-called ice-breakers can be a good use of this time. I call the exercise I use a "Re-membering Liturgy" and that has made all the difference. The name signals a whole other priority and purpose for what is being done. I resist ice-breaker exercises, and I find that many people do, although I usually admit, after the fact, that they accomplish the purpose of warming up the atmosphere for what-ever will follow. A re-membering liturgy has the same effect but as a by-product. Its purpose is to call the church to order, to re-member the body of Christ, to re-cognize the community of faith, to shape a liturgical assembly.

The pattern is always the same. On a blackboard or newsprint I write a fill-in-the-blanks statement like "I'm _____ and one of my favorite foods is _____ . People can always "pass." But few do as the questions are so bland and relatively impersonal. As the group becomes more and more of a community, the questions can become less impersonal ("_____ and the last time I cried was when _____") but always the persons name themselves and they always have the option of skipping any particular question which they find intrusive.

CELEBRATION

Celebration is the unique and specifying activity of a community. A group may come together for a number of purposes: to decide whether a new roof should be put on the church building, to learn about the synoptic gospels, to consider opening a soup kitchen. To the extent that the group is a community however, regardless of what it is doing, it will have a celebratory character.

There are at least three indexes of this character: a democratic environment, a special attitude toward time, a sense of fulfillment.[9]

A Democratic Environment: There are no bosses at a celebration. There may be hosts and hostesses, there may be facilitators, but there are no bosses. A celebration is not necessarily anti-authoritarian. Institutions and organizations may require a line of command, but such lines are antithetical to community. Which is not to say that there is no leadership, but it is the informing leadership which I have been describing and which is everyone's responsibility. Pastoral leaders can model through their affirmation of participatory democracy but efforts to control the outcomes can be counterproductive.

A Special Attitude Toward Time: Worship requires a stately pace. Nothing subverts this requirement faster than a crowded agenda at meetings or too many objectives for a class session. One or two significant agenda items for a meeting, one or at most two objectives for a class session are more than sufficient.

Preparation is the key to achieving a stately, worshipful pace. Much that occurs in meetings can be done outside meetings. Information can be distributed before time, and its study presumed. The presumption will prove to be accurate if the meetings transpire under that rubric. Most pastors have learned that nothing makes people show up on time for meetings as much as the conviction that the meeting will begin on time. So, nothing will make people prepare for meetings as much as the previous experience that such preparation will not be duplicated. Persons can be polled by phone on less-significant decisions. Explanations that offer the rationale for such procedures can foster the preparation and the polling.

Classes do not, or rather should not, offer a similar temptation to clutter. Experienced teachers operate under the conviction that less is more. They trim their expectations and those of the class to *less* than what is feasible. Inexperienced teachers usually learn the hard way that more is less. Rushing disturbs the environment for learning and teaching as well as for worship.

Finally, preparation that has a special attitude toward time plans a closure to the meeting or class. Opening and closing are more appropriate to worship than beginning and ending. Different persons can take responsibility for reminding the community what they have been about, what they are about.

A *Sense of Fulfillment*: In fact this note is directly related to the special attitude toward time. Most meetings and classes and even visitations are instrumental. That is, they occur to achieve some purpose beyond themselves. They are convened to achieve this purpose within a certain time frame. This puts the achievement and the clock in a race against each other. If the achievement has occurred before the clock runs out, there is a great sense of satisfaction. If the clock runs out first, there is frustration. If they both get to the finish line together there is relief.

But community is not an instrumental experience, it is consummatory, fulfilling in itself. As we do not pray, nor listen to a symphony nor watch a sunset to achieve something, so we do not love others instrumentally—for some purpose beyond our loving them. Communion, the experience of community, is a peak experience of existence, a foretaste of shalom. Therefore, in a meeting or class which is an authentic community there will be a certain distance from the race between the achievement of objectives and the running out of time. There will be some unspoken sense that there is fulfullment present regardless of the articulated purpose of the group at this moment.

Wonderfully, this very relaxed attitude contributes to the achievement of the objectives. Relieved of the burden of seeking fulfillment through achievement seems to free the imagination and creativity of a community to accomplish the task it has set itself. Moreover, this seems to happen without the pressure and rush that so often accompanies the attempts to complete a task.

BELIEVING

The belief that structures Christian worship is not some vapid hope in the significance and power of past events. *"Anamnesis"* captures the uniqueness of this believing. Central to the eucharist, the preeminent worship service of Christians, *anamnesis* is a Greek word which is usually translated as remembrance or memorial. Actually the term refers to an almost untranslatable Semitic concept by which an event is not so much recalled as made present. In an authentic Christian worship service the presence of the saving life, death, and resurrection of Jesus the Christ is always re-presented.

But perhaps at this point the belief that dominates the readers' thoughts is that the spiritual education of the congregation that has been outlined here is either too easy to be true or too idealistic to be possible. The portrait of worshipful meetings and classes does not take into account the perennial disruptiveness of Bobby X or the congenital irascibility of Ms. Y. The conviction of a universe saturated with Deity does not account for evil.

The only theology that can be logically reconciled with sin and evil is a deism which portrays God as a creator no longer present or interested in this corrupt creation. However, the Incarnation, passion, death, and resurrection contradicts deism. Yet belief in these events deepens the scandal of evil by portraying our ultimate experience of God's presence to the universe, Jesus the Christ, as defeated and overcome by evil. God does not take away the suffering and pain of evil but shares it. But then there is the resurrection, belief in which persuades us that sin and evil need not have the last word. Moreover, in the resurrection we are convinced that somehow suffering and pain can contribute to the final impotence of evil. It is these beliefs that permeate and shape Christian worship. Through these beliefs we can discover that spiritual formation is neither too easy to be true, nor too idealistic to be possible, but easy *enough* to be possible.

SPIRITUALITY: A MEANS TO AN END

Life is sacred, but it is not an end in itself. That is the reason, for example, that it has long been an accepted moral principle that one need not take extraordinary means to preserve it. Life is a means to an end. To eat and drink simply to sustain our life is a perversion of life. Our life, imaging God's life, is for others. And if spirituality and life are coextensive, then our spirituality is for others.

The spiritual formation of a total congregation as well as its individual members is for others. We are all too aware that this point is often lost in our education efforts.

The picture of John Newman, the captain of a slave ship, retiring to his cabin, over packed and suffocating human beings, to meditate on the Bible[10] warns us that solitary prayer can degenerate to privatized devotions that have no connection to the saving life, death, and resurrection of Jesus.

The caricature of "worship as usual" that took place all over the world while the Holocaust was being perpetrated warns us that the very event which should sensitize us to injustice can be used to mesmerize us so that we are inured to mind-boggling inhumanity. To make present the saving acts of Jesus the Christ and be indifferent to the continuing crucifixions which take place in our families, in our towns, and on this planet is a hypocrisy that calls to heaven for vengeance. "Those who say they love God and hate their neighbor are liars"(1 John 4:20).

In Jesus' class on prayer, after reminding ourselves of the presence of God, we are enjoined to plead that God's realm will be established, that God's best plans for this universe will be achieved everywhere. To the extent that we foster these plans, to the extent that we foment these plans, to that extent can we judge that we have been spiritually formed.

In the beginning of this chapter, I insisted that the spiritual education of a congregation need not and should not be an additional burden on a pastor's time. But I cannot promise that there will not be a redistribution of a pastor's time. Henri Nouwen says that to contemplate is to see; to minister is to make visible.[11] Pastors who contemplate the vision of shalom may feel pressed to reshape their ministry the more urgently to make the realm of God more visible.

Notes

1. Sam Keen, Gabriel Marcel (London: Carey Kingsgate Press, 1966), p. 8.

2. Summa Theologica, I, q. 8 a.1.

3. Confessions, Bk. III, Ch. 6 (11).

4. Cited by Thomas Morrison, "Readings in Spirituality," The Chicago Theological Register 72: 3 (Fall, 1982), p. 43.

5. Summa Theologica, I q.105 a.3 ad.1

6. Anthony de Mello, *Sadhana* (Garden City, N.Y.: Image Books, 1984), p. 8.

7. Actually, this is hardly a new way of praying the scriptures. Ignatius of Loyola proposed such a method. See *The Spiritual Exercises of St. Ignatius*, trans. Anthony Mottola (Garden City, N.Y.: Doubleday, 1964). For a contemporary use of this method see Carolyn Stahl's *Opening to God* (Nashville: The Upper Room, 1977).

8. *The Collected Works of Charles Sanders Peirce*, ed. Charles Hartshorne and Paul Weiss, 6 Vols. (Cambridge, Mass.: Harvard University Press, 1935), Vol. VI, pars. 452-467.

9. Gloria Durka and Joanmarie Smith, "Community: An Aesthetic Perspective," in *Aesthetic Dimensions of Religious Education*, ed. Gloria Durka and Joanmarie Smith (New York: Paulist, 1979), pp. 99-106.

10. Cited in Matthew Fox, *On Becoming a Musical Mystical Bear* (New York: Paulist, 1972), p. 2.

11. Cited in William J. Bausch, *The Christian Parish* (Notre Dame, Ind.: Fides/Claretian, 1980), p. 148.

Bibliography

GENERAL INTRODUCTIONS

Foster, Richard J. *The Celebration of Discipline: The Path to Spiritual Growth*. San Francisco: Harper & Row, 1978.

Foster, a Quaker, has written a classic and easily read text that illuminates the traditional disciplines of prayer, fasting, simplicity, solitude, etc., through the use of scripture. A study guide has been published to accompany the book.

Harris, Maria. *The Dance of the Spirit: Seven Stations of Women's Spirituality*. New York: Bantam Books, 1989.

One of the few general introductions to spirituality written from a woman's perspective. The book contains many exericises that can be done alone or with others.

Nouwen, Henri J. M. *Reaching Out: The Three Movements of the Spiritual Life*. Garden City, New York: Doubleday, 1975.

A basic theology of the spiritual life that is practical enough to provide suggestions for implementation.

EDUCATION AND SPIRITUALITY

Cully, Iris V. *Education for Spiritual Growth*. San Francisco: Harper & Row, 1984.

A broad, ecumenical survey of topics in spirituality which includes a theology, a history of the dominant traditions, and descriptions of various methods.

Palmer, Parker J. *To Know As We Are Known: A Spirituality of Education*. San Francisco: Harper & Row, 1983.

Palmer elucidates in most engaging and practical ways his thesis that all education is spiritual formation.

Lee, James Michael. *The Spirituality of the Religious Educator.* Birmingham, Alabama: Religious Education Press, 1985.

A probing of the optional approaches to spirituality today, including Western contemplative, process, ecumenical, Jesuit, Eastern, etc., and what these mean for the religious educator.

Mid-Life and Old Age

Fischer, Kathleen. *Winter Grace: Spirituality for Later Years.* New York: Paulist, 1985.

This book describes a prophetic spirituality for those whose life must be lived counter to a youth-oriented culture. There are numerous suggestions for prayer, the healing of memories, and ways the elderly can minister to the community.

Brennan, Anne and Janice Brewi. *Mid-Life Spirituality.* New York: Crossroad, 1988.

A readable guide to the journey of our middle years, loosely based on Jung's theories. Many exercises enrich the text.

Children and Youth

Burke, John, O.P. *Bible Sharing Youth Retreat: Manual for Retreat Team.* Washington, D.C.: Word of God Institute, 1984.

Explicit instructions and guidelines for five, five-and-a-half-hour sessions. Includes several types of prayers, a skit, recreation, a letter to oneself, and an evaluation of the retreat.

Doyle, Aileen A. *Youth Retreats: Creating Sacred Space for Young People.* Winona, Minnesota: St. Mary's College Press, 1986.

Ten retreat programs including outlines, materials needed, and other helpful hints. Easily adapted to contexts other than prayer retreats.

Hesch, John B. *Prayer and Meditation for Middle School Kids.* New York: Paulist, 1984.

Offers guidelines and more than one hundred exercises designed to introduce young people to different forms of prayer.

Smith, Judy Gattis. *Developing a Child's Spiritual Growth Through Sight, Sound, Taste, Touch, and Smell.* Nashville: Abingdon, 1983.

Attempts to bring children to a God-awareness through a discovery of their five senses.

Stone, J. David. *Spiritual Growth in Youth Ministry: Practical Models to Help Your Young People (and You) Grow Closer to God.* New York: Group Books, 1985.

Stresses relationships as the key to spiritual growth.

Family Spirituality

Boyer, Ernest, Jr. *A Way in the World: Family Life as Spiritual Discipline.* New York: Harper & Row, 1984.

Shows how "life at the center," that is, in the family, is as authentic as the spiritual life "at the edge," that is, in the monastery. An appendix describes family-centered exercises.

Leckey, Dolores. *The Ordinary Way: A Family Spirituality.* New York: Crossroad, 1982.

Takes the classical monastic categories and applies them to family living.

JOURNALING

Simons, George F. *Keeping Your Personal Journal.* New York: Ballantine Books, 1986.

Valuable for beginners as well as seasoned journal keepers. Contains many exercises that can be done alone or in a group.

Cargas, Henry J. and Radley, Roger J. *Keeping a Spiritual Journal.* Garden City, New York: Doubleday, 1981.

Designed especially for youth, it provides an easily followed program for journaling.

SPIRITUAL DIRECTION

Dyckman, Katherine Marie, and Carroll, L. Patrick. *Inviting the Mystic, Supporting the Prophet: An Introduction to Spiritual Direction.* New York: Paulist, 1981.

Excellent introduction to the art of spiritual direction.

Barry, William and Connoly, William. *The Practice of Spiritual Direction.* New York: Seabury, 1982.

Takes a classic approach to direction updated by contemporary theology and psychology.

VIDEO PROGRAMS

A Way to God for Today. Argus. Six thirty-minute tapes by Anthony de Mello, S.J. which show how to transform daily living. Demonstrates many different forms of prayer.

Genesis 2. Argus. A complete program in spirituality which has been successfully used in thousands of parishes. A separate program for youth.

6

The Pastor as Leader
of an Educational Team

G. TEMP SPARKMAN

Some readers wish to know what qualifies a person for publishing an article or book setting forth ideas and principles for the guidance of some enterprise or activity. This chapter is a case in point. Therefore I want to set forth some salient features of my career which qualify me for reflecting on and writing about religious education in the congregation. This is not intended to suggest that I possess some unique expertise which when transposed to the printed page and by it to the reader's intellection will assure immediate and successful results. To the contrary, I sometimes wonder if I did not spend my years in the basement of educational work, dreaming and struggling, but never able to lead a congregation to own a grand vision for religious education or to work very hard at some readily available dreams and plans.

In the fifteen years after graduation from seminary, I served as the minister of education for four churches—a county seat church in Arkansas, a military base church in Florida, a university church, and an urban church in Kentucky. The ministry staffs in these churches were constituted of anywhere from three to seven career ministers, myself included. I was the religious education leader but also shared in the wider dimensions of ministry such as worship and music leadership, pastoral visitation and counseling, and administration.

In management terms, I was responsible to the pastor of each church for the religious education work of the church and was an associate with other members of the career ministry staff. In the outward management direction (I prefer to say outward rather than upward), I was the leader of a large corps of volunteers. I worked closely with a limited number of volunteer administrative officers who were elected by the church—the director of the Sunday school was one example. I also related cooperatively and in terms of general directional planning to the directors of the age-group departments from infancy to older adulthood, with multiple departments for each group. For example, in one church we had six adult departments in the Sunday school. In addition, I worked closely with teachers in these departments in terms of curriculum and approaches to teaching.

I related to these volunteer leaders individually and in groups. My functions ranged from suggesting to affirming, from informing to listening, from leading to walking alongside. In some of the churches I was perceived and related to as a pastoral figure, a factor which affected positively all of these relationships.

I fully appreciate that the pastor of the church who has no full-time minister of education on the staff cannot invest the same amount of time and energy which I did as the educational leader. The following discussion assumes, however, that the pastor has come to livable terms with the multiple demands of the pastorate and that religious education is among the top priorities.

THE LEADERSHIP TEAM IS CONSTITUTED

Upon assuming a ministry position in a parish, a pastor simply inherits a leadership group. One does not have to begin at the ground and constitute such a corps. Soon after arriving at one of my ministry assignments I was faced with leading a week of training for the educational workers in that church. They had already been enlisted and were waiting for my leadership.

At first, I simply took this inheritance for granted, although eventually this pool of leaders had to be replenished or expanded. In a county-seat church which I served, we typically had to replace persons only once a year, and even then the turnover in leaders was minimal. In a church near a military base, this turnover was constant. However, in either case the point is that religious education leadership teams emerge in the growth and development of the church.

On reflection I came to see the intricate and spiritual origin of these corps of faithful, struggling volunteers and have since identified four factors in their emergence.

First, the leadership team is called into being by the religious education mission of the church. Each denomination has its own terms by which it articulates this mission, terminology which betrays conservative or liberal bent. Some churches speak of faith development, some of teaching the Bible and passing on the tradition, some of appropriating persons into the community of faith, some of nurturing the young and making disciples of the mature, some of radicalizing persons for the work of liberation of the oppressed.

In my own theorizing about the role of religious education in the parish, I have laid down realities which I believe should determine the shape of such education: 1) All persons born into this world are the children of God and therefore are to be told and shown in the earliest years that they are children of God, created in God's image. 2) The children of parents who participate in the life of the church belong to the parish and therefore are to be told and shown that they have a place and an affiliation, and do not have to earn it. 3) Children who grow up within the context of acceptance come to a time, in adolescence I believe, when they must affirm their heritage and make a declaration concerning Jesus Christ, and are therefore to be nurtured toward and encouraged in such a choice of faith. 4) Adults come to a time when they take up the full work of the gospel, that is, they become trustees or stewards for God in the world and therefore are to be nurtured and called out for unique responsibility for the coming generation as well as for the passing generation.[1]

It is this kind of enterprise, this kind of mission articulation which calls a leadership team into being. It is then not simply a sociological phenomenon, or a psychological need among the members which forms the basis for constituting educational leadership. Regardless of the terms which we employ to represent the religious education mission, it is that mission and our understanding of and commitment to it which is basic to the formation and success of any educational leadership team.

Second, the leadership team emerges from persons who are perceived as gifted and committed to the religious education task.
While everyone needs to be better trained for any job, some degree
of giftedness is assumed when we enlist persons for educational
leadership. The degree of this endowment varies with the job and
even with the congregation, but it is nonetheless a constant as
regards its necessity. While commitment varies in terms of intensity
and endurance, it too is a constant in the emergence of the leadership team.

An older study, but still relevant, found that persons accepted
leadership positions in the church for two main reasons: 1) They
felt God's call to the work, and 2) they wanted to help others learn
of God, Christ, the Holy Spirit, and the Bible. These items were
articulated on the survey form and the respondents were asked to
select from among a listing of five reasons for volunteering to work
in the church.[2]

Anyone experienced in enlisting and working with church workers knows that there also are some pathologies involved in dedication to the work of the church. That is true of pastors, professional
church workers, and also volunteers. However, in spite of ill-con-
ceived motivations by which persons are attracted to the work of
the church, good leaders take persons on their own terms and help
them to grow, whether that means facilitating an already healthy
Christian experience or challenging less worthy and unproductive
motives and behaviors. Such is the way it is when we analyze the
emergence of our educational leadership team. It is constituted by
persons whom we perceive as gifted for and committed to the task
to which the church calls them.

Third, the leadership team is commissioned by the congregation.
In every church where I was a minister of education we dedicated
our leaders to their volunteer tasks. Although I will have to admit
that the dimension of recognizing these persons was paramount in
the doing of these installing activities, the act is primarily investi-
tive. It is the church giving the persons the authority to act and
promising them its prayer and support on their behalf.

As a minister of education, I advocated the strengthening of
commissioning activities for religious education leaders. On more
than one occasion I pointed up the discrepancy between the ordination which the church gave to deacons, generally for duties as a

member of the governing board, and that given to religious teachers who were given spiritual leadership among groups in the church. Persons should be ordained for teaching in the church just as surely as clergy and deacons are set apart so appropriately for their work.

The point here is not to revive an old argument (which I lost) or even to suggest the shape of an installation service, but to emphasize that the volunteer leadership team does not authorize itself or proceed on its own volition. Rather, it emerges from and is constituted by the parish for which it functions. The teacher in the nursery who changes infants' diapers is engaged in behalf of the whole community of faith in nurturing children to know and feel that they are children of God and that they belong in the congregation. The teacher in the adult class in teaching the Bible and leading adults to creative trusteeship is serving for the whole church.

This then is our beginning point in examining the role of the pastor as the leader of the educational leadership team. Our team is not of our making or moved by our energy. It is called into being by the church's religious education mission, is composed of persons whom we perceive to be gifted for and committed to the task, and is commissioned by the whole church. In the larger sense, it is powered by God's energy.

THE TEAM IS SOLIDIFIED

The orchestra is a team, and when its professionals play their individual instruments according to the conductor's direction, they transform the dotted score of a symphony into an artistic performance. The anthropological dig is a team, and when the workers function cooperatively at the tell, the past gradually comes to light. So it is with the religious education leaders of a church; they are a team, and when a church is functioning successfully, it is a sign that the team is working together.

Groupness is a chemistry, not a science. Cohesiveness is a phenomenon which we can recognize and even analyze, but cannot really explain. Unity eludes us just when we think we have assured it by our actions, then surprises us when we least thought it might materialize. I once played on a college basketball team and worked on a church staff where a togetherness existed which was uncommon and uncontrived. I have thought much about what brought unity to pass in those situations, but have concluded that the dynamics of my analysis do not add up to the phenomenon in which I participated.

One of the more stable points from my analysis of the secret which pervaded these teams—the one from sport, the one from church—has to do with the leader. Two experiences convince me that the leader is a major dimension in unifying a team. The first experience was a long time ago in my senior college year. Our team qualified for the regional playoffs for the NAIA tournament, but because our outstanding player twisted an ankle and was unable to play, we lost our cohesiveness and the next game. The second experience was on a church staff, which, after the resignation of our pastor, was never the same.

Another indisputable fact about groups is that people participate in them for reasons and not simply by chance, a fact even more evident in leadership groups, such as the subject of this present discussion. It follows that along with these reasons there are various psychological explanations of group-making and group effectiveness. Two of the more prominent theories in management literature are the works of Abraham Maslow and Kurt Lewin.

Under Maslow's hierarchy of needs, which really is not a static pyramid as often depicted, but is a dynamic movement of need and satisfaction, groups are formed and flourish as their corporate character conforms to the dominant motivators operating on the individuals in the group. If my leadership team is predominantly working at the self-actualization level, I can predict that my group will be highly idiosyncratic, independent, critical, and discriminating. It will not respond enthusiastically to hyped and contrived goals and activities or be easily swayed by superficial prerequisites. This is not to deny, of course, that such people also have the need for and will respond to social and esteem dimensions of group life.[3]

In Lewin's field theory a person's relations in a group are determined by a set of forces operative at the time, are circumstantial and complex, and cannot be predicted merely on the grounds of individual needs and motivations or reinforced behaviors. Under this theory I can expect the members of my leadership team to participate according to several factors, such as the present status of their own life space, the present figure of the group and its work, the members' perceived positions and mobility in the group, and the various attempts at the exercise of power in the group process.[4]

Earlier in the discussion I referred to my work with an education committee in a church. Under a cursory field analysis of that group at the particular time when we were working on curriculum reform, I would assess that the group members were stable and reasonably comfortable with their own life space and therefore not threatened by the prospects of change or by conflict in the group deliberations. The context in which the group worked was that of a church committed to being a real church in the late sixties and with a firm sense that such was the direction of the leadership of the ministers. This dynamic matched the intent of the proposed curriculum design. The members' positions in the group followed the usual patterns, but without getting into superfluous detail I cannot describe those, except to point out that most of them seemed satisfied with the range of their roles. In the group, the exercise of power revolved around the strength of ideas more than around political strategy. Therefore, neither the chair nor I enjoyed unchecked power over the committee.

We turn now to a concept of groupness itself as we focus more directly on team building. At least the following eight ingredients constitute groupness, especially as regards leadership groups.[5]

One, participants freely bring their unique gifts to the group. As alike as human beings are, and generally leadership in a church is markedly homogeneous, there is a particular twist which each of us contributes to the team. We play common roles with subtle differences. We bring to the group a phenomenon which is "me," as Mr. Rogers taught us years ago. That we come freely does not mean, of course, that we simply amble into the group or join by accident, or even that we select the group from a host of possibilities. Someone asked us to join the leadership team, and maybe even coerced us, sometimes healthily, sometimes with unjustifiable guilt pressure.

It follows, does it not, that a successful team receives these unique gifts which each member brings and that it builds its life in accordance with such gifts. This is grace in its radical form.

Two, participants affirm each other in their giftedness. This is hard work, because we just naturally take each other for granted, and we sometimes hold the wish that we were in a group or were the leader of a group with different gifts. That is, we wish certain persons were not on our team, and that makes it more difficult for us to relate positively to members of our group. In one such experience a qualified and committed, but abrasive, preschool director resigned her position in our church, and I, though relieved momentarily, realized to my shame that I had not really praised her enough for her invaluable contribution to children and other adult leaders. To the degree that I did not affirm her and that she did not feel appreciated and that other members of the team sensed either or both of these dimensions, our team was less than what it could have been.

Three, participants bring individual ambitions for personal development and willingly invest those in the group. Some persons become leaders in the church because they want to grow as Christians. I have had persons volunteer to teach so that they themselves could become more dedicated students of the Bible. Certainly these persons also wanted to help others, but they volunteered partly in order to fulfill individual needs. After joining the faculty of my denominational seminary, I became a volunteer worker in my congregation. As a religious education teacher I wanted to stay in touch with the dynamics of education in the church. I taught different age groups so that I could better apply the theories of nurture which I was propounding in the seminary classroom.

A leadership team will be stronger if it acknowledges the legitimacy of this kind of need and provides for its fulfillment. The vestedness of this interest is a plus for an otherwise healthily functioning group.

Four, participants share the group's common understanding of the overarching purpose of the group, though they do not necessarily devote themselves with equal intensity to all of the group's goals. The chances are that we will not continue in a group with whose larger aim we are unsympathetic, especially if it is a leadership group. A person can be tangentially related to some group and not even be aware of the group's goals, but such is not the case with participation in leadership teams. While other motives may sustain persons for some time and keep them on the team, as their passion for the chief end diminishes so will their real contribution to the team. I once had a gifted Sunday school teacher who became disenchanted with church and who, when other motivations ran their course as they eventually clashed with his lack of commitment to the overarching purpose of the group, resigned. Although he did not put his resignation in the language of team spirit and group-ness, he conveyed that his detachment from the group had become total. Even the uninitiated know that leadership teams are made of different stuff.

Five, participants are drawn with earnestness, in some cases, passion, into some challenge facing the group. This fact is clearly demonstrated in postseason sporting events, in congressional activity during national crises, and other domains. An educational leadership team might be challenged by some new curriculum design or some new vision of community witness and outreach. Such occasions require an intensity beyond the business-as-usual attitude and the members of the group must sense that to be the case.

Leaders know that it is difficult to maintain intensity or interest in long-term, remote goals. In the same vein, they know that groups cannot be motivated to total investment in a chain of challenging tasks. This means that we operate predominantly with modest but firm commitment to modest but integral goals, but that periodic unusual challenges excite a team and give it a different look at itself and its potentialities. I know a church which proceeded dutifully toward its goal of being a missionary church, among other things, but without any noticeable passion until suburban homes and con-dominiums sprang up all around it.

Six, participants unapologetically disagree with each other and in good spirit confront each other's weaknesses. It might be said that when a leadership group demonstrates no tension or disagreement, it is functioning at a maintenance level. In such cases one might expect that eventually the group will be arguing heatedly over inconsequential matters. Of course, no leader wants arbitrarily to stir up trouble where none exists, but the fact is that groupness is made of diversity of opinion and respectful confrontation. I know a leader who believes that groups exist for the sake of human rela-tions. To the contrary, persons relate in leadership groups in order to proceed with some agenda, which puts the group relations at the service of group goals. Such activity inevitably involves the group in facing its differences. That these are sometimes irreconcilable is simply a point of reality with which leaders have to live.[6]

Seven, participants contribute to and share fully in the group's successes and failures. Nothing is as debilitating to the sense of groupness as the excessive praise lauded on one or a few members of achievement which the entire group made possible. This dynamic is especially critical when the team leader is the one who is receiving the inordinate attention. That is why we career ministers who lead volunteer teams must see that credit is given where it is due.

Imagine that you lead your adult religious education team in an innovative approach to the study of scripture and that its success becomes known in wider circles, whereupon you are cited and invited to speak far and wide. You, of course, have no control over such fortune, and it would be unrealistic to expect that the entire adult team could be engaged to travel around the country to demonstrate their teaching approach. This then means that it is up to you to extend the plaudits to the other members of your team.

Eight, participants recognize and accept that the group and its work impinge on other groups within and beyond the larger organization. This dimension of groupness is simply an acknowledgement that leadership teams need to have a special sense of context, that they are a system within a system. Such awareness prevents the group from building its spirit on activities which go beyond its assigned role. It aids the group with that oldest of human problems—facing one's limitations—and with that ever present threat to any enterprise—misguided competition.

THE TEAM TAKES A LEADER

In the movement of careers which involve the management of organizations or the facilitation of groups, positions and ranks are assigned to us by those in authority. Leadership, on the other hand, cannot be designated; it must be assumed. Positions are hard, cold, static realities which can be created, charted, and described without having any real effect on an organization's purposes. Leaders, on the other hand, can act and stimulate a group toward achievement of its reason for being.

As I ponder the powers and limitations of leaders in various settings and reflect on management literature, it occurs to me that the pastor of the church enjoys a unique situation as regards leadership. Unlike a mayor or head of a business, the pastor is a leader who relates to persons in a holistic fashion. Consider your relationship to the members of your religious education team. You meet with them in planning and effecting the work of the team. But you also are their pastor in the good times and the bad, and you preach before them regularly. What executive really concerned about human relations and productivity would not wish to have such a holistic access to a leadership team?

What I am talking about here provides me with what has been a missing link in my conceptualization of pastoral leadership in relationship to that seemingly alien corpus of material on management and supervision. While we have accepted the term business manager in the church, we are uncomfortable with calling the pastor a manager, although a pastor is required to manage. I would suppose that the term supervisor is even more difficult to substitute for pastor, although a pastor is indeed a supervisor.

I know many pastors who, though disdaining administration, are effective leaders in their churches. How did they ever get employed to lead these complex organizations? Granting intelligence and independence to pulpit committees and good sense to congregations, the explanation seems to lie in the mystique of the office of pastor as requiring a holistic leader.

I hope that this discussion is encouraging to pastors who, without the assistance of career ministers of education, are the leaders of religious education teams. It should communicate to you that you are in a unique position to build a quality religious education worthy of the gospel and the church's mission, and give you some sense of peace that you are not in fact an executive after the mold found in the literature.[7]

The Function of the Leader

Every book on management carries a discussion of the functions of a manager. James Anderson and Ezra Earl Jones list planning, organizing, staffing, directing, and controlling.[8] Paul Hersey and Kenneth Blanchard reduce the list to planning, organizing, motivating, and controlling.[9] I want to narrow the list to three: planning, implementing, and evaluating.

Cooperative planning is the foundational activity of any enterprise, for it is here that the operational mode of the team first shows itself. The style of the leader and the character of the group will be evident in whether the leader brings elaborate plans to the group and requests approval, or brings ideas and asks for collaboration, or brings problems and invites the group to offer ideas and strategies. While all of us have functioned in all of these modes alternatingly, surely the ideal is to develop a team which honestly surfaces problems and cooperatively plans and thereby owns solutions.

Effective planning begins with the leader developing a plan for planning. Namely, scheduling the planning process. The over-involved and over-worked pastor is usually on a short-planning cycle, which generally indicates that the planning is reactionary and stop-gap rather than proactive and considered. A corrective planning process or timetable will indicate on which dates the leader will initiate plans for continuing activites, such as Vacation Church School, training events, census takings, and will provide for regular meetings during which problems will be addressed.

I found it helpful in planning to have a file folder for each major activity in the religious education program, such as training events, and folders for regular meetings, such as team planning meetings. In each folder, I maintained an action sheet on which I listed the actions necessary to that activity and the dates on which I wished to have completed those actions. Also on that sheet I enumerated the problem areas which the religious education team needed to discuss. While this may sound overly detailed for a pastor who has the full range of responsibilities in the church, it actually saves time and focuses one's energies.

The religious education team is responsible for planning in the following areas: organization, grouping of learners, space assignments for the learning groups, curriculum goals and materials, the teaching process, numerical growth, staffing, communication, budgeting, and meetings.

As one follows the plan for planning, each planning area receives attention on schedule. If, for example, the pastor's plan for planning calls for the initiation of Vacation Church School planning at the January team meeting, the pastor gets the folder from last year and reviews the activities, the evaluations, and the notes which that pastor wrote to himself/herself about the school. The team evaluates these and lays broad guidelines for the next school, and then enlists a director to whom the school is delegated. The pastor then works with the director in more specific planning, after which the pastor's planning responsibilities end. From this point on the pastor relates as needed to the director who is now responsible, according both to the pastor's and the director's leadership styles.

Ideally, the pastor should be able to delegate every religious education activity to a church worker and therefore, once the initial planning has been accomplished, be free of further additional planning responsibilities. The degree to which the pastor has to hang on to any of these major activities will influence the pastor's effectiveness in the total work of the church. For example, the pastor who has to plan logistics for the learning groups and the refreshment menu for the Vacation Church School will have to sacrifice some other facet of ministry and will come to resent the demands which the school makes.

The pastor then does the same in April when the planning schedule calls for the initiation of the enlistment of religion teachers for the next year. The pastor goes to the nominating committee folder and sets in motion that particular work. Once in the planning process the team decides on the number of religious educators needed and enumerates any major personnel issues which need to be addressed, the work is then delegated to the nominating committee.

Of course, we all know that it somehow does not always work that easily. But the better job we do at this initial planning stage, the better chance we have of reducing our leadership role to supporting the implementation of plans.

The function of *implementing* is that of organizing and directing the plans; it is the hard work of following through and completing. It consists of budget-making and spending supervision, of identifying and ordering curriculum materials, of enlisting teachers and training them, of detailed scheduling of events and promoting them, of setting up for meetings, of checking on and supporting.

Effective implementation is founded on the existence of structure which clarifies roles, functions, authority, expectations, and accountability. This is labeled formal structuring by Doran McCarty, who recommends it over informal structuring in which traditional and silent agenda determine how a group functions.[10]

Where the delegation of responsibility is complete and efficient, the volunteer worker is really the one who is responsible for organizing and directing the assigned programs and activities. The pastor is still held accountable for organization and direction, but the leadership role now is that of contact and support. This role can best be fulfilled if the leader and the church worker make a contract or covenant concerning mutual expectations, including how often and when they will meet together for talking over the progress of the work. "The covenant," writes McCarty, "is the way the leader structures relationships and goals."[11]

Experienced leaders have learned that this kind of work, even when under contract, often breaks down. In such instances the leader has to attend to the breakdown as one does to pain in the body. In confronting the problem, the leader must be direct and sympathetic and make sure that it is the problem rather than the volunteer that is being addressed. The leader must avoid assuming the debilitating attitude that because the worker is a volunteer the breakdown can be ignored. Obviously, the leader also must avoid simply relieving the worker and taking over the responsibility personally.

Sometimes the pastor, caught in an abundance of such circumstances, simply has to confront the entire leadership team with the problems, and lead the team and church in self-searching whether their ambitions concerning education are too far ahead of their commitments. How easily a church enters upon programs and ministries and then expects the pastor to assure their success. It is humanly impossible, and a church must be told that. Such honesty contributes both to corporate and individual health, and makes the doing of religion more realistic and rewarding.

This leads us to the function of *evaluating*. In this function the leader leads in assessing the value and results of the team's work in light of the goals. The spring training event attracted twice as many teachers as had been projected and made everyone feel good, but did it yield the educational goal which the team had set for it? We might assess that it did not, because of the unexpected attendance, and therefore relay this information back into the planning process for the next training event. On the assembly line, the matter of control is immediate; in the activities with which we work in educational leadership, it is delayed. Still, the leader who is not concerned with it ends up with a defective "product." That eventually comes home to haunt the organization.

A pastor can get heavily into evaluation and find it taking too much time and energy. Minimally, however, the leader can obtain helpful evaluation by two means: One, invite written evaluations from the principal leaders of any activity. Two, learn how to ask leaders in sincerity how their work is going and to ask participants what they think and feel about the activities they are involved in. This kind of conversation could substitute for the idle talk which characterizes many of the pastor's encounters with leaders and other church members.

The function of evaluating raises the question of the systems which influence the success of any activity. Alvin Lindgren and Norman Shawchuck include systems theory as one of several organization theories.[12] A graphic in these authors' book shows a group, in this case a church, with the goals of a balanced budget and of members feeling good about the church's finances but with failure on both. A feedback loop which includes what message the church is sending to the church by nonparticipation in the goals is translated into factors behind the failure. Then all around the chart of this goal-failure-feedback-translation activity is a circle of systems which impinge on the church: lodges, a major league football team, population decline, lack of jobs for youth, depressed community economics, etc.

I served a church which had once attracted double its present Sunday school attendance. The church never realistically accepted that the former large attendances were when the church was the only one of its denomination in the town, whereas at the time there were several such churches and the same population pool. Neither could it accept the social factors which influenced the growth of one of the newer churches across town. The church did not include these factors in its evaluation. Therefore, the reduced attendance was a drag on the church's morale and its causes went unaddressed.

In addition to these systems external to the church, there are systems within the church which influence and are influenced by the work of the educational leadership team. These include groups which by their nature have unusual and legitimate time demands in order to accomplish their work, such as choral groups which are preparing for special musical celebrations. Also, evangelism committees have been known to schedule revivals without considering

the plans of other church groups. Some groups demand a disproportionate share of a church's financial resources and often render
vested justifications for their requests. Youth groups and missions
committees are especially liable at this point. In addition, there are
times when a leader on the educational team is also a leader in
another group in the church, an overlap which is not negative, but
which does represent the influences which internal systems have
on each other.

The Leader's Style

Pastors, though indeed in a unique leadership position, can profit
from management theory where it deals with leadership styles. The
theorists propose the growing conviction that a leader must in fact
employ different styles of leadership according to the context. Especially insightful at this point is the concept of situational leadership,
which recognizes three dimensions of a leadership situation:

> 1) The amount of guidance and direction (task behavior) a leader
> gives; 2) the amount of socioemotional support (relationship behavior) a
> leader provides; and 3) the readiness ("maturity") level that followers
> exhibit in performing a specific task, function, or objective.[13]

Next, the concept is charted on the familiar grid which indicates
the behavior of the leader in terms of the degree to which the
leader is relational oriented and task oriented. Then the factor of
the maturity level of the group is built into the chart, obviously
moving from low to high maturity.

Finally, the crucial entry for our discussion is an overlay which
indicates the style of leading appropriate to the interplay between
relationship, task, and maturity. For high-maturity people, the leadership style is *delegating* which means that the leader's relationship
behavior is low and the task behavior also is low. The high-maturity
person simply needs little direction or support. For moderately
high-maturity persons, the leadership style is *participating*, which
means that the relationship behavior of the leader is high while the
task behavior remains low. The moderately high-maturity person
needs more personal support, but still resists too much direction.
The moderately low-maturity person needs a high-task, high-rela-
tionship leader, thus the leadership style is termed *selling*. The

leader who lays the task out clearly and forcefully and who gives support will lead the moderately low-maturity person to achieve. The final leadership style is *telling*, and it is for the low-maturity persons who need detailed and unequivocal direction and very little support.

In religious education leadership in the church I first assess the level of maturity of my group, as a group in its totality, but essentially as individual members. My primary method of making such judgments is my experience with these persons and what I hear others say about them. By these I learn who can be depended on and for what kinds of tasks. For example, I learn that teacher x is generally a high-maturity person, that she leads her children's department teachers in thorough planning for units of study. However, she gives almost no attention to the care of the children and does not lead her teachers in keeping in touch with the children between Sundays.

As a leader, having judged that teacher x is a high-maturity person, I assume a delegating style of leadership, which on the chart shows as low relationship and low task. I neither have to direct her to do teaching planning nor have to give her a lot of personal attention. She knows what her responsibility here is, and she does it happily and effectively. However, on the matter of the care of children in her department, I must assume a different style, in this case, either participating or selling.

Staying with our example, in using the participating style, I avoid putting pressure on teacher x to visit absentees and otherwise attend to children, and I make sure that when that task is raised that I give her every opportunity to name the terms of the visitation. Furthermore, I support her more than would usually be the case. On the chart this is high relationship, low task. If that fails, I might turn to the selling style of leading, but in this case, it will most likely fail, because she is a high-maturity person generally. The problem is that she is unwilling to engage in the task under consideration. This being the case, teacher x will definitely not be led by the telling style of leading.

There is no need to proceed through the various styles of situational leadership, but I do want to comment on one more insight from that discussion. The experts suggest that the low-maturity person who, you will remember, needs a leader who directs but does not relate closely, might interpret the leader's support as "permissive, easy, and most importantly, as rewarding of poor performance."[14] If this is true, then the pastor has to accept the fact that it is a liability of his or her unique leadership role. For, unlike the business executive or boss, the pastor is also a minister, even to the immature. If the pastor's role did not require this, surely grace would.

A central consideration in this discussion of style is the capacity of the leader of the team to adapt to changing conditions. Can a leader embrace the wide range of styles from delegating to telling? Clearly, the leader will have a dominance in one or other of the styles and some sympathy for those styles closest to the dominant style, but how much can we expect leaders to adjust their approaches? The chances are that most of us do not possess such a wide range of styles and that we therefore either move out of leadership or gradually attract team members with whom we can work according to our style range. Or we and the group simply drift, immobilized by the group's motivational levels and the leader's narrow range of leadership approaches.

My experience has taught me that in addition to the three dimensions of a leadership situation on which the concept of situational leadership is built a fourth is required. Let us name it divergence.

In group leadership, the leader does not have the luxury of dealing only with individuals on a one-to-one basis. Thus the leader must relate to differing levels of maturity within a single group. These differences of maturity are then joined by diversity of background, ideology, and strategic understandings which the leader must help a group to negotiate.

Divergence creates the likelihood of conflict, and when it occurs the leader's first responsibility is to acknowledge it and to be committed to resolving it. That, of course, requires flexibility and empathy, especially in working with volunteer teams. Larry McSwain and William Treadwell discuss five primary styles of handling conflict situations: problem solver, super helper, facilitator, power broker, and fearful loser. The authors recommend that ministers learn the problem-solving approach because it "assumes that attitudinal, substantive, or emotional conflict could be managed if clearer communication were brought to bear in the situation."[15] When this assumption proves false, then the pastor must turn to an alternative style. The facilitator's strengths are when the conflict is around attitudes, the super helper around emotions, the power broker around substantive issues.

CONCLUSION

This chapter raises issues which really deserve more attention, yet I am reluctant to burden the pastor with more resources than one can possibly use to advantage. Therefore, I close with the suggestion that the resources cited in the notes are worthy of additional exploration. Beyond those, I refer you to whatever magazines your denomination publishes around management issues, because many times a brief article satisfies both the pastor's need for insight and the limitations of time. I hope also that this chapter accomplishes the same.

Notes

1. This is the foundation of my theology-theory of Christian nurture set forth in the supposed life-span development of a representative person whom I named Emma. *The Salvation and Nurture of the Child of God* (Philadelphia: Judson, 1983).

2. Reggie McDonough, *Working With Volunteer Leaders in the Church* (Nashville: Broadman, 1976), p. 14.

3. Abraham Maslow, *Motivation and Personality* (New York: Harper & Row, 1970). See Paul Hersey and Kenneth Blanchard, *Management of Organizational Behavior* (Englewood Cliffs, N.J.: Prentice-Hall, 1982), pp. 27ff.

4. Kurt Lewin, *Field Theory and Social Science*, ed. Dorwin Cartwright (New York: Harper and Brothers, 1951); Kenneth R. Mitchell, *Psychological and Theological Relationships in the Multiple Staff Ministry* (Philadelphia: Westminster, 1966), pp. 70ff.; Marvin T. Judy, *The Multiple Staff Ministry* (Nashville: Abingdon, 1969), pp. 86ff.

5. For additional discussion, see Dorwin Cartwright and Alvin Zander, *Group Dynamics Research and Theory* (New York: Harper, 1960), p. 345; Robert Dale, *Ministers as Leaders* (Nashville: Broadman, 1984), pp. 100ff; Douglas McGregor, *The Human Side of Enterprise* (New York: McGraw-Hill, 1960), pp. 231-240.

6. For discussion of conflict management, see Larry L. McSwain and William C. Treadwell, *Conflict Ministry in the Church* (Nashville: Broadman, 1981).

7. See Dale's insight into the catalyst leader, *Ministers as Leaders*, pp. 18ff.

8. James Anderson and Ezra Earl Jones, *The Management of Ministry* (San Francisco: Harper & Row, 1978), p. 83.

9. Hersey and Blanchard, *Management of Organizational Behavior*, pp. 3-4.

10. Doran McCarty, *Working with People* (Nashville: Broadman, 1986), p. 77.

11. Ibid., pp. 79-80.

12. Alvin J. Lindgren and Norman Shawchuck, *Management for Your Church* (Nashville: Abingdon, 1977), p. 33. Also Judy, *The Multiple Staff Ministry*, p. 81f; Hersey and Blanchard, *Management of Organizational Behavior*, pp. 6-8.

13. Hersey and Blanchard, *Management of Organizational Behavior*, p. 150.
14. Ibid., p. 153.
15. McSwain and Treadwell, *Conflict Ministry in the Church*, p. 181.

Bibliography

Adams, James B. and Hahn, Celia A. *Learning to Share the Ministry.* Washington, D.C.: Alban Institute, 1984.

Argyris, Chris, and Schon, Donald. *Theory in Practice: Increasing Professional Effectiveness.* San Francisco: Jossey-Bass, 1974.

Browning, Robert L., Foster, Charles R., and Tilson, Everett. *Looking at Leadership Through the Eyes of Biblical Faith* (tapes and guide). Nashville: Discipleship Resources, 1978.

Dudley, Carl S., ed. *Building Effective Ministry: Theory and Practice in the Local Church.* San Francisco: Harper & Row, 1983.

Greenleaf, Robert K. *Servant Leadership.* New York: Paulist, 1977.

Heusser, D. B. *Helping Church Workers Succeed.* Valley Forge: Pennsylvania: Judson, 1980.

Howe, Leroy T. "The Pastor As Educator" in *Quarterly Review* (Fall 1983), pp. 18-32.

Killinger, John. *The Tender Shepherd: A Practical Guide for Today's Pastor.* Nashville: Abingdon, 1985.

Lindgren, Alvin J. and Shawchuck, Norman. *Let My People Go: Empowering Laity for Ministry.* Nashville: Abingdon, 1980.

———. *Management for Your Church.* Indianapolis: Organization Resources Press, 1984.

Whitehead, Evelyn, and Whitehead, James. *Method in Ministry.* New York: Seabury, 1980.

7

The Communications Revolution and the Religious Education of the Congregation

WILLIAM PHILLIPS

When Karl Barth proposed an image of the preacher of his day as one who stands in the pulpit with the Bible in one hand and the newspaper in the other he was recognizing the importance of integrating text with context. Preachers, as well as teachers of the faith, have found the task much more difficult than the simple image would suggest.

To integrate text with context in Barth's time, as now, demanded of the interpreter the highly developed discipline of the exegete, and the complex set of skills needed to discern "the true" context from that particular expression of it offered by a given newspaper.

In using a similiar image today, we create a picture that is both cluttered and comical. The preacher, Bible in hand, is surrounded in the area of the pulpit by a number of instruments of electronic equipment providing a continuous stream of mediated experiences from many contexts. Each electronic device is itself a symbol of part of the new context in which the pastoral work takes place.

A series of T.V. monitors display news, commentary, entertainment, documentaries, rock videos, game shows, old movies, violent dramas, and endless commercials simultaneously. All are relayed to the pulpit from one or other of the many commercial or government-owned communication satellites strategically hung in orbit

146

around the world. The T.V. monitors symbolize the multiplicity and diversity of mediated contexts and the orbiting satellites connect us in a way that makes McLuhan's image of a global village a reality.

A computer station with added modem links the preacher with a dozen or more interrelated networks of information data banks. The stack of floppy discs containing mega bytes of images, information, and reference material seems to grow as we watch it. Both computer and storage discs are symbolic of the impact of the knowledge and information explosion.

A new compact disc player, and an unopened box containing a digital tape deck provide another symbol of the relationship between media and context. The digital tape, which is considered superior in quality and technology, is unavailable in North America. Its importation has been restricted in response to the lobbyists' work since the millions of dollars expended in the development of the compact disc technology would be lost if it did not have time in the marketplace before the superior new technology arrived. All are symbols of technology, politics, control, economics, and the rapidity of change.

The video player/recorder attached to yet another T.V. monitor is narrowcasting a prepackaged 'how to . . .' program of educational significance for some carefully selected audience. Narrowcasting is a symbol of the specialization which is developing within the mass media, and of the highly developed educational resource libraries of audio visual materials.

The old slide projector which was once used to show scenes from the mission field narrated by a tired itinerate missionary is now integrated into a multiple projection and multi-image presentation network activated by a computerized control panel to a dual drive stereo audio system. The mission field seems closer somehow.

In the background are the banks of audience referenced magazines and stacks of newspapers all of which are published through a complex web of electronic wire services, satellite transmission of print and picture, laser printing, and electronic mail services. The newspaper is simply not what it used to be.

Karl Barth would probably decide not to use the image at all.

The changes in the image have not all been on the side of media. The biblical text is being examined through lenses which, if not new in quality, are certainly new in quantity. Imagination and the interplay of conscious and unconscious as it affects the writer and the reader are matters of concern to the contemporary exegete. So is the insight developed by research into the bicameral nature of our thought processes. The ever-expanding discoveries of linguistic and historical research, the very useful knowledge that emerges from interfaith dialogue, the profound influence of science and mathematics on various aspects of literary critical work, all contribute to making the task of the contemporary preacher, religious educator, and interpreter of faith more complex and difficult.

On the other side of the image the change is nothing short of overwhelming. Not only are we surrounded by multiple mediated images bringing contexts to us which may or may not influence the way we interpret the biblical and theological tradition, but we are situated in a new context, neither of our making nor within our control.

The new contexts do not irradicate the traditional ones. The roles of pastoral ministry in communicating faithfulness to the gospel are far more extensive than those limited by the potential from electronic media.

Like the Christ whom the pastor represents, the pastor is a person who embodies faith and personal response to the gospel. Such embodiment is both sign and symbol and, as such, is powerful in the fullfillment of those tasks which are not, nor can be, mediated impersonally.

Pastors experience many opportunites for immediacy, spontaneity, flexibility, and responsive compassion not available to the media minister. There is also a degree of responsibility inherent in the personal ministry which is less evident and often problematic in those ministries mediated through communication technology. The levels of reciprocity in relationships between pastor and parish where each is simultaneously teacher and learner, servant and one served, interpreter and enquirer is never possible to those who are removed because of technology from the interpersonal engagements of ministry.

Contemporary pastors however cannot escape into an interpersonal oasis and disregard the impact of the communications revolution on our ways of relating to one another.

In addressing the subject of the nature of the interface between technology and our understanding of ourselves and context, J.

David Bolter suggests that the computer is a "defining technology" which as well as other aspects of the technological revolution serve to alter and influence our self-perception. "It is certainly not true," he says, "that changing technology is solely responsible for mankind's changing view of nature, but clearly the technology of any age provides an attractive window through which thinkers can view both their physical and metaphysical worlds."[1]

Jacques Ellul goes further. He suggests that to define the situation in terms of the impact of technology upon the culture is futile because technology is already culture. Technology, he suggests, can be comprehended accurately only if it is equated with the contemporary environment.[2]

It becomes necessary, therefore, for the thoughtful Christian to decide which perspective he or she will use in relating text to context. Whether a window through which to see culture or a cultural context in and of itself, electronic media in general, and particularly television and the computer, are now clearly positioned to influence the interpretation of the text. Because of the diversity and omnipresence of mediated images reflecting the global village, and because we are engaged by the media at so many levels, the logical linear tradition no longer functions as the norm.

The pastor's personal self-understanding and his or her sensitivity to the contexts in which ministry is called for is both influenced by and interpreted in the media. As William Fore, in his essay on theology of communication states: "The mass media are not mere message carriers. They also confer power, legitimate systems, and provide ways of looking at the world. They supply the context in which information is learned, attitudes are formed, and decisions are made."[3]

Therefore the new image of the pastor goes beyond a model for integrative preaching. It raises important issues for all aspects of pastoral leadership, especially when teaching and learning are intentionally designed.

CONTEXT AND COMMUNITY

One of the most obvious issues is the challenge presented by the media to the church's attitude toward context and community. Alvin Toffler may have contributed a major insight in suggesting that the future approaches us. Such an attitude changes the way in which we consider the future and live in the present. It also raises questions as to the nature of community and of context when they are being approached by the future.

Coupled with such an idea, the descriptive term employed by William Fore years ago in describing the effect of television on the acculturation and socializing processes takes on double meaning.

> T.V. is not merely entertainment. It is not even primarily an advertisement for mass produced goods—although that is the primary interest of its overseers. T.V. is first and foremost an education. From it children learn more about the realities of citizenship and politics than from all their school's civics courses combined. From it adults learn how to consume, how to play, how to be family members and even how to think. From it we develop our perceptions, so that we now expect more excitement, originality, and creativity in everything we see. From it we learn to apprehend our world in great gulps, so that a new word—allatonce—has entered our vocabulary.[4]

Partly because of the allatonceness of the mediated contexts in which we live, and partly because of the interpenetration of contexts made possible by the immediacy of electronic networks, the concept of context itself is as much subjective as it is objective. The levels of empathy and engagement with the concerns of persons and places separated from us is heightened to a level that allows for displaced contextual thinking and reflection even when the contexts are not, in the traditional sense, our own.

Neither can we expect to control the nature and dimension of the contexts in which we do our thinking. The most fearful among us say that the issue is out of control. The less fearful simply acknowledge the limited control individuals or institutions have over the contextual choices people make and with which they must deal. By extension, it is clear that we are not in control of the experiences that will be the basis of the creation of contextual frameworks against which theological reflection will take place. We are, however, confronted with the question of the relation between the ideal and the real in the matter of the place of context in ministry.

The transmission of context from one generation to the next can no longer be assumed. After describing traditional communities of faith as effective agents for the handing on of the traditions and heritages of that faith, Norbert Mette acknowledges, "It can no longer be taken for granted that the rising generation will be made familiar with the heritage of experiences preserved in these traditions. In fact, it is increasingly a case of a break in tradition."[5] The further statement of an ideal context for religious education by socialization, seems antithetical, "What therefore are indispensable are close-knit and durable networks of social relationships in which those involved can still mutually recognize each other as 'complete human beings' without already being reduced to partial roles."[6] Such an ideal has a chilling emptiness when considered alongside the image of the multimedia "fast-track" image-makers of the contemporary society. As Barbara Hargrove observes, "The media have undermined the power of local communities to reinforce a common lifestyle and set of values through the kind of personal contact that gives a human face to social control and that interprets the world in ways that incorporate the individual into the larger society through the agency of local groups."[7]

Our lack of control over the complexity and immediacy of contemporary contexts challenges James Michael Lee's description of the elements of a total teaching structure which presupposes a system that 1) shapes experiences for individuals and groups, 2) tests them in situations "close to the normal," and 3) adjusts them to suit instructional objectives.[8] Such a system must allow for the fact that while we "shape," "test," and "adjust" numerous new factors have been added by a mediated environment which is neither predictable or intentional.

The communications revolution raises yet another basic question about context—namely, who sets the agenda? Frequently the church is confronted by the need to make public statements, clarify positions, and determine theological, religious, and biblical responses to issues that are not of the church's choosing, nor timed in such a way as to be suitable to, nor reflective of, the church's agenda. The issue then becomes one of courage. Will the church and its educational leaders accept the role of irrelevancy suggested by the media response to their silence?

The context, like the newspaper, is not what it used to be.

CONTENT

In some ways it is fair to say that contents come to us with such speed and quantity that the task of the church's teaching and preaching ministry has become less a matter of preparing content than of responding to the contents which are so efficiently communicated. There are problems. The contents projected toward us are often without reference to the values, communities, concerns, and traditions that form the basis of faith to be communicated by religious educators. The second problem is that any response must compete with an ever increasing cacophony of media messages for the attention of those to whom it is addressed. James Michael Lee and other religious educators are therefore concerned with the need to communicate in a way that will itself reveal an awareness of the new contexts and contents. Ronald Sarno approvingly writes of Lee, that he "is wholeheartedly in tune with McLuhan's central position that the process by which people communicate is an essential component in the overall message of what is communicated."[9] Sarno goes on to say that "when religious educators fail to realize that the medium is indeed the message, they get lost in replicating (or when creative, in adjusting) print formats that no longer possess optimum power to communicate with contemporary learners."[10]

We are called to learn both from the content provided by the media and through the media itself. To learn from media we need to overcome our fixation with print. To learn through the media we will have to engage in the efforts required to appreciate the multileveled impact of the media on our learning activities. We also need to allow ourselves to be influenced at all eight content levels described by James Michael Lee.[11]

Mediated learning, when appropriately set in contexts which provide for reflection and community reaction, is capable of effecting us significantly, but the content of our learning may be both conscious and unconscious.

Research which supports the cultural norms theories of communications indicates that there are three ways the media can influence norms and the definitions of both situation and individual. Mass communications can *reinforce existing patterns* and leave people to believe that existing or given social norms are being maintained.

Second, the mass communication content can *create new shared convictions* with respect to subjects of which the public has little prior experience, and third, mass communications content can *change existing norms* and thereby convert people from one form of behavior to another.[12]

The reader will recognize that such learning products are not only cognitive, not strictly affective, not necessarily verbal nor non-verbal, may well be unconscious, and are the result of a lifestyle learning.

We learn such norming content through a process which engages us both in and through media.

Both the substantive content—Lee's term for the subject matter; and structural content—his term for the fashioning of material into a teachable form; will have "come at us" without either our planning or bidding. In considering therefore the content of the educational resources offered by the instruments of the communication revolution, it will be important to recognize the socializing effect of media and to establish some education objectives based on the power of the content. This was once a major factor in the role of the church community in religious education.

For persons increasingly feeling isolated from communities which share their particular values, norms, and sensitivities, media may provide the kind of content support that is encouraging. Many believe this is the fundamental factor explaining the massive support of the Electronic Church.

Many churches still seek to teach through the print medium assuming that the communities will provide the necessary social contents. But if print is coming to be seen as an isolating medium, then there are mixed messages and countervailing forces in such a practice.

Ronald Sarno makes a similar observation about the content of process.

> In this information environment, literate people, on the one hand, focus on the *content* of change and evaluate change's worth on the basis of what is happening now in relation to what happened *in the past*. On the other hand, audio visual people attend to the *speed or process* by which change comes about. Audio visual people evaluate change's worth on the basis of how *relevant* it is to their *present* experience.[13]

EXPERIENCENVIRONMENT

To recognize the new symbol of the preacher, with its electronic and multi-imaged projection of contexts, is to perceive a more complex interplay between environment and experience. That interplay has profound effect on the church's religious education efforts.

To name the issue one way is to attend to the matter of focus. Contemporary pastors and religious educators will recognize that what is cast into the foreground and what provides background is the result of a complex set of decisions made on the basis of bias, priority, assumption, and purpose. The media so forcefully engage us with the issues of foreground and background that we should no longer be unaware of the impact of the decisions that set the focus.

Picture a group of four or five ten-year-olds in a small church school classroom with an inexperienced religion teacher reading together from the printed paragraphs of a prepared study book.

Leave that scene now to recall that what is experienced through the media is not so much distortion of fact, as distortion of focus. Now recall the ways in which cultural norms are influenced by the mass media and recognize that viewers of television and users of the mass media for information gathering may be unevenly influenced. The influence is not so much by the critical mass of opinion, attitude, or experience but by a "perception" of critical mass which gives undue weight to the opinions, attitudes, and experience of specific groups, segments of the population, or certain leaders.

The interplay between the environment and experience in our understanding of value can be illustrated by the fact that for the media and their objectives, a large audience is a priority. When religious events or matters of religious importance are cast in a setting of isolation or seen as being of interest to a small community, the subject itself is affected. Thus there is a significant difference between the scene of a T.V. evangelist preaching in a sports arena to an audience of thousands and a televised worship service from the local church. The significance is not in the sermon as much as in the perceived "critical mass" of appreciation, acceptance, and support.

Focus again now, on the tiny church school classroom. the medium is itself a message of background/foreground significance since the four or five people gathered there have difficulty overcoming the effect of a perceived lack of "critical mass."

Randolph Crump Miller is right in his statement that "we bring habits, skills, techniques, and expectations to our experiences; perception becomes recognition and discovery, but the discovery comes to the sensitive and trained mind and is akin to revelation or disclosure."[14] The issue here, is to develop an awareness of the interplay between the leadership of the church and the mediated environment which creates habits, teaches skills, provides techniques, and sets expectations. In such an environment the kinds of experience used by pastors and teachers are brought to focus. In the interplay between the foreground and background, what is "recognized and discovered" may be seriously distorted.

DIMENSIONS OF HUMAN LEARNING AND TEACHING

Because we are aware of the new complexity within the task of interpreting the faith in context, we must also deal with the ever-widening dimension of the human learning and teaching activity.

One aspect of this is the importance, for contemporary pastors, of the insights of those inquiring into the interdependent relationship between subjective and objective learning. John Westerhoff asserts that "a healthy understanding of religion in human life necessitates an acknowledgement of the bicameral mind (and) a comprehension of its functioning."[15] He calls religious educators to attend to the subjective as well as the objective aspect of learning with increased intensity and intentionality. "My plea is that we affirm both the sacred, symbolic, nonrational, and mystical as well as the profane, discursive, rationalistic, and prosaic dimensions of human life."[16]

Today's pastor must be aware that a second aspect of the teaching/learning relationship made explicit by the impact of the mass media is the emerging new role of the individual in the work of religious learning. Because there is no control or even limit on the flow of data, experiences, and expressions of reality through which individuals must sort to develop their own perspectives, the individual learner has a peculiar new function. The learner, in a significant sense, becomes his or her own curriculum advisor. What choices are made from among the many alternative symbols, experiences, and other contents will be made by individuals with less help from those who would assist in the establishing of norms.

What has become one of the fundamental intentions of mass media—an intention that serves the media's purposes well, but not necessarily those of religious interpreters—is the creation of a dialogical or confrontational stance. By opposing one view with another and leaving the viewer or reader to try to decide what to use as criteria for evaluating the two or more opposed views, the media may not appear neutral. In fact however, in the guise of objectivity a reporter, panel host, or interviewer becomes almost normless. In an effort to report—some would say "feature"—an opposing view, much of the media suggest that all issues are "up for debate." This is the case even if those debating the issue represent a minority of a minority.

This leads however to a situation under which many, if not most, of those whose attitudes are shaped and strongly influenced by such a media mentality no longer believe that there are established norms of behavior and/or fundamental assumptions of values against which to measure a given new initiative.

The issue for the church's religious education in general and the preacher and pastor specifically is to learn to reflect an understanding of basic beliefs, norms, and values in a context systematically being conditioned to "hear" such teachings as relative.

So what if Jesus said "love your enemies." Our government does not think we can trust them and besides some people think we need the jobs that the munitions industry provides.

Preaching, teaching, and learning activities all take place in an increasingly normless society. The church and those within it, endeavoring to offer teaching and learning opportunities, must be concerned with how groups and individuals are provided with sanctions or approved modes of conduct toward objects, events, and issues which are brought to the individual's attention.

If religious values and assumptions are to have any appreciable hearing in society there is need to establish methods and models which both critique the trend toward normlessness and establish the credibility of those structures and spokespeople who make decisions on the basis of solid and conscious norms. This explains in part one of the grievances in the recent developments in the world of the T.V. evangelist. What was projected as a "normed" community is discovered to reflect the growing normlessness of society in general.

The Christian church needs obvious, mass-communicated examples of individuals and communities of people who live out normed, valued, and consistent lifestyles. Without these examples the teaching and learning activity of the church is carried on in a context of relativity—a context which sets minorities, basic communities, and the local church at a serious if not crippling disadvantage.

Pastors and other religious educators know that contemporary teaching must include activities which involve the learner in doing, observing, evaluating, critiquing, assisting, and experimenting. What is now important is the *direction* of all that activity.

A class of seminary students researched, redesigned, wrote, and performed a series of educational television programs entitled "Portraits in Spirituality." The research involved the study of a number of characters in church history who symbolized both the spirituality typical of their time and a personal experiential expression of human spirituality. The work of *designing* put the students into a cooperative and, indeed, dependent relationship with communications specialists. The *writing* involved a struggle to engage the bicameral aspects of learning. *Performing* demanded a level of excellence and attention to detail which taught respect for the power and complexity of the media. Debating the relation between "truth," "dramatic license," "poetic justice," and the limits of time and television all contributed to a learning experience that was penetrating and compelling. It should be noted however that all of this says nothing about the learning experience of the audience. We may assume however that the content of learning for the audience was, in a large part, quite different even if significant from that of the seminary students. The experience was, and is for those involved, a case of the ever-broadening nature of teaching and learning possibilities created by the electronic media.

EMBRACING THE NEW MEDIA

The ministry of the church is enhanced where persons responsible for preaching, teaching, interpreting, and modeling the faith are

able to embrace more technique than those of the verbal and
literary media.

Randolph Crump Miller states the problem clearly: "The problem of method is technical. If we once develop a relationship theology which has the possibility of relevance at every level of human
experience, the educational problem becomes that of finding methods which will bring this relevance into focus."[17] Miller further
warns against the false antithesis—often perpetrated by the
church's religious educators—between content-centered and life-
centered teaching.

A major shift in educational methodology, made possible by the
technological revolution and media-based education, is the trend
toward individualized instruction and individualized learning. Computers, video and audio cassettes, and various forms of "programed" learning resources allow for the development of targeted,
specific, and learner-referenced teaching materials. However, the
church's commitment to certain assumptions about community and
the community's role in teaching and learning are in conflict with
the priorities which would create and make available such resources.

There are some examples of "technological tutoring" wherein
individuals in their own time and convenience work at discovering
the meaning and content of scripture and the church's tradition
while being "supervised" by a computer or a programed learning
video tape. The commitments needed within the church to plan,
produce, and distribute such materials are, as yet, weak and tentative.

For many within the church, the issue about the use of technology for proclamation, instruction, and nurture is not a "how" question but a question of whether to do it. The knowledge of technique is available. The source of resistance is deep.

In his urging of the church toward the many new techniques of
teaching and learning offered in the new information environment,
Ronald Sarno recognizes that all the past structures formed by the
technology with which the church is so comfortable (print technology) are all challenged by the new media. His pleas, however, may
reveal the sources of resistance even as they describe the directions
of the new forms and structures.

There is an urgent need for all the Christian churches to break with the characteristics associated with the past print age and to assimilate the forms of structures of the contemporary audio visual media. Incorporations of the forms and structures of the media revolution will lead the churches to become less hierarchial and more participatory, less centralized and more local, less authoritarian and more democratic, and less monolithic and more pluralistic.[18]

Sarno also points out that the learner as well as the teacher needs to move to a more active, involved engagement with modern technology. The problem is nevertheless primarily that of the attitudes of those responsible. "Once religious educators recognize their primary task is not verbal communication about a past message but a holistic communication about today's church, they should find eager learners at their doorstep."[19]

NEW OCCASIONS AND NEW DUTIES

Many within the church share Marshall McLuhan's view that technology of mass communications itself is a value creator as well as a transmitter of values. McLuhan held that mass media can be empowered with religious values. Others believe the cultural roots from which the new media have sprung imbued them with values which are often antithetical to those the church would advocate.

In discussing the ways in which church leaders approach the computer revolution in particular, Kenneth Bedell acknowledges the internal conflict of values and effectiveness. Some look to the computer to provide a captivating and motivating new dimension to old religious education tasks. They believe the computer can make religious instruction and learning both exciting and efficient. Bedell asks the hopeful questions:

Have computers arrived just in time? In an age when the average congregation is almost biblically illiterate and knows even less about traditions of the church, will the computer make it possible to convey religious information so that people are better equipped to apply religion to daily life? Imagine a congregation that is not limited by geography, size, culture, or history because it has immediate access to a computerized library. Can computers universalize knowledge and information so that each individual has access to the best answer for every question? Could large computerized data bases of religious information be available to every church school, so that every question can be seriously investigated? Can computer-based communication systems make it possible for individuals to share and grow in new ways?[20]

Such questions, are born, as Bedell rightly states, out of the dreaming and imagination of those who hope for some kind of media savior in the present malaise of ministry. The questions, however, do contain elements of the very kinds of new opportunities and possibilities provided by the media. Other students of the relationship share the optimism and the caution inherent in the thoughtful pursuit of the interface between communication media and the church's task. Ronald Sarno's optimism is tempered by an awareness of the large preparatory work needed if the church is to engage creatively in a future where educational ministry is enhanced by the media.

Religious education needs to wholeheartedly participate in the media revolution with all its realities and benefits. . . . Catholic teachers and learners must come to recognize that the verbal language of the catechisms is not the universal experience of the faith community. Protestant teachers and learners must come to recognize that the theological language of critical interpretation is not the original religious language of the ancient biblical authors.[21]

Both Sarno and Bedell explore the relation between the four theoretical approaches to religious education found in Harold Burgess' work, on the one hand, and various elements of the communication revolution, on the other hand.[22] Both clarify the differences of opinion and some of the fundamental causes for these differences.

What is at issue here is not that the church is divided as to its response and approach but that the very fact of the delay in responding creatively to the potential and possibilities of electronic media and mass communications is itself a message, and one that is being "heard" by those who are predisposed to assumptions of the church's irrelevance in contemporary society. This situation—an ever-exploding media revolution and a church experiencing difficulty shifting its priorities in order to participate in it—is creating a pressure within the church. The result is the development of powerful organizations outside, or at least on the edge of traditional church structures. Private businesses managed by religious people are entering the religious media field, and other entrepreneurial activities are uneasily located within the bureaucratic structures of the church. Some of the most powerful expressions of the values and lifestyles the church would advocate are coming from commercial production houses, film and television productions, and ad hoc communities of concerned media people.[23]

All of this further relegates the institutional church to a "background" position.

PROBLEMS AND NEEDS

Part of the institutional church's difficulty in responding creatively and effectively to the communications revolution is related to the fundamental differences of approach taken by "schools of thought" within the church's educational community. Using a variation of Ian Knox' categories or "metaperspectives" that form and shape religious education,[24] Ronald Sarno summarizes the relationships and attitudes.

Transcendist religious educators are those, especially some Evangelical Christians, who "witness to the historical unity between the Christian faith and the doctrinal verbalization of that fact as it is found in the printed Bible."[25] That link between faith assurance and the printed page leads them to "steadfastly refuse to accept modern communication theory's imperative to leave behind the product-content orientation of the print culture."[26]

Sarno divides the second group into two categories. The immanentist-theological approach is aware that theology is a changing process challenged by culture and updated by new knowledge. Persons taking this view "are most receptive to modern communication theory. They insist however, that modern communication cannot be allowed to strongly influence or alter the cognitive substantive context of contemporary theology."[27]

The other immanentist group—Sarno calls them immanentist-educational—"tend to make use of immanentist theology as a resource and an aid for what is basically understood as a pedagogical enterprise."[28] Sarno believes these theorists are "the most willing to integrate modern communication theory into the teaching act."[29]

With this approach the alleged duality between method and content is refuted and thus a freedom of method ensues.

The last group, the integrationists, attempt to synthesize transcendism and immanentism in the hope that such an incorporation may benefit from the insights and advantages found in the other positions. According to Sarno, "Integrationist religious educators show no interest in modern communication theory. Contemporary language studies are more applicable to their agenda."[30]

While the categorization of a number of religious education theorists is dangerous at best, it does point to the internal difficulties within the church's religious education community as it approaches the interface with media.

A second problem is related to the fact that a pastor today must respond to issues much more quickly than in the era of the print media. He or she must also develop the ability to prepare materials rapidly for consumption by an ever-accelerating educational need. If the Christian interpreter is to be responsive to the context, and the context changes with the speed of light, then those who prepare resources for ministry within the church will need to accelerate their capabilities and develop the structures that support such rapid responses. Computerized networks of clergy who "meet" regularly to do their exegetical work together over an electronic party line are having some of the desired effects.

Both at the local congregational level and throughout denominational and interdenominational structures there is need for a level of media literacy that allows mental and emotional access to the influential media. It will not be enough for pastors, church leaders, and religious educators to think they know what is happening to them in and through the media. It is crucial that we have some competence in the skills of media systems analysis, content analysis, relational critique, values clarification, and mediated context assessment.

Further, in order to engage effectively in religious media activities in response to rapidly changing needs, the church needs to accelerate its ability to create symbols and images that reflect the values and purposes it holds. The church must learn to create media events that authentically reflect the depth of emotion, conviction, and purpose it would convey.

At its national meeting, the delegates of The United Church of

Canada struggled with both the historical and contemporary dilemma of strained and broken relationships with that nation's indigenous people. A mood of contrition and regret was translated into an act of apology with an appropriate symbolic visit to the native people encamped nearby. Such an authentic expression of the mood of the meeting was both a media event and a powerful symbol. Individual congregations can and should undertake to symbolize their values, purposes, and mission goals.

Another element relating to the factors of acceleration is reflected in the many ways new structures can be established "within" the church which make use of contemporary media. Computerized national church offices are linked by modem to regional offices and even to individual pastors and congregations offering the promise of the high-speed transfer of:

- educational resources
- background documents for congregational study
- support for sermon preparation
- news about recent church-related issues
- assistance to congregations in various stages of development or redevelopment
- financial and administrative data
- links between persons, task forces, and interest groups

Each of the above demands new human and technological structures which give persons in the congregation a sense of support and a tangible confirmation of the existence and value of the wider Christian community.

Desktop publishing, the child of the marriage of computer with laser technology, is making appreciable changes in the church's ability to deliver quality print products to serve the religious education needs of constituent members.

While little has been done yet to make use of the communications satellite technology, those efforts that have been undertaken have proven highly encouraging. The Vancouver School of Theology produces an annual telecourse delivered via satellite to over a hundred learning groups in the Province of British Columbia. The groups are formed in advance, given reading material and study guides, watch the video program simultaneously, and then are linked via telephone network to the teachers in the studio for responses, questions, and clarifications.

Once again new structures are designed to serve new needs.

It is now evident that as the church's ministry enters the new world of media with intentionality and conviction there is need to continue to broaden understanding in two fields; communication theory and communication process. An increasing number of authors and researchers are addressing these subjects, but it is interesting to note that few are using electronic media methods in teaching the church about its relationship with the eletronic media.

EMERGING STRATEGIES

New strategies are being developed by pastors and others responsible for the task of integrating text with context on behalf of the church.

A strategy of *consciousness raising* assumes the need for increased knowledge and understanding of the process of communications and the implication of that process for discernment of the context. The process has a number of elements which can have the effect of changing the concept being sent by a communicator.

A concept in the mind of one person is influenced on its way to another by:
1) the motive of the sender (to persuade, teach, inspire, inform, close or open discussion, challenge, suggest, interpret, etc.)
2) the code chosen (words, music notes, pen strokes, color, dance gesture, body language, etc.)
3) the delivery system used (human voice, radio, T.V. film, canvas, a letter, telegraph, etc.)
4) the filters that function in all communications exchanges (preconceived images, language usages, cross purposes, prejudices, etc.)
5) the degree of acceptance of the delivery systems employed
6) the skill of the decoder
7) the interpretation of the motives of the sender on the part of the receiver.

Contemporary pastors and other interpreters of the faith need to understand this process both as receivers and senders of messages which influence discernment.

A second strategy is that of *consultation* with a new set of experts. Recognizing that reporters, news editors, film and video makers, and writers have unique and well-developed gifts of discernment, a number of pastors have identified these as valid consultants to assist in the determination of those issues within the contexts which call for response from the pulpit.

A third strategy involves *experimentation*. Using sound communication theory, pastors and others are experimenting with various forms of media as alternatives for the traditional preaching and teaching functions. When care is taken with the insights from the theories used, this experimentation proves time-consuming and at times frustrating. The development of the appropriate skills and sensitivities needed to use the new media does not come easily. A simple example will suffice. Recognizing that the medium of radio, or its less-flexible counterpart the audio cassette, is received as a one-to-one form of communication and, unlike a sermon, a message sent by radio or cassette is heard by persons alone, some clergy are experimenting with new efforts of preaching to one person at a time. The Sunday sermon is rewritten for the individual listener and read onto an audio tape for persons who will receive it in the privacy of their own home or car. Those pastors who have undertaken the discipline of such an experiment have found the responses both revealing and instructive.

Some pastors, theological students, and theological educators are taking an approach which employs a method similar to the urban plunge used in both urban training and field education programs. Based on the assumption that one is likely to learn about the city by plunging into a microcosom of it, the urban plunge sends participant-observers into a subsystem of the city—usually the innercity—in order to reflect upon the systems, contexts, power structures, values, compromises, tensions, and relationships that make up the larger entity. Actually to make the metaphor more accurate, a plunge into the "world of mass media" is more likely entering the wealthy old part of town where the power brokers, decision makers, developers, government leaders, and lawmakers live. To understand the city from that point of view is to see it from the vantage point of those who not only live in the context but have power to change it. To plunge into the "world of media" is to discover that it is neither a subsystem nor adjunct to the society in which we live. Mass media are themselves system-makers. They form and reform institutions, reflect and project values and icons, create impressions and replicas of the societies of which they are part. Mass media set agendas for other elements of the community and become themselves an item of the agenda. To plunge into the world of mass media is to discover the dramatic interplay between initiator and respondent, merchant and customer, value maker and value maintainer.

Like the urban plunge, an experience first-hand of the mass media can be deeply disturbing, not only because of what it reveals concerning the nature of power, the sources of values, and the shape of communities, but also because of the new, difficult, and challenging questions it leaves unanswered. A confrontation with mass media also lays bare some of the reasons for the difficulty pastors and other leaders have in coming to terms with the challenges of contemporary culture.

WHAT NEXT?

The following, while not an exhaustive list, is reflective of the variety and depth of the task before those who will take the lead in the relationship between the church and the media. The pastor as religious educator would do well to act on many and, if possible, all of the following.

1. A serious exploration of our sensibilities toward the use and understanding of symbols and metaphors is needed. While this is of course an age-old issue, it now moves at interstellar speeds since new metaphors and captivating images both of meaning making and meaning maintaining are developed for the insatiable appetite of the mass media. The dramatic presentation "Jesus Christ Superstar" and a film "Rainbow Wars" prepared for Expo '88, Vancouver's World Fair, are examples that point to the possibilities. "Rainbow Wars," using symbols of color to identify three different types of "world," demonstrates the danger of self-centeredness and nationalism as opposed to inclusiveness and an open worldview.

2. Attention must be given to the matter of *motivation* within the church, particularly in advance of our need to respond or react to contemporary media-created agendas. Too frequently the institutional church responds to the media agendas rather than

persist in pursuit of its own. The reason may often be traced to the church's confusion as to what it actually wants; media coverage of its meetings and events or the articulation of specific theological premises.

3. A search must be undertaken for ways to embrace the use and values of mediated experiences and relationships in order that the interpretation of the faith may have a wider audience. Since so many of the resources and energies of the church are turned in the direction of the local congregation, little energy is left for the development of interpretive material for those who are unrelated to the church generally and unconnected with the local congregation in particular. Recent efforts at understanding the task of Christian interpretation when directed toward "persons with no Christian memory" are encouraging examples.

4. New networks are needed. A careful but accelerated effort to develop networks of people with resources, knowledge, and experience within the various interest areas and mission foci of the church would allow for increased information-sharing, sharper critique, more widely circulated interpretations, and more inclusive involvement of those who could assist in the church's task. Both efficiency and appropriateness are important principles here.

5. Some new strategies are needed. The intentional empowering of "need centers" by providing both the means and methods to use the newer media to express and interpret need in a highly competitive milieu has now reached the proportion of a "justice issue." The electronic media provide both access to and delivery of the kinds of information that increase the likelihood of responsible, informed, efficient decision making about the application of decreasing or scarce resources. For those with greatest needs to have little or no access to the powerful and effective media is an issue of inequality to which the church could, and must, address itself.

6. Some risk taking in the area of self-censorship is appropriate. The church has been able to censure South African leaders,

South American dictators, coffee growers, employers of itinerant workers, and many others, but is not as articulate on matters of theological, biblical, and ecclesialogical "corruption." The fear of conflict and of alienating some whose attachment is tentative at least often leads the church to be silent about its own internal struggles and mute on the subject of heresy. By its silence the church often appears normless to those who look to it for norms.

7. New relationships are needed. Church leaders could well create intra- and inter-dependent relationships with the experts of electronic media similiar to those developed over the years with print editors, publishers, print technicians, graphic designers, and artists. "Amateur" media productions sponsored by the institutional church are themselves a message sender, suggesting that it is indifferent to, or unaware of, the power and potential of the medium. The church will benefit from the recognition that to use modern communication technology effectively and well is an expensive and creative task requiring a high commitment of energy and funds.

8. A clarification of agendas is required. Increased effort should be expended to clarify and articulate the church's social and attitudinal agenda so that it will not so easily expend energy in response to the agendas set by the media. There is, of course, the risk of being considered irrelevant since the media agenda is usually powerful in establishing community expectations. There may also be some reprisals from within the congregation when agendas begin to call members to choose rather than remain neutral on issues of public import. Such a clarification may also result in the realignment of the structures both within and between existing denominational forms.

In one sense, to "go public" through the mass media with interpretations, metaphors, messages, and challenges is to be called to account, to come to terms with priorities, and to be expected to be precise and clear about agendas. It is suspected that the use of mass media or other forms of educational technology is avoided by some because of a reluctance to be precise, pointed, succinct, and unequivocal.

PRINCIPLES OF PARTICIPATION

When pastors, church leaders, and religious educators intend to interact with media in an effort to enhance ministry, some principles are useful.

A. *Reciprocity/Reflection*. It is important to be cognizant of the fact that, like all human organizations, the institutional church is capable of using others for its own ends. While we deplore that in others, it is an attitude and response for which we may be guilty especially when it comes to matters of the use (and abuse) of media.

To the degree that media provides only *methods* the church may feel free to employ technology for its own ends. Where the relationship between the church and institutions of media production and distribution are concerned however, we do well to maintain a high level of reciprocal commitment. The basic question to ask is "how can we serve T.V. (radio, the production houses, etc.), while they are serving us?"

B. *Authentic Motivation*. Church media users do well to ask "why are we using additional media support?" There are good reasons for using it, but there is need to be clear about them. Some shallow ones include:
—"We didn't have time to prepare otherwise."
—"We need something to catch people's attention."
—"We've done it the same way so long we need a change."
Some deeper motives are evident in these more reflective statements:
—"The multi-imaged presentation we're planning recognizes the complexity of the problem we're trying to portray and the speed with which it changes."
—"The eucharist is both a symbolic event and a personal experience and the use of lighting and special projection in our program helps to clarify the ways in which both symbols and emotions are involved."
—"The edited version of the video tape of our annual meeting helps people who are isolated or unable to attend and participate to continue to experience the dynamics of our congregation's life, even though they cannot be part of it in the way they have been in the past."

To ask the deeper motivational questions is to press congregations and individuals toward theological and religious reflection
on issues of the nature of the church, community, and gospel.
To clarify our motives is also to clarify our mission.

C. *Multiple Impact/Single Concept.* The church, both in its local and
denominational expressions often makes the mistake of trying
to do too much with one media exposure. Communication
experts know that there are many reasons for diversifying the
medium methodologies which simplify or specify the content.
Multiplying media exposures and targeting specific segments of
the audience with appropriate variations of the same general
theme is a more productive and creative way to interpret the
church's understanding of ministry and mission.

D. *Targeted Communication.* The author possesses an audio demon-
stration tape with the same commercial message prepared with
appropriate rhythm, voice intonation, musical sound, etc., for a
variety of radio stations; country and western, light rock, hard
rock, easy listening, classical, and the middle of the road (mor).
    The difference is so notable when heard in serial fashion that
it raises consciousness to challenge the simplistic assumptions
made in the church about the "audience."

E. *Informed Participation.* If church leaders are to engage creatively
in the use of communications media it is important that they be
informed not only about the nature of the media itself but about
the effect of such media on various audiences. It is possible now
to use well-prepared books, articles, even television courses to
become better informed about the media itself. Media literacy in
general, and television awareness in particular, has been an agenda item for denominational Communication Divisions for some
time. Most major denominations have materials for their con-
stituencies use. Some local congregations, many theological
schools, some district or regional gatherings of clergy and other
church leaders have undertaken a "plunge" into aspects of media production and resource creation for the purpose of learning more about it. Such an experience can open important new
avenues of communication between the church and the various

forms of mass communication and media technology.

Thanks to the work of Ronald Sarno, Kenneth Bedell, and others, it is now possible for congregations to acquaint themselves with many more of the resources available for effective use within the church.[31]

A reflective process helps church leaders to recognize and become more clearly aware of the bias the church projects and the images that form both the collective attitude within the church and the conscious and unconscious perspective of those outside of it. Distorted perceptions of the significance and effectiveness of ministry are often troublesome in as much as they reinforce negative attitudes toward the church among those predisposed to such attitudes.

Informed participation in the media should also be based on an informed attitude about the global nature of the content of religious education. James Michael Lee's definition of eight different types of substantive content (product, process, cognitive, affective, verbal, nonverbal, unconscious, and lifestyle) establishes a level of caution for those planning media presentations. Such planning demands intelligent and intentional preparation of both substantive content and the delivery system. The complexity of the task is recognized more fully when the diversity of content is also recognized.[32] An example of the latter point can be seen in the complexity of planning and broadcasting a worship service. In fact all of the eight content areas are integrated in a liturgical broadcast, but the T.V. audience does not experience the physical community of a congregation, has not prepared for worship in the same way as the congregation, and does not possess the same sense of belonging. Therefore the broadcast of a worship service is quite a different experience from the service itself even though all the content areas are being covered.

F. *Shared Needs.* Just as we have come to recognize that publishers and editors have needs that reflect the goals and purposes of the publishing institutions, so we will need to acknowledge the needs of those involved in the broadcast media and in other aspects of media production. The manager of a local, privately owned radio station was addressing a group of clergy, all of whom had some interest in broadcasting. After acknowledging the demands for public service laid on by regulatory bodies he addressed the subject of shared needs and mixed motives.

You need to understand that the purpose of commercial radio is to make money. In order to do that we identify a segment of the population, program directly to the perceived interests, needs, and attitudes of that audience, create a sound and a media environment that will gather and hold the audience so that they can be counted. On the basis of that count we can establish the fees we charge to those who want to address the audience commercially. The larger the audience, the larger the fees. If your broadcasts on our station diminishes that audience, we lose. That's why we charge many religious organizations who want to address our audience. If by your broadcasting on our station you contribute to the growth and expansion of our audience, then it would be legitimate for you to expect us to contribute to your costs and to the development of your programs.[33]

It is precisely this combination of motivational factors and or recognized need that has led in some cases to creative religious broadcasting. In other cases it leads to an extremely high cost for religious programing on commercial radio and television stations. Always, however, there is a danger of the commitments and convictions of the religious community being compromised for the sake of reducing or reversing the cost of communicating through the mass media.

G. *Clear Objectives.* We can learn much from experts in the media about the definition of communication objectives and the selection and utilization of media materials and resources to meet those objectives. We can also learn about the value of single concept programing. Frequently the church's use of mass media has been a form of "electronic eavesdropping" where we expect the media to "cover" something we are doing for a specific and predetermined audience elsewhere. Pastors and other church leaders resent the media personnel if they recommend appreciable change in their planned format, changes which would alter the direction and focus of the material. The point is that the media people are concentrating on a "different" audience and "their" needs and seek to put pressure on would-be broadcasters to address the audiences according to the audience's need.

H. *Critical Distance.* As has become the custom of pastors and other church leaders, a certain critical distance from any media is an important principle to observe. One of the most helpful recent books on the subject of newspaper journalism contains the kind of documentation that should alert clergy and concerned lay leaders to the need for critical distance. David Broder, himself a national political correspondent, states clearly, and with exceptional illustrative support, that the "news" is often produced in "ignorance and haste" and reflects newspeople's "ingrained values and biases."[34] The critical distance will be enhanced by adherence to some of the above principles, most notably authentic motivation, informed participation, and clear objectives. Critical distance is a major factor in maintaining perspective in those who become "media personalities" as well as church leaders.

I. *Search for Discernment.* It is important at times to examine what is said, when there is nothing to say. The media often force us to create news or establish something as newsworthy which under normal circumstances would not be considered so. Radio and television institutions are in fact often responsible for the sponsoring of popularity polls, political polls, surveys, and instant opinion taking. The purpose of most of that is to create news. On the strength of the political poll, news reporters are then able to spend their time asking newsmakers to respond to the polls, to describe their feelings and their attitudes toward the findings and their implications. Without the polls there would have been no news. Whether or not the response of individuals to the polls is news is questionable. For pastors and educators, a fundamental question arises because of this and similar phenomenon. How can we clarify the important from the unimportant, the relevant from the irrelevant, the substantial from the mundane. Some discernment questions may be useful.
—"Who says this is important?"
—"Who will be affected by the answers and who benefits from the question?"

—"What change is being recommended, by whom, and for what purpose?"

—"Is there an obvious bias in the question?"

—"Is the question hypothetical or the context contrived?"

It is also helpful to turn those same questions on ourselves as we think about developing, creating, or projecting, through media, elements of ministry and mission. "Who says this issue is important?" etc.

J. *Attitudinal Principles.* Church leaders do well to attempt the maintenance of two attitudes toward mass media and the communications revolution. The first is to avoid cynicism. The second is to avoid naivete. When pastors glimpse the power, manipulative strength, and resourcefulness of men and women within the media it is possible at times to become cynical about both those who project and those who accept media messages. It is equally possible to assume naively that nothing important is happening and that the resourcefulness of human beings is strong enough to overcome and cast-off the effect of the meaning-making and value-creating media. Both attitudes would appear to be unhealthy for the creative interaction between church and media. A recent National Council study recommends five strategies "to help religious groups transform themselves from passive receivers to active participants in media life and in the shaping of culture."

—"Consider religious institutions as both reproducers and challengers of prevailing views of reality."

—"Develop religious communities as facilitators of human interaction."

—"Examine religious precedents for resistance and positive means of communication."

—"Encourage subjective interpretations of experience."

—"Generate critical analysis of media."[35]

K. *The Principle of the Three-Way Process.* The pastor as religious educator will want to remember that the process of planning, designing, projecting, and evaluating media presentation is a three-way process involving programers, audience, and tradition. The *programers* include not only those with theological, biblical, and ecclesiological concerns but also those with creative and technical commitments. The *audience* is different when its participation is mediated through technology even if it includes the same people with whom we worship, study, and share communion. *Tradition* both of the church and the media carries its own message and its own significance and each example of the combination of church and media carries its own meta-message. To be specific, some people are turned off by the church because of some residual message they carry about the tradition the church represents. Some are "turned off" by television for the same reason. Conversely, others are drawn to the church because of experiences that strengthened and enriched their lives. Others are drawn to television because it has been useful, entertaining, and comforting. When church leaders plan to utilize media they need to be aware that the third element in the process of communication provides a filter which may allow messages through or block them significantly.

CONCLUSION

In their central role as religious educator, pastors are surrounded by high impact, intensive image-makers, and context-creators. There are new skills and sensitivities needed if the contexts to which the biblical, religious, and theological traditions apply are to be discerned.

The media, while capable of delivering a "message from the word," will also influence both the way it is sent and the way it is received. While projecting the old and new images of faith and faithfulness, the media also project images of those who proclaim, interpret, and symbolize the community of faith. Simultaneously the contexts to which messages of faith are proclaimed are themselves interpretive and not necessarily as the church understands or embraces them.

The messenger and the message are entwined, the content and the contexts interpenetrate, and the individual often feels overwhelmed by the complexity of it all.

Yet there may be, in this new situation, opportunities beyond any past dream because of the power, influence, and possibilities of the media to interpret the word more clearly, share the faith more widely, include God's people more fully, and embrace with integrity the "whole inhabited earth."

Notes

1. J. David Bolter, *Turnings Man* (Chapel Hill, N.C.: University of North Carolina Press, 1984), p. 10.

2. Jacques Ellul, *The Technological Society*, trans. John Wilkinson (New York: Vantage, 1964).

3. William F. Fore, "A Theology of Communications," *Religious Education* 82: 2 (Spring 1987), p. 235.

4. William F. Fore, *Image and Impact: How Man Comes Through in the Mass Media* (New York: Friendship Press, 1970), p. 8.

5. Norbert Mette, "The Christian Communities Task in the Process of Religious Education," *Concilium, Religion in the 80's*, ed. Norbert Greinacher and Virgil Elizondo (Edinburgh: T & T Clark, 1984), p. 70.

6. Ibid., p. 70.

7. Barbara Hargrove, "Theology, Education and the Electronic Media," *Religious Education* 82: 2 (Spring 1987), p. 222.

8. For the complete presentation of Lee's description of the total teaching structure see James Michael Lee, *The Flow of Religious Instruction* (Birmingham, Ala.: Religious Education Press, 1973).

9. Ronald Sarno, *Using Media in Religious Education* (Birmingham, Ala.: Religious Education Press, 1987), p. 152.

10. Ibid., p. 152.

11. For a description of these eight types of content see James Michael Lee, *The Content of Religious Education* (Birmingham, Ala.: Religious Education Press, 1985).

12. For an explanation of the various theories of Mass Media (New York: David McKay, 1970).

13. Sarno, *Using Media*, p. 35.

14. Randolph Crump Miller, *The Theory of Christian Education Practice* (Birmingham, Ala.: Religious Education Press, 1980), p. 65.

15. John Westerhoff, "On Knowing: The Bi-cameral Mind," *Concilium*, "The Transmission of Faith to the Next Generation," ed. Norbert Greinacher and Virgil Elizondo (Edinburgh: T & T Clark, 1984), p. 64.

16. Ibid., p. 64.

17. Miller, *The Theory of Christian Education Practice*, p. 160.

18. Sarno, *Using Media*, p. 78.

19. Ibid., p. 80.

20. Kenneth B. Bedell, *The Role of Computers in Religious Education* (Nashville: Abingdon, 1986), pp. 11-12.

21. Sarno, *Using Media*, pp. 78-79.

22. For a full exploration of the theoretical approaches see Harold William Burgess, *An Invitation to Religious Education* (Birmingham, Ala.: Religious Education Press, 1975), pp. 127-165; and for the comparisons with communities issues see Sarno, *Using Media*, pp. 24-37 and Bedell, *The Role of Computers*, pp. 15-21.

23. Some helpful advice in the identification and use of this type of material can be found in the book by William B. Levenson and Edward Stanhoff, *Teaching*

Through Radio and Television (Westport, Conn.: Greenwood, 1952).

24. Ian Knox, *Above or Within: The Supernatural in Religious Education* (Biringham, Ala.: Religious Education Press, 1976).

25. Sarno, *Using Media*, pp. 87-88.

26. Ibid., p. 156.

27. Ibid., pp. 156-157.

28. Ibid., p. 125.

29. Ibid., p. 157.

30. Ibid., p. 157.

31. Sarno's book contains excellent bibliographic references as well as indices for Motion Pictures, Television Titles, Photography, Popular music, Radio, Video Recording and Computers. Bedell lists computer software designed for church uses. The spring 1987 issue of *Religious Education* (The Journal of R.E.A. and A. P.R.R.E.) contains an extensive annotated bibliography on Electronic Media prepared by James A. Capo.

32. Lee, *The Content of Religious Instruction.*

33. Dennis Fisher notes to author, 16 February, 1984.

34. David S. Broder, *Behind the Front Pages: A Candid Look at How the News Is Made* (New York: Simon and Schuster, 1987).

35. Report of The Study Commission of Theology, Education, and the Electronic Media. Division of Education and Ministry, National Council of the Churches of Christ in the U.S.A., 1987. Printed in *Religious Education* 82: 2, (1987), pp. 163-184.

Bibliography

Brooks, Peter. *Communicating Convictions.* London: Epworth Press, 1983.

Cummings, H. Wayland, and Somervill, Charles. *Overcoming Communications Barriers in the Church.* Valley Forge, Pennsylvania: Judson, 1981.

Davis, Dennis M., and Clapp, Steve. *The Third Wave and the Local Church.* Champaign, Illinois: C-4 Computer, 1983.

Ellul, Jacques. *The Technological Society.* New York: Vantage, 1974.

Emswiler, James P. *Using a Computer in Church Ministry.* Denville, New Jersey: Dimension, Inc., 1986.

Hopper, Robert, and Whitehead Jack L. Jr., *Communication Concepts and Skills.* New York: Harper & Row, 1979.

Kelly, John C. *A Philosophy of Communications.* London: The Centre for the Study of Communications and Culture, 1981.

Lowe, Kathy. *Opening Eyes and Ears: New Connections for Christian Communications.* Geneva: World Council of Churches, 1983.

McLuhan, Marshall. *The Guttenberg Galaxy.* Toronto: University of Toronto Press, 1962.

——. *Understanding Media.* New York: Signet Books, 1964.

Sarno, Ronald A. *Using Media in Religious Education.* Birmingham, Alabama: Religious Education Press, 1987.

Soukup, Paul A. *Communication and Theology.* London: The World Association of Christian Communication, 1983.

Sumrall, Velma, and Germany, Lucille. *Telling the Story of the Local Church. The Who, What, When, Where, and Why of Communications.* New York: Seabury, 1979.

8

Black Pastoral Leadership in Religious Education: Social Justice Correlates

GRANT S. SHOCKLEY

INTRODUCTION

Since the tumultuous years of the civil rights movement of the 1960s, including the Free Speech Movement and the Women's Liberation Movement, there has been a renaissance of interest in social justice concerns and intentional education for social change. This concern has been noticeable across the entire religious community. It can be attested to by church pronouncements, a growing literature, and in some cases professional staff provision. The source of this interest, however, generally has not come from religious education practitioners or local church clergy but rather from the academe, researchers, professionals, youth, and laity.[1] Even more interesting than this are two other observations. Religious education formats in the vast majority of local congregations have few intentional social justice progams, excepting perhaps denominational curriculum resource-oriented ones. Second, most clergy are not significantly involved in these programs, nor indeed in most educational programs excepting church membership or confirmation education. This observation was confirmed in researching this chapter. One seeks almost in vain for pertinent experience or literature pertaining to the role or concern of pastors in social justice ministries.[2] It is therefore the writer's opinion that despite the "priority" reportedly given to social justice ministries by many denominational bodies, such programs that do exist are either ad hoc, the result of the effort of concerned individual members of congregations, or the product of commissioned, short-termed projects. Almost totally absent from the vast majority of churches (black or white) are viable religious educational programs or structures dealing with social change or social justice concerns. If such programs do exist they are not indigenous or related to the area of the community the parish serves. Most disturbing of all is the reluctant and often negative attitude of pastors of local congregations toward the initiation, development, sustaining, and administering of comprehensive social justice ministries. The rationale for this chapter is the need to explore this enigmatic situation and, hopefully, to define and delineate the possible shape and content of a usable program of Christian social justice ministry.

Purpose

Given the situation-description above, the purposes to be achieved in the chapter are several: 1) to discern and conceptualize the nature, purpose, and mission of the church with a particular concern for a social justice ministry; 2) to delineate several rather specific objectives that will fulfill that mission; 3) to develop an educational strategy that can reasonably be expected to carry out the objectives; 4) to design an implementing model or miniature system for a social justice ministry; and 5) to derive a complementary leadership component implied by the model and supplemented with insights from the black religious experience.

Methodology

A modified case-study method will present the data of this chapter. Selected examples in the development of the church in the United States (black and white) will be used to illustrate principles and factors that determined (and determine) the emergence and effectiveness of pastoral leadership for an intentional ministry of social justice.

Thesis

The thesis that is being advanced in this chapter is simple: an examination of the evolution of pastoral leadership, in ethnic and black churches (in response to past, continuing and present needs and demands for justice, equality, and liberation in the church and in the general society) provides a paradigm of an integrated social justice ministry for local congregations that is prophetic, holistic, and transformational.[3] Unless and until churches (black, white, or other) commit themselves to these elemental presuppositions the integrity of their total design for either ministry or education must be questioned.

MISSION AND MINISTRY

The typical lack of concern and indifference for social issues in Protestant churches in the United States (and probably elsewhere in North America) today has historical roots. The churches may have gotten their religion before getting their social ethics. Franklin H. Littell has insisted for a number of years that most North Americans never had religion. His statement is, "The American people (are) but slowly being won from heathenism to faithfulness and the process is far from complete."[4] In terms of social problems, the picture he gives of the Colonial period was bleak. Instead of the idyllic image of a flourishing religious nation in a high moral state, there was "slavery, concubinage, limited suffrage, indentured servitude, religious persecution, and widespread illiteracy."[5] It was also true of this period that while pre-Civil War antislavery impulses did come from the churches, it was these same churches that instituted racial segregation. They did this before the war and after it as well. The most devastating criticism of the churches during this period, however, was their ethical duplicity. They achieved phenomenal growth, statistically, for almost a century following the North-South conflict based on segregated churches and domestic programs of missions and social uplift. The cost in integrity to the churches for this was enormous. Again Littell points out, "One large church after another formalized the abandonment of church discipline . . . smaller churches broke off from the major bodies to reestablish some measure of internal integrity."[6] A third factor contributed to the difference of Protestants in social justice ministries as the nation became urbanized (1875-1914). Following its period of growth into the "Establishment" it was challenged by non-Anglo-Saxons. F. Nile Harper reports that E. Digby Baltzell found that this challenge to Anglo-Saxon Protestant power was met by retreating from political leadership but maintaining itself as an aristocracy of wealth, prestige, and privilege.[7] It did not lend its enormously powerful influence to social justice causes as it could have done. Harper makes this point clear in the following statement. "The Protestant Church has grown economically comfortable and socially privileged. It has not encouraged its people to seek a vocation in politics as a means of working for social justice."[8]

The point of this brief, introductory historical exercise is clear. Churches in America, especially Protestant, had not "fallen" from some originally high state of responsibility for the maintenance of social justice. There is grave doubt that they ever aspired to it or achieved it.

A plea for faithfulness to the implications of the social teachings of the Christian churches in America's past, then, except on the basis of selected exemplary pastors, leaders, and churches, would not be productive. As a matter of fact it would be difficult to find the development of a significant social conscience in the centuries preceding American colonization excepting perhaps the English antislavery crusade. Of course, no social historian would wish to regurgitate the history of the centuries that bred the mentality that introduced the slave trade and chattel slavery of which John Wesley said was "the vilest that ever saw the sun." It is a sad but true commentary on the history of American Christianity generally and Protestantism specifically, that apart from its inspiration of individual leaders and "missions" there is little institutional development of social justice not born out of the "civil rights" struggles which the churches joined lately and weakly. More will be said about this later. In summary, the witness of the churches to social justice causes must be declared still-born.

Currently the churches are still failing to have any significant impact on the critical social issues that face vast numbers of their members and parish communities. This ironic situation may be called an "identity crisis," i.e., the church not identifying with the radical character of the gospel which calls it to action and faith to live and decide as Christians, responsibly, under a future-in-the-present style of existence in a world of permanent revolution. Even a brief examination of the Christian "presence" today raises serious questions about its understanding of and commitment to the need for basic social change. It appears, also, to be operating on the basis of a dubious principle of mere "personal salvation" with a minimum of radical biblical realism, theological analysis, or secular sophistication. In other words, it has failed and is failing, almost utterly, to come to terms with a major "identity crisis" in its life in relation to the time in which it lives. For example, excepting pronouncements, church think-tanks avante-garde resources, and an increasing number of religious activists on behalf of refugees, liberation, women's rights, and a sane ecology policy, the churches as churches seem both impotent and paralyzed in the face of the voracious changes of recent years. Jürgen Moltmann refers to this situation as an "identity-involvement dilemma": "The more theology tries to be relevant to the social crises of the society, the more deeply it is drawn into the crisis of its own Christian identity."[9]

What would resolve this crisis? It is suggested that the church again confront itself with the forthright, critical insights of its own neglected Reformed tradition. Among other things, this tradition emphasizes the kingdom of God as the goal of the human community and the prophetic word as the conscience of the nation. It offers the challenge of proactive social engagement and warns against succumbing to the paralysis of conservative reactionism. Again Littell identifies the issue. It is what he calls the lack of radical Christian discipline or the willingness to witness to a belief despite the vulnerability or cost.[10] This, he believes, is the "root and stem" of the fundamental problem facing the church and the churches. The recovery of such a discipline should precede any attempts to deal seriously with social justice issues.

SOCIAL JUSTICE ISSUES

A new consciousness of ministry and a new understanding of the urgency for social justice as a priority for church education emerges as the result of the foregoing critique of the church's general lack of concern for and neglect of the persistent cries of the oppressed for justice, equality, and peace. The situation is so acute that it might be said that "faith should withdraw from full interaction with contemporary life if it cannot authentically confront the full range of the concerns of the men it addresses."[11] The evidence is convincing and practically overwhelming. We are not inculcating in children, youth, or adults, to any appreciable degree, the kinds of knowledge, attitudes, or skills that will constructively contribute to the building of a more just social order in the United States, Canada, North America, or elsewhere. Jesse Ziegler, an eminent religious educator, would be correct is his estimation of the state of affairs on this issue when he wrote in *Religious Education* in 1950: "We remain almost 100 percent a segregated church and continue to teach more potently by example our real attitude about race than all our words can deny. . . . We support the cause of capital as over against labor. . . . We seem completely unable to achieve any unanimity in the rejection of the single greatest denial of . . . social order . . . war. . . . Totalitarianism is utterly abhorrent to many Christian people who nevertheless find no rallying center within their educational resources to resist this movement toward the suicidal destruction of a war against Communism. There is no prophetic lead being given by Christian education forces as to how Communism can be stopped without war."[12] While much has changed since 1950, Ziegler's perspective is still descriptive of many of our problems.

Clearly, these "realities" of our age and our world call us to shape or contextualize ministry to become the "servant church" in order to redeem and liberate God's people and equip them for ministry to others.

In the remainder of this section of the chapter several suggestions of key social justice issues will be made in response to Ziegler's challenge. In the case of each issue an attempt has been made not only to identify a social justice issue that the churches should be concerned about and "pray for" but issues that must be engaged at the deeper levels of both motivation, mission, and social change. In other words, the church must practice a single moral standard. It must speak, teach, and act consistently, coherently, and congruently in helping persons to make moral, social, economic, and political decisions in the spirit of the Christian faith they acknowledge and follow. Without a doubt pastors have a crucial role in generating such a vision for the church. *Peace with Justice*, the Roman Catholic U.S. Bishops' Pastoral Letter on war and peace (1983), succinctly poses for all human beings the "supreme crisis," nuclear war. It does this in drastically frightening words: "Nuclear war threatens the existence of our planet; this is a more menacing threat than any the world has known before."[13]

In the face of this ominous threat, pastors as religious educators are confronted with a fourfold task. First, teaching and learning about war must identify the enemy as injustice, hate, greed, national pride, and fear. It must communicate that other people and nations are not ultimately the enemy. Second, it can and must be taught that there can never be real peace without real justice, i.e., respect for human rights, differences among people, religions, and cultures, economic justice, protective civil rights and liberties, and interdependent development in and among nations. Third, church-oriented informal and formal education and public dialogue must begin to influence national foreign policy formation on a basis that is humanistic rather than militaristic. Fourth, concurrent with maturing understandings of the nature of peace, justice, and the responsibility to protect life, the churches through religious education must seek to influence decisions to reduce and eventually abolish the instruments of war and produce instruments of peace.

Ecology/Nonhuman Resources: Second only to the threat of a nuclear holocaust as a potential destructor of our planet and all of its life-forms is the critical ecology, environment, nonhuman resources issue. This problem which must claim much more of the attention of religious education than it has is basically one of pollution. It is also interrelated with food, hunger, technology, and population growth. The ecology issue, according to Kenneth P. Alpers,[14] confronts theology and religious education with two questions: What is a theology of the natural environment and what is a responsible ethic that complements it? In referring to the latter issue, Alpers suggests the following approaches: 1) the technological, i.e., mechanical interventions and 2) lifestyle change, i.e., adjusting lifestyles to the limits of the environment. Speaking to the "limits" approach, Kenneth Boulding[15] indicates that a new approach is mandatory, including: scale models of life-support systems that are austere yet reasonable; monitoring of population growth; evaluation of technological interventions; and disciplined consumership.

There seem to be four implications for religious education here. First, the churches must recover (or develop) a theology of the natural (or of creation) and teach it. Paul Tillich, Joseph Sittler, and others, have done work on this. Second, an ethic of managing the environment efficiently must go beyond the "conservation" concept. Pastors and laity must become involved in teaching the principle of maintaining ecological balance in all ecosystems. Third, the "web of life" or the interdependence concept must be emphasized with its "mutually supportive" notion of cooperation to meet the needs of the whole human community. Fourth, religious education must articulate with more deftness and explore zealously ways to communicate the principle that we must live "with" rather than just "on" the land or in the air and sea (the "crucial crucible"—or God's place of encounters with us as unique creatures).

International Development: Granted a world in which there is some will to work for the things which make for peace and some effort to interrelate the limits of the natural environment with the requirements of a sustainable and habitable human future, the issue of international development arises. What, then, is development and what does it mean in international terms from a Christian perspective? There are several ways to look at it.

Gunnar Myrdal would define development as the upward move-ment of a system of interdependent conditions—social, economic, political, etc. Benjamin Higgins opts for a more limited economic interpretation of the term. Denis Goulet selects a broader spectrum of interpretation including improved "optimum life sustenance," "esteem," and "freedom."

The World Council of Churches' definition suits this chapter best. It describes development as a "liberating process," emphasizing "the need for radical changes in social, economic, and political structures which oppress, enslave, and dehumanize men [and wom-en]."[16]

Church involvement in a ministry of international development as it has been defined above lays down certain assumptions which religious education may or may not initially be able to make in most local congregations. Clarification may be needed on the following:[17]

1. All persons were created by God and are entitled to every possible opportunity to become who and what they are in that divine image.
2. Christian vocation is to love God and neighbor, to share God's gifts of creation, and to enhance the quality of life for all.
3. Churches, through corporate witnessing and giving, should seek to promote and support local national and international development.
4. International development is a central and indicative mode of missional expression.

5. Churches must strive to demonstrate in their own common lives what they are requesting the "secular" society to do.

Human Rights: The basic entitlement of every human being is the right to be a person, i.e., to be recognized, affirmed, and treated as a "person of intrinsic worth before God . . . and . . . a right to the fullest possible opportunities for the development of life abundant and full."[18] This declaration is broadened in the preamble to the Universal Declaration of Human Rights and offered to the churches as a pivotal guide in human relations. It declares "recognition of the inherent dignity and of the equal and inalienable rights of all members of the human family (as) the foundation of freedom, justice, and peace in the world."[19] More specifically, the Universal Declaration of Human Rights affirms human entitlement to freedom, equality, dignity, the right to life and faith, security of person, privacy, and recognition before courts of laws. It is incumbent upon the churches to be concerned about the abridgement of these entitlements anywhere, i.e., in the United States, South Africa, in the yet unliberated areas of Africa, and in totalitarian societies in any part of the world. Max L. Stackhouse suggests that there are several other warrants for the church's advocacy of this social justice ministry. They are found of course in the Bible but also in Judaism, church history, and the liberal church tradition. He might also have mentioned the Black Church tradition.

Where would the human rights advocacy ministry stimulate pastors to lead the churches? Certainly it would lead to the treatment of human beings as more than "statistics, pawns, common fodder, or units of labor/consumption."[20]

The clue for religious education in the area of human rights is more implicit than explicit. While not prominently stated in the Bible or in the unfolding of the Christian faith, it is of the very essence of the central teaching of the prophets and the parables. Supremely revealed in the sacrificial death of Christ for humankind, it continues in the ministries of the saints and martyrs of the church from Paul to Perpetua—to Martin Luther King Jr.

Civil Rights: The civil rights movement of the present era began with the historic *Brown v. Board of Education* decision (1954), declaring unconstitutional the concept and practice of "separate but equal" treatment for black youth in the public schools of the nation. This was the beginning rather than the end of litigation toward the achievement of civil rights in the federal government, public accommodations, education, housing, voting, and employ-ment for black people. Undeniably, some significant progress has been made in specific and limited areas of civil rights amelioration, principally in the area of reducing visible symbols of racial discrimi-nation in public sector institutions, i.e., armed forces and restau-rants, schools, etc. Basically untouched are two fundamental issues: 1) the provision of equal legal protection of recently acquired civil rights and the provision of equal advantages to exploit the newly achieved civil rights; 2) a racist attitude toward black people (and other color minorities) which neutralizes legal resolutions and ren-ders much of the progress in this area counterproductive.

Essentially, the response of white churches to these issues has been disappointingly ineffective. While generally responding with appropriate theological rhetoric, pious pronouncements, selective funding, and even personal participation in protests and advocacies, they have usually not ventured beyond the relatively safe confines of national policy, legal courses, or local and congregational custom in confronting the causes and the "principalities and powers" of oppression and racism that are both endemic and systemic in the civil rights struggle and throughout the general society.

Educationally, the least that the church can be expected to do is to know, affirm, teach, and evangelize its own ethic of Christian community which is trans-racial, trans-cultural, trans-class, and trans-historical. This can be done, however, only through sincere and committed involvement and at the cost of real discipleship "holding up the plumbline of justice tempered by love" [and] "free-dom tempered by order."[21]

Women's Rights: A discussion of women's rights is necessary and germane to the contention of this chapter that certain aspects of the message and mission commanded by the gospel have been long and acutely truncated in the churches, generally, and in church programs of religious education, specifically. Letty Russell did not hesitate to make this point clear about women in her critique of the 1975 World Council of Churches meeting. The statement about this was, "The unity of humankind includes in it women as well as men, yet women remain invisible in its dossier."[22] Dorothy Jean Furnish in probing further into that "invisibility" would suggest, I think, that it could also be the work of pernicious stereotyping which women "in their efforts to affirm their whole humanity. . . are desperately trying to avoid."[23] The thrust of these statements is clear. The basic issue is sexism. This was defined at the World Council of Churches Consultation on Sexism at Berlin in 1970 as "any attitude, action, or institutional structure which systematically subordinates a person or a group on grounds of sex."

This vignette on women's rights and sexism concludes with several suggested strengths that the churches should welcome from women in the religious education of the congregation:

1. Exemplary models of prophetic teaching as well as nurturing as they bring the pain and growth of former minority status and the strengths of new identity.
2. Exemplary models of independency, creativity, and resourcefulness for visioning a future unfettered by a past and present of false starts.
3. Exemplary models of leadership based on a new paradigm of cooperation, cocreativity, mutuality, open-endedness, and mutual trust rather than competition.
4. Exemplary models of venturesome creativity in visioning scenarios of hope rather than despair.[24]

Pastors, both women and men, have unique opportunities to inaugurate such education.

Economic Justice: Trend data comparing absolute and relative economic well-being in the U.S. (based on selected leading indicators, i.e., income, consumership, poverty. and employment when examined in relation to race, gender, class, and status) reflect inequalities that are "a moral scandal" to the nation. White, middle-class and upper-class males/families "have and hold" a grossly disproportionate amount of the country's wealth, buying power, and financial control. This same sector of the population, incidentally, overlays much of the white Anglo-Saxon Protestant and Roman Catholic church membership. Conversely, the poor, ill-fed, ill-clothed, and ill-housed constitute a growing population of millions unable to avoid sub-subsistence levels of economic existence with little or no corrective power or viable political influence.

The gospel challenges this situation of inequality and lack of access to the commonweal at several points: 1) the denial of the inalienable right of all persons to enjoy a full human life; 2) the denial of the right to work through forced unemployment thus abusing self-esteem and human dignity; 3) the disallowance of a benign work ethic to generate wealth and contribute to the general welfare of the society at large.

The social responsibility of the churches in this situation seems clear. In the words of Paul VI in his 1971 apostolic letter, "It is up to the Christian communities to analyze with objectivity the situation . . . to shed on it the light of the Gospel's unalterable words and to draw principles of reflection, norms of judgment, and directives for action from the social teaching of the Church."[25] More simply, "the Church is responsible for the personal and corporate life of Christians in the world. Since this is the case, Christians must respond to any act or institution that disregards the sacredness of persons."[26]

In terms of action, the questions of redistribution of wealth and the reallocation of the national budget with less emphasis on national security and more on social securities for all of the people is on the agenda.

Public Education: In the past and until quite recently, churches and public schools had a practical relationship with each other in terms of model-sharing and technical assistance. Since the revival of the principle of church-state separation in the public school area, however, the churches in our country have shown little concern for the public education establishment itself. That attitude is changing. A social justice approach to ministry is increasingly claiming a legitimate role in the status and role of public education and the public schools. Robert W. Lynn who gave this challenge some years ago states the case for the new perspective the church should have in relation to any and all child and youth serving agencies: "The first of our new duties . . . is to become aware of the widening breach between traditional convictions and the demand of the future that is now breaking in upon us."[27] More specifically, these "new duties" constitute a concern on the part of the churches relative to their role in strengthening and supporting the public education endeavor. Four issues come to mind immediately:

1. Universal, compulsory public education, a necessity for "an enlightened citizen" in a representational democracy, is an issue in which the church has both a stake and a moral responsibility.

2. Quality public education which often leaves much to be de-

sired, must become and remain a highest priority for church
and state as a fundamental base for religious teaching and
democratic living.

3. Multiracial, mulitcultural, and multiethnic schools need to be
   viewed as highly positive elements in any society that pro-
   fesses to be open and for any religious faith that claims pluralistic inclusiveness.

4. Cost-free universal public education, enormously expensive at
   best but actually inexpensive if its alternatives are considered,
   must increasingly become a matter of both commitment and
   support in the churches.

Again, the attitudes and actions of pastors and laity can have a
profound impact on important decisions ahead in our society.

STRATEGY DEVELOPMENT

Thus far in this chapter we have attempted to do three things:
1) relocate the warrants for social justice ministries in the historic
mission of the church; 2) indicate the need for and scope of those
ministries, and 3) critique, generally, the noninvolvement of most
churches, clergy, and religious educators in them. Prior to discussing model building and a specific model for a social justice ministry
it is necessary to develop a theoretical base. The elements of such a
base are: a radical vision; a radical commitment; a radical awareness;
a radical holism.

A New Vision

The construction of a viable social justice ministry in the average
church program will require a radical biblical vision of a just
world—one in which there is respect for the personal and social
rights of all; full freedom and participation for every racial, religious, and cultural group; economic justice for the poor and disad-
vantaged; priority-regard for the civil rights of women and black
people; a more humane system of public education; and a deeper
concern for a sustainable physical environment. Together with this
new vision there needs to be a new sense of "radical historicity," i.e.,
an acute awareness of the historical situation of the churches and
the redemptive word that must be spoken by them and enacted in
their communities. Vision and historicity form the basis for creative

and hopeful involvement requiring "action toward the establishment of justice," often despite the limited correctives that can be
induced. Vision, historicity, and involvement equate to prophetic
leadership to be assumed by the churches, i.e., proactive rather
than reactive stances on issues denying social justice. Finally, this
new paradigm for church ministry requires a new view of the
church as a "committed Christian community, one that seeks to
unite theological and biblical reflection with social analysis leading
to action for justice."[28]

A New Approach

The new approach that is suggested for a social justice ministries
program is holistic. It seems to integrate social justice ministries into
the life of the whole congregation as it relates to the church in
mission, to the whole person at every age level, intergenerationally,
in every conceivable relationship and setting, inside as well as beyond the United States. An important advantage in using this
approach is the fact that it gets away from a rather separatistic
"issues-oriented" approach and moves us toward a truly corporate
approach. Susan Thistlethwaite feels strongly that this is most necessary. She says, "We have to rethink the whole approach to peace
and justice issues in the churches and reject the concept that justice
is an issue. It is not an issue, it is an identity for the church."[29]
More simply, the aims of religious education are personal and corporate and religious development occurs within the context of the
whole believing, worshiping, learning, serving, community of faith.
We are not "called" to a particular area of "church work" or program or specialized concern. We are called to ministry. The educational mission of the church is derived from the whole mission of
the whole church. Thus, the basic strategy for developing a social
justice ministry is a holistic one, i.e., the conceptualizing of social
justice ministries as an integral aspect of ministry—"a hermeneutic
of ministry" or one that "uncovers the public significance of all
aspects of congregational life."[30] This concept has important implications for the theory behind the model to be discussed in the next
section. It also has several important things to say to us now:

- Social justice ministries are implicit in each and all of the ministries of the church. Nowhere in scripture can it be correctly

implied that the "personal" and "social" or the "church" and "society" are separable.

- Social justice ministries are ministries done by the whole congregation. Just as the whole church worships or teaches or witnesses, so the whole local church is to involve itself in social justice ministries.

- Social justice ministries are carried on in relation to the church ecumenical. One, several, or many churches of different denominational backgrounds may and should witness to the unity of the church in the community, in the schools, and in the world of the work place with respect to social justice concerns.

In pursuing social justice ministries holisticly, churches will address the whole person. The various identities of the person (parent, spouse, student, citizen, and so on), should be observed for growth, development, and the actualization of potential in home, school, church, community, and occupationally. Influences and factors that enhance growth will be promoted and those that threaten growth will be circumscribed.

Recognizing that persons learn throughout life, life-span education should be provided and encouraged to assist adaptation to changing conditions and a rapidly changing world. Proportionately, as much time will be spent on adults as on children and youth as they face increasingly complex and difficult decision-making situations.

Through social justice ministries the churches should seek to identify, analyze, interpret, and correct factors and forces that impinge upon the various networks of meaning, support, and assistance that children, youth, and adults depend upon for wholesome and abundant growth and development with dignity. This would particularly include civil rights, women's rights, economic justice, public education, and ecology issues.

Finally, social justice ministries will include: 1) the education of persons to create and cherish a sustainable environment for as large a population as can reasonably be supported; 2) the development of international relations and foreign policy relations that are peacemaking rather than just peace-keeping; and 3) human rights protocols that affirm life, privacy, security, legal protection, and freedom of belief and worship.

MODEL BUILDING

The search for models that embody the radical visioning, commitment, awareness, and integration that are necessary for the development of an intentional program of ministry for social justice in congregations as well as in denominations is probably the most puzzling quest in religious education today. There are several sources of this dilemma: questionable assumptions; unsure objectives; nonpertinent theory; unclear guidelines; and the lack of viable alternative designs. Prior to suggesting a social justice ministry model for consideration these problematic issues should be briefly discussed.

First, it cannot be assumed universally that the mission and purpose of the church is to be a revolutionary force in society. Paul Lehmann points out that the "Christian should have known about revolution all along . . . and only the non-Christian . . . [be] surprised at revolution. . . . The church has repeatedly succumbed to silence about the authentic connection between its faith and this tumult."[31] For examples of this, the typical Christian wants peace but means "peace-keeping" rather than "peace-making." Christians want a sustainable environment but allow ecology legislation reflecting only modest restraint. Civil rights are guaranteed by the law but affirmative action is taken reluctantly. Lehmann states further that "revolution" is "the natural environment of the Christian." It was born out of God's response to a revolutionary situation."[32] Its genius is to relate "stability and change," "decay and fulfillment" through the Incarnation. In our tradition, at its best, every Christian inherits the right and the obligation to be a change-agent of God. Again in the words of Jürgen Moltmann referring to Ernst Bloch's comment about the Bible and revolution: "It is difficult to wage a revolution without the Bible, says Bloch. It is even more difficult not to bring about a revolution with the Bible."[33]

Second, the lack of commitment to the revolutionary intent of the biblical witness has led to compromised and often truncated objectives. In successive periods of pre-Christian and Christian history, the churches have proclaimed, taught, and with varying degrees of integrity, pursued social justice ministries. The central ethical motif in Hebrew religion was enlarged and refocused in the "kingdom of God teaching" of Jesus. The early church validated this teaching and articulated it in communal living. In the Middle Ages, charitable impulses carried the social concerns of the church beyond its parish boundaries and into the wider community. The Protestant era witnessed the advocacy of the social concerns of the public which in many cases motivated the national governments in Europe to both reform, endow, and in other ways provide for the less advantaged and indigent. Despite these evidences of social sensitivity, however, the churches today, almost universally, are experiencing difficulty and ambivalence in inculcating a categorical ethic of personal moral perfection and revolutionary social justice. In an increasingly complex and pluralistic society, "the church has been far more inclined to respond sensitively to individual problems and to condemn personal practices of injustice than it has to see clearly how broad social conditions incorporate responsibility for personal casualties."[34]

Third, few theories of religious education contain or articulate explicit constructs that can serve as the foundations for a social justice ministry. Excepting the work of George A. Coe[35] and the socio-cultural school of thought,[36] little of the why, what, or how to educate (religiously) can be found. Theory in this field has essentially moved in other directions. In secular education the situation, interestingly, is similiar. Individual Fulfillment theories based on "Third Force" psychology are concerned that the "unique is activated and strives toward expression and fulfillment." Scholarly Discipline theories emphasize "developing the curriculum for the underlying principle of the academic discipline." Educational Technology theories stress the production of desired behavior by determining what is to be achieved, programing its achievement by reinforcement, and evaluating its results for further reinforcement. The work of John Dewey practically stands alone in its insistence that the school "not merely [provide] the means by which students could 'fit into' the existing society, but also . . . [become] . . . a laboratory which would provide them with what they needed to change society for the better."[37]

Fourth, guidelines for church social justice programs, where they do exist, usually leave much to be desired in terms of integrity.

Often they are "utilitarian" or "pragmatic," i.e., making religion the means to personal or social ends rather than "objective" and "transcendent" standards of justice. Otherwise, they reflect a double-standard of their own social ethic. They do not speak, teach, and act in congruence with the biblical and theological basis of their faith. Finally, they often fail to respond to the immediate problems and issues of their communities but rather choose to "flee the scene" via diversionary rhetoric or "white flight."

Guidelines for a social justice ministry model should fulfill at least the following requirements: biblically prophetic; educationally sound; laity empowering; change-agency; replicable; and generative. Briefly described this connotes that they should be:

Biblically prophetic—neither social reform or revolution can be divorced from biblical faith without compromising both.

Educationally sound—education cannot be neutral. It domesticates or liberates;[38] real learning cannot be divorced from action.

Laity empowering—recruiting and equipping laity to enact the gospel and witness to it in and through its structures.[39]

Change-agency—basic to social justice ministries are concurrent efforts to change intransigent social structures.

Replicable—the test of an effective social justice ministry model is its capacity to be effective in its host community.

Generative—the ultimate worth of a social justice ministries program is its capacity to generate and renew community self-efforts toward liberation.

INTENTIONAL ENGAGEMENT:
TRANSFORMATIVE MODELS

The foregoing assumptions and guidelines bring us to the consideration of exploratory models of ministry which reflect "action toward the establishment of justice." They may be referred to as intentional-engagement models or strategies. They were generated

in situations in which varying degrees of oppression existed, to
enable and empower churches to realize and pursue transforming
ministries of social justice more effectively. Somewhat more specifically they also respond to certain fundamental questions which
arise as churches seek to institute social justice ministries. Included
in such questions are usually the following:

1. Is there a basis on which religious education and liberation
   theologies can functionally unite?
2. Are the objectives of religious education contradictory to the
   need for the oppressed to become aware of their oppression
   and their humanity and engage in whatever struggle might be
   necessary to achieve liberation?
3. Is religious education to be concerned about the social, economic, and political liberation of other persons, groups, communities, and nations?
4. Is the involvement of church members and others in social
   justice ministries, including liberation ministries, a viable religious education task?
5. Must religious education be action-oriented to be relevant or
   transforming?
6. How can people at different levels of "religious readiness" be
   brought to accept the radical implications of biblical social
   justice?

Guidelines and Steps

The intentional-engagement models to be suggested as potential
approaches to social justice ministry programs generally follow certain guidelines. The remainder of this section of the chapter will
delineate these models, enunciate some guidelines, and suggest
some implementive steps. Common in each of the models to some
degree is the influence of Paulo Freire's transformative education
concept.[40]

Guidelines

Theological Basis: Religious education and liberation theology can
find a common base in their common task, namely, to respond to
the call "to social engagement by God who is fully social and
radically present in the world."[41] Such a response frontlines social

and political involvement and gives the church an "identity" as an advocate of social justice.

Church Involvement: If it is granted that God acts in history and has acted decisively in the Incarnation, to demonstrate that concern, church involvement in the liberation struggles of minorities, women, and the oppressed is obligatory. Nothing, therefore, that impedes or imperfects that liberation can be tolerated and anything that genuinely contributes to that liberation should be given priority on the agenda of the churches.

Role of the Laity: The "worldly" emphasis alluded to above, projects a new role for the laity, i.e., "the people of God." That role is to share in the ministry of Jesus Christ in the world. Randolph Crump Miller interprets this to mean that "one finds his vocation at the centers of power, that the ministry of the laity is crucial in terms of the religious issues in political action, economic decisions, and social concerns."[42]

Praxis Learning: The educational foundation for a liberation-oriented social justice ministry is praxis learning, i.e., interactive reflection and action toward the actual transformation of the world. The basic contention of this chapter is—if this motif in the basic design of the church's ministry is not articulated and intentionally pursued, the central teachings of the churches are being denied and their essential ministries truncated. The prophetic word of the gospel is meant for more than hearing and understanding or analyzing. It is meant for doing. Freire speaks eloquently to this point, "Within the word we find two dimensions, reflection and action, in such radical interaction that if one is sacrificed . . . the other immediately suffers. There is no true word that is not at the same time a praxis. Thus, to speak a true word is to transform the world."[43]

Five Models

The foundation of Paulo Freire's "transformative" learning model is a Christian humanistic belief that education should be an instrument to liberate the oppressed and the oppressor in order to experience the power of their authentic humanity. With this new power they can "name" their world, discern heretofore unrealized options, and voluntarily pursue courses of action to obtain and maintain

their freedom. Methodologically, this can be accomplished by nego-
tiating four aspects: 1) coming to an acute sense of awareness of
one's oppression and oppressors; 2) realistically analyzing the extent
and impact of the "limit-situations" imposed and the "limit-acts"
required for liberation; 3) praxis, an articulation of the critical
action that must follow analysis if education is to be more than
"intellectual emptiness"; 4) verification or ascertaining that the new
person "born" in this process is "no longer oppressor nor oppressed, but . . . in the process of achieving freedom."[44]

Dieter Hessel develops an "integrated" or "holistic" model for
the implementation of a social justice ministry in the church.
Agreeing basically with Susan Thistlethwaithe that justice must become an "identity" for the churches and not just a panel of issues,
he contends that each ministry of the church, e.g., proclamation,
teaching, worship, fellowship, witness, and service, "has at least
some social character for those that have eyes to see." Hessel's
implementing methodology is a lectionary commentary, *Social
Themes of the Christian Year*, exploring an ecumenical lectionary in
relation to social justice ministries. It's avowed purpose is "to utilize
a socially liberating hermeneutic in preaching and teaching and to
achieve more dynamic integration of the congregation's worship-
nurture witness."[45]

There are five foundations for Hessel's holistic approach: 1) critical reflection on ministry as a whole including linkage "between
worship, teaching, and public engagement"; 2) scriptural grounding
"in the biblical story of the social God" who "creates us with
promise, commissions us by grace, and sends us into mission";
3) insistence that no distinction be made between the personal and
social aspects of the Christian faith; 4) faithfulness to the gospel
involving "public engagement simultaneously with personal integration" consonant with Freire's conviction that, "there is no true
word that is not at the same time a praxis"; and 5) participation in
the life of the "church redemptive" as the singular and authentic
center of "God's transforming activity."

Sara Little's "discipleship" model for social justice ministry raises
an important and difficult question for religious education. She
asks, "How does one include actual acts of effecting social justice as
teaching—not motivating action, nor raising consciousness about
issues, nor applying biblical mandates in verbal formulations, but

acting?"[46] She goes on to question whether just "doing" is "doing the truth" to use a phrase of Thomas Groome. She believes that "simulating," "planning," and "contriving" experience is not too meaningful or helpful. She is convinced that it is important to work with persons and/or situations which have need of help or liberation, "to help . . . [them] . . . relate the gospel to their situation, learning with them, and working to move toward 'responsible freedom.' "[47] Toward the achievement of this goal she shares a four-phase process known as AAAR: Awareness, Analysis, Action, Reflection:[48]

> *Awareness*: a learning process phase designed to increase levels of awareness and understanding in reference to "God's intention and purpose for human life" and "the Christian's responsibility to be involved."

> *Analysis*: a learning process phase in which information and facts are gathered, explored, and perceived in relation to goals, resources, alternatives, urgency, and the integrity of the gospel.

> *Action*: a learning process phase in which participative individual personal and/or corporate action "consistent with the Christian ethic" and directed toward the establishment of social justice is enacted.

> *Reflection*: a learning process phase in which planned-for theological reflection on the praxis experience is held "to test the ethical assumptions of our perception of God's will on which the action was based."

Working from within a somewhat different educational construct, James McGinnis projects a "relational" model, i.e., one that "moves from awareness to concern to action" in a program "to educate for peace and justice," premised on the belief that peace (and other social justice concerns) is not simply a concept to be taught, but a reality to be lived. Awareness, concern, and action are deployed as the basis for conscientious decision making in the following way:

Awareness of social justice issues and the disposition to work for change would be encouraged by "promoting a sense of self-esteem" and a feeling that our "gifts" should be shared with others for the good of all.

Concern about social issues is to be nurtured into a sense of solidarity with the victims of injustices. Such a link is crucial for action.

Action itself should eventuate from concern. It may take the form of direct service, action on local issues, and/or action within one's "zones of freedom."[49]

In a courageous attempt to confront and answer the question, "What would it mean to respond seriously to the turmoil and suffering of our world," Suzanne Toton is convinced that religious education must go beyond the domestic issues of church education and even beyond "consciousness raising" and "value change" learning. Her insightful thesis is "that if justice is to be central to religious education, it must play a role in effecting structural and systemic change."[50] More explicitly, educational efforts to change individual attitudes and value systems must be realistically viewed in relation to "the nature of social structures and the web of structural relationships that make up the social order."[51] In her food crisis research, for example, she found that national policy on this issue "is structured primarily to meet the economic interests of our country and only secondarily to meet the needs of hungry people." Implicit in this critique is a basic issue for religious education in reference to social justice. Can structures and systems be placed beyond criticism and succumbed to as a patriotic duty? Further, can Christians do this?

Toton offers several suggestions toward engaging the problem of the systemic nature of injustice. Commencing with a distinction between religious and general or public education, she asserts that the peculiar task of religious education regarding injustice is to stand with those who seek "to create a world of justice, peace, and love (and) to remove whatever breeds oppression, be it personal, structural, or systemic." Additionally, religious education can do some other things: 1) move from the "anecdotal" to the "analytic" with the development of social analysis skills to more clearly discern directions and tasks; 2) identify and define "concrete economic, political, and social changes" that must be made and intentionally work to bring them about; 3) integrate education for social justice into the church's entire program.

Limitations of Models

In black perspective, the models for social justice ministry that have just been discussed evoke two reactions. From the standpoint of theory they are fresh, provocative, and even exciting. In practical terms, however, they have distinct limits in several areas. First, does religion, the church, or religious education generally perceive itself to have social revolutionary intent? Is Peter Berger incorrect in saying that religion is "functional" rather than "dysfunctional" in reference to conserving the status quo and that religion will tend to provide "integrating symbols rather than symbols of revolution?"[52] Second, is there really sufficient evidence to believe that the churches are willing to go beyond ministries of "helpful intervention" and seriously challenge the structures and systems that are the root causes of the injustices, oppression, and suffering of the masses? Third, is the church willing to look at some of the implications of change for its religious education programs? F. Nile Harper[53] indicates that several changes are needed at this point, namely: focusing religious education for social justice on adult as well as children's ministries; reevaluating the realism of denominational curriculum goals now expected to "change" social justice attitudes through education alone; reexamining the premise of the all-importance of small group methodology; and neglecting the nature and potential impact of corporate strength and witness. Fourth, are members of churches, usually remote from the struggle against injustice, willing to become participants in groups that are in "life and death" struggles with poverty, hunger, abuse, and/or criminal injustice?

AN INTENTIONAL-ENGAGEMENT MODEL

This final section of the chapter will suggest a social justice ministry perspective and model that has grown out of the black church. Basically, it is one that "worked" as the black community in

concert with the black church cooperated to initiate and support
the unprecedented revolution in civil rights for black people during
1955-1970. This model has the potential for adaptation by any
church if it becomes committed to and intentionally involved in a
social justice ministry in solidarity with the oppressed. Essentially, it
is a model that relates mission and ministry in "praxis" through the
change agency of the church. The characteristic-objectives of this
"intentional engagement model" are six: 1) biblical integrity; 2) radical contextuality; 3) systematic engagement; 4) educational change;
5) programatic integration, and 6) laity empowerment. Prior to
describing this intentional engagement model, two distinctions
should immediately be recognized as significant variables in relation
to its evaluation and/or deployment. First, black people needed
justice ministries because of their immediate and existential situa-
tion(s) of oppression and their deathless determination to correct
and transcend it. Whites and white churches while deploring the
oppressive situation of millions of black people were not directly
the victims of oppression. Their involvement in liberation acts was
qualified and different. Second, generally white churches have difficulty relating faith and social action. Their people may participate
in "studies," "research," and "mission" projects but seldom in movements for systemic change, i.e., for the correction of the root causes
of the problems themselves. Actually, very little in their background
prepares them to engage the many "principalities and powers" that
cause systemic injustice. Third, church members find it difficult to
interrelate personal faith and social change. Regarding this dilemma, however, Gustavo Gutiérrez maintains that it is not possible
for a Christian to say that, "he lives on the level of liberation from
sin or sonship and brotherhood if he is disinterested in economic,
social, and political liberation."

Characteristic I: Biblical Integrity

The biblical story and witness has perennially been a prime
source and central foundation for black Christians in their quest of
freedom, dignity, and equality. It has also been a mainstay in black
church preaching, worship, music, and teaching, as well as the
motivator for evangelism, mission, and service.

The black religious experience is replete with Old and New

Testament references and images of God's concern for justice, right-eousness, and their freedom from slavery. In the life, teachings, and ministry of Jesus, black churches stress his concern for human need, his solidarity with the poor, his association with the outcast, and his identification with the marginal people of society.

Crucially important in the understanding of the black church in relation to the Bible are its convictions: that God is the Lord of history; that God is concerned about and involved in history; that God is the God of the oppressed whom God came to liberate in Jesus Christ, and now through the black church.

Characteristic II: Radical Contextuality

The black church, historically and currently, has held reflection and action in creative tension. It acts, believing that the activity of God primarily occurs in the midst of the trials and tribulations of the poor, oppressed, prisoners, and outcasts. Theologian James Cone makes this the basic definition of black theology referring to it as "that theology which arises out of the need to articulate the significance of black presence in a hostile white world. It is black people reflecting religiously on the black experience, attempting to redefine the relevance of the Christian gospel for their lives."[54] William Jones makes this same point when he says, "Each black theology presents itself, implicitly or explicitly, as a specific strategy for black liberation. From this perspective it must be regarded as an 'engaged' or committed theology, for it makes a prior commitment to an ultimate goal, i.e., transforming from oppression to authentic humanity."[55]

Characteristic III: Systematic Engagement

Biblical integrity and radical contextualization lead to another characteristic of the intentional-engagement model for social justice ministries—systematic engagement, i.e., identifying, analyzing, correcting or eliminating, restraining destructive structures and/or systems that support and sustain oppression, racism, and sexism. Herbert Richardson indicates that this was a major concern for Martin Luther King Jr. throughout the civil rights struggle: "King's perception of the human problem . . . led him to emphasize . . . that his struggle was directed against the forces, or structures, of evil itself

rather than against the person or group who is doing the evil."[56]
The authenticity and effectiveness of the civil rights movement,
largely the fruit of King's leadership, was due to this assessment of
the fundamental problem and the development of a complementary strategy of nonviolence to resist evil and witness to good.

Characteristic IV: Education for Change

Two basic issues emerge whenever the educational philosophy
that is implicit in the civil rights movement or Martin Luther King's
leadership is discussed. Those issues are purpose and method. Can
a religious education that resists social change, as frequently
charged,[57] be useful in initiating, advocating, and inculcating social
justice teachings and action? If this issue can be resolved, what
methodology best serves this purpose?[58]

Religious education can become an ally of social justice ministries
rather than serving merely as "social cement" or "legitimization" for
the maintenance of a traditionalist religious establishment. According to Peter Berger what is needed to reverse this anomalous situation is a religious education that challenges—through praxis—and
remains "dysfunctional" rather than "functional" for those who
would domesticate its radically prophetic message. Berger makes
this point quite clear in the following statement: "The family-
centered and child-centered religiosity of many of our suburban
middle-class churches contributes greatly to this problem. The ideology of religious education . . . gives intellectual rationalization to
this constellation. . . . There occurs a process of religious inocula-
tion by which small doses of Christianized concepts and terminology are injected into consciousness. By the time the process is
completed, the individual is effectively immunized against any real
encounter with the Christian message."[59]

Donald Miller suggests a fourfold educational methodology to
meet this challenge. Some of this was/is non-self-consciously done
by black churches in the rapprochement between the Black Revolution and Black Theology, viz., 1) develop in persons, through their
ongoing involvement in a social justice praxis, an awareness of the
radical social mission of the biblical message by indicating both its
positive and negative responses in past/present history; 2) develop
in persons, through their ongoing involvement in a social justice

praxis, a sense of hope and expectancy that "God confronts us in the present as One who shall fulfull in the future what he has promised and begun to establish in the past";[60] 3) provide for persons, through their ongoing involvement in social justice praxis learning situations, "contrast experiences" or encounter experiences with injustice in other forms and contexts and/or "contrast experiences" in their own context; 4) develop in persons, in and through their ongoing involvement in a social justice praxis, a sense of community and a quality of commitment that will call them to and sustain them in social change roles and ministries.

Characteristic V: Programatic Integration

Black churches or congregations, generally, historically and presently but more particularly since the Black Revolution in the late 1960s, have viewed themselves as having varying degrees of accountability not only to their local church families, constituents, and their denominations but also to the black communities in which they are located. Further, this relationship to the community has usually been one of humane concern for the general health and welfare of its children, youth, and adults and for its family, economic, social, and political life as well. This has resulted in a communal-type experience of church relationship style that has allowed the black church to view its ministry holistically, both locally and in a community sense. This perspective has meant that the black church tends to consider the whole person in all of his/her varied relationships as the necessary and proper focus of ministry.

Social justice ministries in the black church, then, tend to be congregation-oriented rather than committee-oriented and mission-directed rather than externally influenced.

By contrast, many nonethnic constituency churches tend to make or draw distinctions between personal and social aspects of the gospel, private and public witness to its teachings, and individual rather than corporate responses to the challenges of the collective issues of the public domain. Dieter Hessel firmly believes that a strategy for a social justice ministry in congregations like these should be a broad and pervasive qualitative endeavor that includes the whole gamut of the life of the church: individual and corporate; cross-model, e.g., social justice ministries and liturgy; interdisciplinary, e.g., biblical-ethical; contextual or focused through congregational issues; missional and integrated.[61]

THE PASTOR'S ROLE IN RELIGIOUS EDUCATION FOR SOCIAL JUSTICE

Pastors have an exciting opportunity to model and stimulate others to become engaged in social justice ministries. It is clear that the pastor is the key person in this development of a vision and strategy for the education of members of the faith community concerning the genuine problems and issues facing our society.

To avoid involvement is testimony to the pastor's lack of faith. To become involved creatively is testimony to the pastor's attempt to be an authentic interpreter and teacher of the whole gospel. Such a social justice ministry must be undertaken in community with the laity who are involved in the very structures of society where they can make a difference.

Notes

1. Dieter T. Hessel, *Social Ministry* (Philadelphia: Westminster, 1982), p. 14.

2. Suzanne Toton, "Structural Change: The Next Step in Justice Education," *Religious Education* (Summer 1985), p. 447.

3. Dieter T. Hessel, "A Whole Ministry of (Social) Education," *Religious Education* 78:4 (Fall 1983), pp. 525-556.

4. Franklin H. Littell, "Religion and Race: The Historical Perspective," in *Race: Challenge to Religion*, ed. Mathew Ahmann (Chicago: Regnery, 1963), pp. 31-32.

5. Ibid., p. 32.

6. Ibid., p. 37.

7. F. Nile Harper, "Social Power and the Limits of Church Education," *Religious Education* 64:5 (September-October 1969), p. 392.

8. Ibid., p. 392.

9. Jürgen Moltmann, "Christian Theology Today," *New World Outlook* (November 1972).

10. Cf. Littell, "Religion and Race," p. 39.

11. William A. Beardsley, "Frontiers in the Interpretation of Religion," *Religion in Life* (Spring 1960), p. 228.

12. Jesse H. Ziegler, "Is Religious Education Fulfilling its Function?" *Religious Education* (November-December 1950), p. 360.

13. *The Challenge of Peace: God's Challenge and Our Response: A Pastoral Letter on War and Peace*, May 3, 1983 (Washington, D.C.: U.S. Catholic Conference, 1983), Introduction.

14. Kenneth P. Alpers, "Starting Point for an Ecological Theology: A Bibliographical Survey", in *New Theology No. 8*, ed. Martin E. Marty and Dean G. Peerman (New York: Macmillan, 1971), Ch. VI.

15. Kenneth Boulding, *Human Values on the Spaceship Earth* (New York: National Council of Churches, 1966).

16. Robert E. Reber, Monograph #3: *World Development as an Aim of the Church's Educational Work* (Nashville: Board of Discipleship, The United Methodist Church, 1974), Ch. 1.

17. Ibid., p. 6.

18. "Human Rights: A Pronouncement": *A Policy Statement of the National Council of the Churches of Christ* (December 3, 1963).

19. *Universal Declaration of Human Rights* (New York: United Nations Office of Public Information, 1948).

20. Max L. Stackhouse, *Creeds, Society, and Human Rights: A Study in Three Cultures* (Grand Rapids, Mich.: Eerdmans, 1984).

21. This familiar quotation is the basis of Martin Luther King Jr.'s Christian social philosophy (see: William D. Watley, *Roots of Resistance*. Valley Forge, Pa.: Judson, 1985), passim.

22. Letty M. Russell, "Women: Education Through Participation," *Religious Education* (January-February 1975), p. 45.

23. Dorothy Jean Furnish, "De-Feminizing Religious Education: A Double Bind," *Religious Education* 71:4 (July-August 1976), pp. 355-362.

24. *Women's Issues in Religious Education*, ed. Fern M. Giltner (Birmingham, Ala.: Religious Education Press, 1985), Preface, pp. 1-2.

25. Drew Christiansen, "Americanizing Catholic Social Teaching," *Quarterly Review* (Winter 1987), p. 17.

26. This statement reflects a new seriousness about humanization issues as well as Catholic social and theological teaching.

27. Robert W. Lynn, *Protestant Strategies in Education* (New York: Association Press, 1964), p. 52.

28. Donald E. Miller, "Religious Education and Social Change" (an unpublished paper presented at the Professors and Researchers in Religious Education, February, 8-9, 1969), p. 6.

29. Susan Thistlethwaite, "Peace and Justice, Not Issues but Identities for the Church," *Engage/Social Action* (January 1987), p. 33.

30. Hessel, *Social Ministry*, p. 16.

31. Paul L. Lehmann, "The Shape of Theology for a World in Revolution," *Motive* (April 1965), p. 9.

32. Ibid., pp. 9 ff.

33. Moltmann, "Christian Theology Today," p. 487.

34. Haskell M. Miller, *Compassion and Community: An Appraisal of the Church's Changing Role in Social Welfare* (New York: Association, 1961), p. 47.

35. George Albert Coe, *A Social Theory of Religious Education* (New York: Scribners, 1917).

36. Harold William Burgess, *An Invitation to Religious Education* (Birmingham, Ala.: Religious Education Press, 1975), Ch. III.

37. John Dewey, *The School and Society* (Chicago: University of Chicago Press, 1900).

38. See: Paulo Freire, *Pedagogy of the Oppressed* (New York: Herder and Herder, 1970).

39. Alvin J. Lindgren and Norman Shawchuck, *Let My People Go: Empowering Laity for Ministry* (Nashville: Abingdon, 1980), p.10.

40. Freire, *Pedagogy of the Oppressed*.

41. Hessel, *Social Ministry*, p. 18.

42. Randolph C. Miller, "From Where I Sit: Some Issues in Christian Education," *Religious Education* 60:2 (March-April 1965), p. 101.

43. Freire, *Pedagogy of the Oppressed*, p. 75.

44. Ibid., pp. 33-34.

45. Dieter T. Hessel, ed., *Social Themes of the Christian Year* (Philadelphia: Westminster, 1983.)

46. Sara Little, *To Set One's Heart: Belief and Teaching in the Church* (Atlanta: Knox, 1983), p. 76.

47. Ibid., p. 77.

48. Ibid., p. 79.

49. James B. McGinnis, "Educating for Peace and Justice," *Religious Education* (Summer 1986), pp. 446-465.

50. Toton, "Structural Change, p. 449.

51. Ibid., p. 62.

52. Peter Berger, *The Precarious Vision* (New York: Doubleday, 1961), p. 111.

53. F. Nile Harper, "Social Power and the Limits of Church Education," *Religious Education* (September-October 1969), pp. 390-398.

54. James H. Cone, "Black Consciousness and the Black Church: A Historical-Theological Interpretation, *Annals of the American Academy of Political and Social Science* (January 1970), p. 53.

55. William R. Jones, "Assessment of Black Theology" (a published but undocumentable paper).

56. Herbert Richardson as quoted in *Roots of Resistance: The Nonviolent Ethic of Martin Luther King Jr.* (Valley Forge, Pa.: Judson, 1985), p. 15.

57. Miller, "Religious Education and Social Change," p. 1; also see his *Story and Context: An Introduction to Christian Education* (Nashville: Abingdon, 1987).

58. Bennie E. Goodwin, *Reflections on Education: A Christian Scholar Looks at King, Freire and Jesus* (Atlanta: Foodpatrich, 1978), Ch. 2.

59. Peter L. Berger, *The Noise of Solemn Assemblies* (Garden City, N.Y.: Doubleday, 1961), p. 116.

60. Miller, "Religious Education and Social Change," p. 3.

61. Hessel, "A Whole Ministry of (Social) Education," pp. 525-559.

Bibliography

Berger, Peter L. *The Noise of Solemn Assemblies.* Garden City, New York: Doubleday, 1961.

Brueggemann, Walter. *Living Toward a Vision.* New York: United Church Press, 1982.

Fenton, Thomas P., ed. *Education for Justice.* Maryknoll, New York: Orbis Books, 1975.

Frazier, E. Franklin and Lincoln, C. Eric. *The Negro Church in America/The Black Church Since Frazier.* New York: Schocken, 1974.

Freire, Paulo. *Pedagogy of the Oppressed.* New York: Herder and Herder, 1971.

Greenleaf, Robert K. *Servant Leadership.* New York: Paulist, 1977.

Groome, Thomas, H. *Christian Religious Education.* San Francisco: Harper & Row, 1980.

Hamilton, Charles V. *The Black Preacher in America.* New York: Morrow, 1972.

Hessel, Dieter T. *Social Ministry.* Philadelphia: Westminster, 1982.

Lindgren, Alvin J., and Shawchuck, Norman. *Let My People Go: Empowering Laity for Ministry.* Nashville: Abingdon, 1982.

Russell, Letty M. *Christian Education in Mission.* Philadelphia: Westminster, 1967.

Schaller, Lyle E. *The Change Agent.* Nashville: Abingdon, 1972.

Thompson, Daniel C. *The Negro Leadership Class.* Englewood Cliffs, New Jersey: Prentice Hall, 1963.

Warford, Malcolm L. *The Necessary Illusion.* Philadelphia: United Church Press, 1976.

Wilmore, Gayraud S. *Black Religion and Black Radicalism.* Garden City, New York: Doubleday, 1973.

Wynn, J.C. *Christian Education for Liberation.* Nashville: Abingdon, 1977.

Young, Henry J. *Major Black Religious Leaders.* Nashville: Abingdon, 1979.

9

Case Study I: Pastors As Religious Educators At Work In Middle America

C. JOSEPH SPRAGUE AND PAUL MILLER

INTRODUCTION

Epworth United Methodist Church, a 1600 member reflection of Middle American United Methodism, was in trouble as 1982 dawned. And so was Marion, Ohio, the once thriving county seat of 36,000 in whose increasingly shoddy, nearly abandoned downtown area Epworth's steeple had towered for more than a century and a half.

Marion's difficulties were and are indicative of the plight of many small cities in the industrial heartland. Four major railroads, whose intersections were once the hub of the town's momentum, long since had been sidetracked. The industrial giants, which once employed thousands, and the smaller plants with their hundreds of employees, were closing, relocating, or cutting back so drastically that unemployment soared to 15 percent. The real estate market was glutted with fine, unwanted houses. Many of the more mobile white-collar workers left the area, while countless blue-collar families staggered and sometimes broke under the strain of deflated jobs and shrunken budgets. A pervasive miasma of gloom enveloped this paradoxically picturesque "Our Town," located only forty-five minutes north of Ohio's vibrant capital city.

But Marion's malaise, poignantly depicted in the bumper sticker—"Would The Last One Out Of Marion Turn Off The

Lights?"—was not the only painful reality which greeted C. Joseph Sprague when he was appointed pastor of Epworth in May, 1982.

Sprague, an urban cleric with teaching experience in university, ecumenical, cross-cultural, and interfaith settings, was assigned to Epworth to help heal the wounds and tend the scars which resulted from the tragic circumstances of his predecessor's departure. A once proud congregation was battered and badly bruised. To be a part of Marion in 1982 was painful; to be active in the life of Epworth was doubly so.

Additionally, Sprague, who was representative of those clergy who take seriously biblical criticism, modern currents in theology, religious education, and demanding calls for discipleship, quickly discovered that, despite Epworth's religiously astute legacy, the seven years of neo-fundamentalistic leadership which preceded his coming had created a theological and religious hodge-podge. Epworth was stripped of missional goals, nurturing programs, and an administrative structure through which to be a vital part of Christ's body in the needful setting that was Marion, Ohio.

A small, energetic core of lay persons, who were reflections of the theological stance of Sprague's predecessor, occupied nearly all of the few leadership spots still extant. Nonetheless, despite these enervating factors and the anger and pain associated with the departure of his predecessor, things went well in the early months of Sprague's pastorate. The diverse people of Epworth rallied as one as they tapped the Spirit's wellspring of understanding, love, and forgiveness to temper their anger and assuage their hurts. The people of Epworth displayed sacrificial charity in their behavior and were amazingly graceful in their attitudes.

Thus, a sense of euphoria settled over the congregation in late 1982 and into 1983. Worship attendance increased markedly, and, due largely to Epworth's historic prestige and remarkable music ministry, two hundred new members were added in 1982 and 1983. But by mid-1983 Sprague knew, as did a growing number of lay people—both veterans of better days and newcomers who were attracted by Epworth's increasingly discernible actions in the community—that beneath the smooth veneer of the high steeple there was too little substance and even less intentionality regarding internal nurture and external mission. Finances were in a jumble; theological juxtapositioning was increasing within the congregation, and between Sprague and the neo-fundamentalistic leadership; and there was no unifying vision, no common dream. Epworth possessed neither the intention for a journey inward nor the means, theological or practical, for a journey outward.

What to do? For Sprague the choices were clear, if the expected results were not. On the one hand he could leave: he had accomplished what he had been asked to do; the wounds were healed or healing and the scars were fading. Perhaps someone better suited for a county-seat town, someone more attuned to the fundamentalistic theological proclivities of the area should come and guide the needed next steps of congregational renewal. Or, on the other hand, he could stay and face the battle which certainly would rage. Sprague wanted to stay, as he had been at Epworth only a brief, albeit hectic period, and, more importantly, the genuineness of the people and the potential of Epworth to reclaim its legacy in order to respond to the needs of Marion had impressed him deeply. But to stay would mean radical congregational surgery. Sprague had some sense of what that would mean. He had been in other processes of renewal; he had fought other battles with institutional sickness unto death. Radical surgery would hurt before it could begin to heal given the atrophied parish structures and the growing recalcitrance of those who controlled them. Many good and well-intentioned people would be touched by surgery; some would feel cut loose and leave. Nevertheless, in large measure because of the growing support of many Epworthians for whom the church was coming alive again, Sprague decided to stay. As he did, Epworth embarked on a faith journey which would be marked by painful, radical surgery as a dying parish and a groping pastor reached for new life.

Shortly after the pivotal decision, Sprague experienced some nagging doubts about his choice when forty or so of the increasingly resentful, erstwhile leaders left Epworth for one or another of the neo-fundamentalistic congregations which abound in the area. Sprague wondered about his decision when it was said, "What right does he have to do that to our church?" and, "He is a nice person, which makes him all the more dangerous given his secular humanism." To be the topic of gossip in a town like Marion was an unenviable experience. This whisper campaign became public with published letters of criticism to the editor of the local newspaper following Sprague's involvement with several local political issues and his public work at United Methodism's 1984 General Conference. But the decision for significant change and a possible new day at Epworth had been made. Thus, in the midst of the resultant furor, which touched the parish both in purse and heart, a needed pastoral staff change occurred.

Sprague had determined with the counsel of newly designated lay leaders that in addition to much that he was doing there was a glaring need in the life of Epworth which had to be addressed if the surgical procedure underway were to have long-term therapeutic results. That need: the revitalization of the ministry of Christian education for adults and children.

Once upon a time, Epworth had been a conference, even a jurisdictional, leader in the quality of its total program of religious education. But by 1983 that program was in disarray. The religious education building, built in the early 1960s to house the overflow crowds so characteristic of that period in midwestern Methodism, was in dire need of physical attention and wider use. It was both shabby in appearance and too often found empty. The religious education program for children, while it had a few bright spots, was crying for direction and innovation. Programs of study and nurture for adults were few and far between: The few were located in five historic Sunday morning classes which were passively resistant to the "new"—whether people or curriculum; and far between were occasional retreats for women and several devotional studies which were attended by the diligent.

Given this scenario, Sprague made two fundamental decisions regarding the religious education program at Epworth. The appropriate lay leadership prodded, shaped, and supported these decisions whole-heartedly. The decisions:

1) Sprague would assume a major role as a religious educator of adults. That is, he would lead at least three and often five adult classes weekly; and,

2) Sprague, through traditional United Methodist channels, would seek help in the form of a new pastoral staff colleague with expertise in childhood religious education.
(The youth and young adult religious education programs were in a process of positive change, which had been initiated

by the enthusiasm of some of those who left, and then carried forward by a youth religious educator who stayed with Epworth until the new religious education team was in place. Presently ten lay persons, a part-time Youth Co-ordinator, and the Rev. Deanna Self-Price, Student Minister for Youth and Young Adult Ministries, lead a religious education program for youth that has turned the corner and is a vital aspect of Epworth's life.)

Thus, in January, 1984, Rev. Paul E. Miller was appointed as the church's childhood religious educator. With Paul came an additional bonus for Epworth. Patricia Miller, Paul's spouse and a registered nurse, who, in December of 1983 had completed her baccalaureate degree with a major in psychology and counseling and would enter seminary in September, was available for employment at Epworth, full-time until September and part-time thereafter while a seminarian. Hence, the Millers came on board as Epworth's first clergy couple.

Given Patricia's maturity and experience as a care-giver, she began at once to assume a major portion of Sprague's heavy pastoral load, thus enabling him to devote increased time and energy to the tasks set for him in preaching, community involvement, overall administration, and adult religious education. Additionally, Patricia was given the administrator's role for the entire adult religious education program. She began immediately to work closely with the existing Sunday morning classes while Sprague created new adult learning options for non-aligned individual adults and the long-standing adult religious education classes.

Paul Miller, while an experienced pastor who came to Epworth from a nine-year stint as the pastor of an innovative rural parish, is committed to and expert in religious education for children. This is his specialty both by inclination and professional preparation. As he entered Epworth in the frigid winter of 1984, Paul was handed the portfolio for children's ministry and asked to guide its revitalization, no holds barred.

What follows are narrative accounts by Paul Miller and C. Joseph Sprague of their ministries as religious educators at Epworth United Methodist Church in Marion, Ohio.

THE PASTOR AS RELIGIOUS EDUCATOR OF CHILDREN
(PAUL E. MILLER)

Working with the children of the Epworth congregation has been challenging and rewarding. They are eager to learn, ready for new approaches and responsive. Each child is unique and wonderfully made. Within each, sometimes hidden deeply within, is a gift from the Creator. Together, we discover and share those gifts. And in the process, I believe, we also work with God to create new gifts.

There are four main expressions of my religious education work with the children. First, there are opportunities for direct involvement with children. Second, there are the administrative responsibilities for religious education programs that relate to our children. Third, in a variety of settings there is a need to be an advocate for children's needs. And fourth, there is the responsibility to involve children in meaningful ways in the corporate worship service.

The opportunities for direct involvement with children are what I cherish the most. At times, I teach a church school class of elementary age children. I enjoy taking an active role in the Vacation Bible School program, either as a classroom teacher or in leading the opening and closing exercises. I lead the older elementary children's church during the sermon portion of the Sunday worship service. I observe and substitute teach in the weekday preschool program, and, whenever possible, I plan and lead special events for children. These opportunities allow me to know the children personally, to learn from them, to discover new things with them, and to be in touch with their cultural daily life and faith experiences.

The administrative responsibilities are tedious at times and seldom filled with instant rewards. However, they provide the territory in which creative programs and opportunities for ministry with children take place. When understood as such they become far more than just tolerable.

Epworth United Methodist Church has owned and operated a weekday preschool program for more than twenty-five years. There are one hundred and thirty-seven children enrolled and eleven paid staff members. Serving as the administrator of the preschool is a tremendous responsibility which requires a great deal of time and energy. There are also the usual administrative tasks for the ongoing church school program, which involves nine classrooms, six paid leaders, and more than a dozen volunteer workers. Hiring, evaluating, planning, training, resourcing, and supervising are normal daily tasks of administering the program for children.

The need to advocate for children would not occur to some but must be done in a variety of settings in the local church. Sometimes it requires arguing with trustees about the comfort of infants in an unair-conditioned nursery. Other times there is the need to challenge adults who schedule three-hour meetings and expect little ones to remain in a confined babysitting space for the duration of that time. On occasion older adults have needed to be reminded that behaviors which are considered to be "childish" are, in reality, "childlike." Most often, the culture of children (their daily experiences, desires, hurts, and hopes) must be lifted up as the beginning point for meaningful planning for ministries with our children (rather than a fondly remembered or still-wished-for culture). "But what about children?" can be the most important question asked in the church and someone must be asking it. Why not the pastoral educator?

Corporate worship can be an endurance test for children and for their parents. When the little ones are seen as "adults in process of becoming" they can be forced to sit quietly and pay attention to words and concepts that are far beyond their comprehension. The challenge is to involve them in the worship service in ways that are meaningful to both the children and to the adults who are present. To keep them interested, involved, and anticipating more is a challenge to any leader. But it is one that is filled with rewards for the entire family of God, gathered for worship.

What makes all of this so important? Each of these aspects of my role as the parish's religious educator of children relates to an understanding of the role of the religious educator as the enabler. My call is to equip the laity to be about their ministry with each other and to others. And the laity includes the little children. In the United Methodist Church we baptize the little ones into membership at an early age, since Jesus very clearly identified the little ones (either understood as babes in the faith or as children) as being the examples of faithful members of God's reign on earth, pastors and other religious educators need to respect all the children in our parishes as important and fully participating members of the body of Christ. Our equipping for ministry happens in at least three ways: modeling, training, and providing appropriate settings.

Learning happens best through doing. It is most effective when it involves all the senses. So, modeling an effective religious education program for children becomes vitally important as we work to equip the laity. Seeing the pastor as religious educator wearing the preschool teacher's apron says clearly that children count and that the teaching role is important. Knowing that the pastor spends all morning on Saturday preparing a room for the Sunday school hour communicates that this experience with children is top priority. Knowing that a pastor genuinely loves to be with children suggests that there is a lot to be gained from the little ones among us. When it becomes as natural to see the minister holding a baby as it is to see the pastor in the pulpit, then the equipping of the laity has progressed greatly. Not many of our parishioners would begin to imagine that they could preach a sermon, but many would like to be given permission to enjoy the little ones. Modeling an excitement for children helps others to express more freely what is perhaps deeply buried within them—a love for children. And thereby the opportunities for being the whole church begin to unfold.

Training leaders of children has a strange and very challenging beginning point. Often those who most love children and have the genuine God-given gifts to work with them do not realize it. An awareness of the gifts has been hidden deep within them, perhaps covered over by stereotypes of age, sex roles, class, or schooling. Calling forth those gifts is the first challenge in training workers with children. An effective way of doing this is "naming." To say directly to persons that I believe they have the gifts and graces to be in ministry with children often comes as a shock to them, but it also can be a meaningful eye-opener and the beginning of a rewarding relationship with the children of the church. There is also the need to dispel the myths that still surround leadership in the church. Myths like: You must have the Bible memorized, you must have the answer to any question that may arise, your life must be a shining example of Christian perfection, and that if you agree to substitute in the two-year-old room this Sunday you may not be relieved for the next ten years. Once the realistic expectations are identified, the task of recruitment becomes more manageable. Training leaders today requires fewer meetings and planning sessions and more identifying and establishing connections. Answering questions about resources (both material and human) creates confidence. Being in touch on a regular basis to answer questions and to offer reassurance builds a sense of belonging to the total children's ministry. Celebrating together and recognizing workers strengthens commitment. Things as simple as mentioning the work of the church school department during the worship service solidifies the importance of the educational ministry in the minds of leaders, participants, and worshipers.

Often neglected but equally important is the task of providing the appropriate settings for the educational ministry with children. In a time when we are very much aware of the influence of color, space, and environments, it seems only logical that these learnings would be applied to our work in the church. When we begin to plan for a new program with children we must ask about the space in which the program is to take place. Is it appropriate to the age level? Does it communicate the importance we place on this program? Will it assist in accomplishing the goal or will the environment hinder what we hope will happen? We would never think of having a choir rehearse in a room without a piano, yet we often wonder why children do not feel as if they are a vital part of the church while meeting in a quickly madeover furnace room. There is a subtle but significant message being communicated by the space that is required for adults on Sunday morning and that which is provided for the various religious education activities with children. These understandings relate not only to the actual room and the condition of it but also to the equipment that is found within the classroom. Often the space for adults is ample and pleasant—the space for children is filled with broken and outdated materials. In the electronic age in which we live, the absence of up-to-date equipment communicates an undesirable message about the relevancy of our Christian faith. Today, we must push toward the expectation that televisions, video cassette recorders, and computers are the norm in our church school classrooms (even as at one time flannel boards, slot charts, and puppets were the norm.)

These ways of equipping the laity to be about their ministry with children are found in the example of Jesus. Jesus modeled his teachings. His lifestyle communicated a consistency with his words. Rather than suggesting that teaching is a high calling—he taught! Remembered more vividly than his words about children is the fact that he drew the little ones close to him and set them on his lap. Pastors as religious educators find a challenge in the example of our Lord. We move toward rich and meaningful ministries as we model the church's commitment to religious education with children. Jesus invited his friends to follow him. He did not hold a Saturday morning training session and then send them off on their journey. He believed in the long and often difficult task of equipping through continuous training and learning together. The invitation to be in relationship with him was an invitation to "come and learn of me." Questions of the master were often turned around and given back as deeper meanings. The training for discipleship and for leadership became an ongoing challenge and an invitation to an exciting journey of growth. So it is for the training of our leaders today.

Jesus utilized the most powerful of all settings for most of his teachings—the everyday life settings of the learner. Nature became the opportunity to discover a lesson in stewardship. The marketplace was the setting for learning about prayer. Fishing was the opportunity to teach about commitment. And in each of the settings, the genuine hospitality of the teacher was communicated with openness and love. Jesus not only provided but also seized the richest of environments for the teaching-learning exchange.

The opportunities and the rewards for working with children are truly unlimited. But so are the challenges and frustrations! If we begin with a genuine love and appreciation for the way in which God created each little one, and if we have a sincere openness to children, we have discovered the path for a rich ministry with children. If we follow the example of our Lord in providing for the equipping of the laity and for a positive learning environment, we can journey down that path with confidence.

These specific examples of Epworth's religious education efforts with children are shared with the hope that they will spark the reader's imagination. Programs which are responsive to one setting may not be helpful in another. But the sharing of ideas helps to create new and relevant models for a wide variety of settings:

1. *The Children's Liturgical Art Day.* The summer months bring a

lot of excitement for children, but by the time August rolls around the days seem to drag on. It is a good month to do something special. Our parish had just recently restored a nearly one-hundred-year-old sanctuary. As a part of the project, a member of the church was commissioned to create new paraments for the altar. As each new set was unveiled there was a genuine excitement and curiosity: excitement for the newness of design and variety of colors, and curiosity about "liturgical" art. All of this combined to create a very exciting summer event for children. In our weekly newsletter we invited any elementary age child who enjoyed art to call the church office. Fifteen children responded. A letter was sent inviting them to come to the church for a Children's Liturgical Art Day. They were encouraged to learn all that they could about the word "liturgical" before coming. Our resident fabric artist and a parishioner who is a graphic artist were invited as resource persons. The paraments of the church were on display. Together we discovered the seasons of the Christian year and the appropriate colors and symbols for each season. The artists shared their experiences. Each child was invited to select a liturgical season and begin thinking about and working on an art project (drawing, painting, etc.) to be displayed in the church entrance during that season. Laity Sunday was designated as the target date for turning in the artwork. (This gave the children two months to complete their projects.) A reminder card (including liturgical season and target date) was sent out in September. On the second Sunday in October thirteen of the fifteen children had their liturgical art on display during the fellowship time before the morning worship service. All the liturgical seasons were represented. A fourteenth piece was turned in later. Each season of the church year we display one or more of the children's liturgical art pieces. The two important unexpected benefits were: A lot of families began talking with each other about the meanings of the liturgical year, and the children of the church began to get positive feedback from the older generations. This is a project that is likely to be repeated again each summer.

2. *The Peace With Justice Quarter.* Our congregation formed a Peace with Justice Task Force in response to the request of the General Conference. After studying the issues for a period of several months, they asked the Education Committee if it could designate an entire quarter of study on topics related to the issues

of peace with justice. Several of the adult church school classes and all of the elementary classes agreed. We ordered a wide variety of printed and audiovisual resources, recruited teachers who were especially interested in the topic, and followed a prepared curriculum. The age-level departments began by grouping several classes together for introductory work and then met separately for several weeks before regrouping for another departmental time of sharing. Some of the benefits of this quarter of study were: beginning conversations across the generational lines, having a focus that carried over into other aspects of the church's life, getting in touch with the cultures in various other parts of the world, and focusing our attention upon ways that our daily actions can effect peace for others. While not all of the adult classes chose to participate, those who did gained a great deal from sharing this study with the children. The teachers appreciated working together on both the departmental meetings and on their individual session resources.

3. *Children's Moments During the Worship Service.* Each Sunday morning during our corporate worship service we have a special time just for the children. It usually happens about a third of the way through the service. The children are invited to come forward and sit on the steps of the chancel area. Three years ago this was virtually impossible. The chancel area did not have adequately open steps for the children and it was surrounded by a communion rail that did not allow for accessibility. There just was not enough space down front for the children to gather. We removed the front center pew and installed some carpet, but still the space spoke of confinement rather than hospitality. With the opportunity to renovate this space, we opened the center of the communion rail, added the steps to the chancel platform, and changed the whole potential use of the space. Generally about sixty children, primarily elementary age, gather on the steps facing the congregation. They are ready for their time and anxious to share in the dialog that happens. Usually I focus the conversations on the text of the morning, making the application appropriate for their experience of life. Often the format is question and answer. On occasion, it is the opportunity to lift up the liturgical season or what is happening in school. Always it is focused on worship and generally ends in a brief prayer of thanksgiving. This is not a time to talk to children, it is not a junior sermon, and it is not an object lesson. It is a moment of spontane-

ous (yet well-planned) dialog with the children (with adults listening in). It is their moment of identification and worship. These moments last only three to five minutes but they are cherished by the adults as well as the children. One of the most frequent responses I hear from the adults (of all ages) in the congregation is how happy they are to see so many children who are excited about being in worship. It is a challenge to be fresh and relevant in what we do each Sunday, but it is probably the most consistently rewarding aspect of my job as Christian educator with children.

4. *Elementary Children's Church.* Following the children's moments in the morning worship service, except on Sundays in which holy communion is shared, the children go from the sanctuary to their own children's church. We have divided the elementary-age children (the preschool age children and younger remain in their church school classrooms for an extended hour program) into two groups which parallel the age groupings for the children's choirs. The kindergarten through second grade children are across the hall in the third and fourth grade classroom. As the minister with children, I feel it is important for me to take an active leadership role in the older age group. A seminary student leads the younger age group. We meet monthly to plan our activities with the children—often following a similar outline but adapting it to the abilities of our children. The format varies with the use of audiovisuals, special guests, crossword puzzles, word searches, and discussions. We focus the children's church experience on the same text that is being used by the preacher of the morning for the adults. This allows for Sunday noon discussions on a common biblical passage when the family regroups following the worship service. One of the benefits of this approach has been the opportunity that we, as leaders, have had to get to know the children on a more personal basis. We discovered that former discipline problems have disappeared due to the continuity of the leadership, the focus on the morning text, the variety of approaches used, and strict discipline. We feel very positive about the experience that we are having with children in elementary children's church. (We do have helpers because there are often more than thirty children in each room.)

5. *"We Are the World" Sunday.* When the popular song "We Are the World" hit the top of the chart in the mid-1980s, one of our older children came to me with an idea. She wanted to have an

entire worship service focused on the song and on the issue of world hunger. We explored the possibilities together. Her ideas included: singing the song as a congregation, hearing a sermon on the story of Jesus feeding the multitudes, receiving a special offering for hunger in Africa, and using slides to show the living conditions of others. We discussed doing such a service with the senior pastor and found him excited about it. The young person invited several other children to a planning meeting in which she shared her idea and encouraged the others to add to it. The result was a summer Sunday worship service that focused on our responses to the famine in Africa. The popular song was played over the PA system and the congregation was invited to sing along (words were printed in the bulletin). The sermon challenged us to follow Jesus' example of feeding the hungry. The children participated in the worship leadership. (It was not a "children's" event—it was for everyone.) A special offering was received for the Bishops' Appeal for Africa. And, both before and following the worship service, people were invited to purchase handmade items from a variety of African countries. These crafts were ordered on consignment from SERRV, a self-help supplier sponsored by the Church of the Brethren. We sold all the crafts and had to reorder. A total of $3,000 was raised for famine relief by this special Sunday emphasis, which was suggested by a child. Most importantly, our children connected their everyday lives with the gospel and found concrete ways of responding to a real issue in their world. This experience was also a beneficial religious education event for the adults as well.

6. *Trash to Treasure Auction.* One of our Boy Scouts came to me a couple of years ago, interested in doing a church project toward his Eagle Award. Together we examined several possibilities. The one that he liked most was organizing an auction of old and unused items in the church. We had accumulated a wide variety of furniture, toys, equipment, and materials that were not being used. It seemed that no one was willing to throw it out even though no one had used it for a long time. Permission for the auction was secured from the Board of Trustees and the project itself was approved by the scouting committee. Several other scouts were recruited to help with the gathering, moving, sorting, and preparing of the items for the auction. An auctioneer was engaged and the work began.

Before the auction, the members of the Board of Trustees examined the items collected and gave their approval for the sale of each. There were games, old record players, pews, stained glass windows, wood, pictures, and many other items. Good advertising brought an eager crowd. When the money was counted, the project had netted over $4,000 (after paying the auctioneer and treating the boys to a steak dinner). The proceeds from the auction were used to purchase new audiovisual equipment (including a VCR), and tape recorders (including a boombox), to redecorate several of the classrooms, and to buy small items that were needed to enhance the church's religious education efforts. In the process, the Boy Scouts learned a great deal about the workings of the church and the Eagle Award recipient decided to become a full member of the church. In addition, the adults who worked on the project came to know several of the boys of the parish on a much more personal level.

7. *Vacation Bible School.* We recruit Bible School directors two years in advance. Three teams of codirectors work together. One team is in charge, the other two teams are in training. Vacation Bible School is one of the most successful and rewarding opportunities for working with children at Epworth. We have age-level groupings beginning with three-year-olds and continuing through junior high. Sometimes we must divide a class by birthdays because we know that we will have too many for one room in that grade level. We have the largest number of children in the preschool ages. Our curriculum materials vary but usually we have used one particular program more than the others. Each year we emphasize a special mission project. One year it was the Oklahoma Indian Missionary Conference. We ordered handmade crafts from the native Americans and sold them to the children. We also invited a local "expert" on the American Indian culture to share with the children in the opening and closing exercises. (We have the younger children come together for an opening and the older children for a closing. We found that the age span from three-year-olds to thirteen-year-olds did not allow for a meaningful time together as a total group.)

The mission project that has generated the most excitement centered on Grace Children's Hospital in Port-au-Prince, Haiti. We began this emphasis about six weeks before Bible School. That year we borrowed a canoe from a member of the church and placed it in the sanctuary. Children at Bible School and all the members of the church were encouraged to bring in hospital, personal, and school supplies for the children in Haiti. (A list of approved items had been published.) We also set up a sewing network to make dresses, shirts, and shorts for the children at the hospital. During the week of VBS, we had a sewing room with several ladies working on the clothes. Further, handmade items from Haiti were ordered from SERRV and sold all week long. There was a feeling that the entire church was supporting this mission project. Over $3,000 was raised for Grace Children's Hospital, and, through slides and special visitors, both compassion and excitement were generated for our friends in another part of the world.

8. *Organizing for Church School.* Our ongoing religious education work with children through the church school program generally follows traditional models. We age-group the children as follows: infants, toddlers, two's, three's, four's, kindergarten/first grade, second grade, third/fourth grade, and fifth grade. These groupings change from year to year depending upon the enrollment in each. We have paid workers in the infant through two-year-old church school classes. We also pay the workers in the extended hour (worship hour) classes for preschool age children. The other religious educators are volunteers and are recruited on a quarterly basis. When possible, we try to have more than one leader in a room. During some quarters, we have had a man and a woman in each class. One quarter we had a senior-high helper in each room. There are age-level coordinators who are responsible for the supervision of no more than three rooms each. They assist in recruitment and locating substitutes. They stay in close and regular touch with the teachers. We have a meeting of all the children's coordinators during the church school hour on the Sunday before the Education Committee meets (every other month).

9. *Children's Specials.* Occasionally the opportunity presents itself to do something very special with the children of our congregation. Recently, the church school lesson for the fifth-grade class focused on the Methodist mission at Upper Sandusky, Ohio, with the Wyandot Indians. Almost spontaneously we decided to take a trip to the mission site. The following Saturday, a vanload of children and teachers explored our Wyandot Indian mission. The experience included doing some rubbings of the Indian and missionary gravestones. These "specials" offer an opportunity for a closer relationship with the children and for enrichment of the learnings about

our faith that are so important to the children of our churches.

These are a sampling of the ways in which we work together in the religious education of the children at Epworth Church. There are many other opportunities and a variety of settings in which we learn together. I keep several key words in mind as I work with our children and with the other leaders of children: involvement, taking risks, and being responsive. *Involvement* means being with the children. It takes time and patience. It means listening more than talking. And it often means going to where they are, rather than waiting for them to come to where I might be. *Taking risks* means being willing to try something that might fail. Not every "children's moments" makes it. Sometimes a question gets a most surprising answer. Sometimes there is little or no response to a program or project. But always we must be willing to try, to evaluate, and try again. *Being responsive* means recognizing that often the suggestions of children are the best. Some adults assume that the ideas of children are silly. I have discovered that most of the suggestions that children offer are very serious, and more times than not they have an excellent handle on how they can best learn. Hearing their concerns, understanding their culture, and responding to their questions are the ways of being most responsive to children.

When the religious educator with children has a genuine appreciation for children you have found the right path. Add to that a commitment to ministry and a supportive attitude toward the total church and you are well on your way to an exciting ministry with children. At all times, lift high the excitement for children—they are a part of the church today!

THE PASTOR AS RELIGIOUS EDUCATOR OF ADULTS
(C. JOSEPH SPRAGUE)

Two working presuppositions have guided me as I have engaged in the work of pastoral educator with adults in the revitalization process underway at Epworth. They are:

1) *Ministry is holistic and cannot be segmented.* As Jesus the Christ paradoxically was fully human and fully divine, through the gift of grace and the response of ultimate trust, so is the ministry one in its paradoxical, even disconcerting, mixture of the mundane and the magnificent. Hence, that which is enacted at the Table and pro-

claimed from the pulpit is tied inextricably to the classroom and is integral to administration, pastoral care, social witness, missional outreach, evangelism (which is the subject of all the foregoing), and the daily lifestyle of an authentic parish as modeled by clergy and laity alike. Religious education work is not separate from the pastor's overall ministry. Rather religious education work is necessarily an integral part of the pastor's overall mission. We at Epworth are learning that what affects one facet of ministry directly affects all indirectly. We either practice what we preach, teach what we live, handle the lives of others as we handle the Bread and Cup, or the whole enterprise crumbles. In short, while religious education is a distinct function, it cannot be isolated from all that I do, from all I am, and all we are as a called people.

2) While the revitalization of Epworth is centered in worship, we believe we will find staying power in the careful nurture and risky equipping of adults for their own lifelong ministries within and without the congregation. Thus, I approach the task of adult religious educator as an intentional pastor, prophet, and priest who is seeking to subvert the powers and principalities of this present age. Teaching adults at Epworth is a vital pastoral, prophetic, and priestly action of subversion; it is the act of confronting the idolatries of our age, our town, our parish, and ourselves with the authority of the victory won in Christ that Christ's victory might be recognized, celebrated, and incarnated in personal and corporate expressions of wholeness and liberation.

Given these two presuppositions, I organize my religious education work around the classic scholarly subjects of scripture, theology and ethics, and church history. Often, I will be teaching a class in each of these arenas simultaneously. Such a procedure forces me to correlate and integrate constantly while I try to guide others to do the same. For the sake of clarity and particularity, I shall describe the teaching I have done and am doing in each arena. While doing this, I write knowing that each emphasis, while distinct, is a part of the whole; together these parts provide me with pliable settings for the subversive tasks to which I am called.

Scripture is the unifying component in Epworth's worship life. The Bible serves as the basis for our preaching ministry. We plan music and liturgy around the weekly themes of the ecumenical lectionary; one of the appointed lections is the text for the Sunday sermon. In order to help prepare for worship and to engage pastor and congregation in a shared approach to the biblical basis for next Sunday's music, liturgy and sermons (as has been noted the Children's Moments and Children's Church are empowered by the same text), I lead a "Sermon Shaping" session each Wednesday morning from 7:00 a.m. to 7:45 a.m.

Fifteen to twenty-five laypersons, who, given their pronounced differences, are representative of the congregation, gather faithfully week after week to struggle with me on both an emerging exegesis and an initial exposition. The designated texts are selected seasonally from the lectionary and published well in advance for the parish's information and study.

Prior to Wednesday morning, I have done my homework and am equipped to present a brief overview of the text and its context. Then, after clarifying discussion, the text is read aloud. We seek to hear the text with both mind and heart; we seek God's Word for us as we work to understand the words of historic witness in the text. Sometimes we react through group discussions to the language of judgment and grace within the text; occasionally, in more meditative personal postures, we will see images and frame visions in order that we might be fed and challenged at transrational levels.

Often our sharing helps me structure the sermon's germinal idea with specific implications for the people of Epworth. The whole process is dialogical: God and the Word, Word and text, text and preacher, preacher and people, people and text, Word and us— engaged, pushed, confused, mystified, empowered.

I cannot imagine preaching week after week without such a teaching and learning context. A vital spark for the increased energy within Epworth is struck weekly in "Sermon Shaping." Interestingly, two weekly breakfast groups, seeded by participants in "Sermon Shaping," replicate this process without this writer.

"Sermon Shaping," important as it is, is not sufficient in regard to our need at Epworth to study the Bible. "Sermon Shaping" touches too few, and the selected lections preclude a systematic, comprehensive study of the whole Bible. Thus, I offer a survey course in the Old Testament for nine months duration every other year. The class meets weekly in the evening, holidays excepted, and we read our way through the Old Testament, while also studying Lawrence Boadt's excellent and inexpensive, paperback commentary, *Reading the Old Testament.* The class outline is drawn largely from the Boadt book, but the lectures and discussions reflect an attempt to correlate the textual materials with the practical realities of our lives and the issues at hand in Epworth, Marion, and the world.

During alternate years, when I am not teaching the Old Testament course, I offer three New Testament courses of six to eight weeks duration each. These are in the Synoptic Gospels, John, and the Pauline Epistles. These are offered during the church school hour. In addition to reading the New Testament, we use Jack Kingsbury's *Jesus Christ in Matthew, Mark, and Luke* for the synoptics course, and for the course on Paul, Robert Jewett's *Christian Tolerance* and Victor Furnish's *The Moral Teachings of Paul.*

An early frustration in all of this was the initial reaction of several of the longstanding classes. Quite simply, they were resistant to anyone teaching adult options during church school. They feared that their classes would be weakened or ended. But, by virtue of the careful work done by veteran class members, several of the classes now invite me and other "outsiders" to lead specific courses for them. These have worked remarkably well. Hopefully the day has come when these classes are no longer threatened by optional opportunities for growth. To facilitate this hope, our pastoral staff is quite careful about the options we offer on Sunday morning; we process them carefully with the Education Work Area. Additionally, I offer myself as a resource person for these classes regularly. It is important that they see me as "theirs."

I was delighted when our Young Parents' Class invited me to do two major pieces with them in 1986. It was intentional subversion at its best as forty-plus eager, affluent, bright, young adults were exposed to Jim Wallis' *Agenda for a Biblical People* and the "Gospel According to St. Mark," with the help of Werner Kelber's commentary, *Mark's Story of Jesus.*

Positive results continue to emerge, not only as members of this class assume more and more positions of leadership at Epworth, but also as they converse with their friends, co-workers, and families about life's meaning and the call of the gospel for them. While the class disagreed vehemently with much that Wallis advocates, and while some of the members were perplexed by Mark's radical nature, there is a creative restlessness stirring among them.

Periodically, we bring before our adult constituency outside resource persons of considerable ability. This is especially true in biblical studies. For example, large groups of our adults studied on two separate, extended periods of time with Van Bogard Dunn, a professor at a nearby seminary. Dunn exposed us to the "Book of Revelation" in a way that T.V. evangelists could ill afford to affirm. His stirring narrative presentation of Mark's account of the gospel, followed by a clarifying exegesis and exposition, helped us to hear anew the call to discipleship which Mark the evangelist issues.

Advent and Lenten studies dot our historic landscape. We are encouraged by what can happen in these settings. For example, an Advent study I led in 1985 with one of Epworth's long-established classes provided a surprise breakthrough both to some individuals for whom the church was marginal, at best, and to the ongoing ethos of that class. As a result of the honest struggle in which we engaged, several new persons from the class stepped forward for witness and service in Epworth's task groups and as elected officers of our parish. The new teacher of the class is encouraged and supported as he offers the kind of substantive material which nurtures and empowers discipleship. After forsaking the tried and tired for a season, this long-standing class of middle-aged adults has opened itself to processes of spiritual formation which are still underway. They now choose their curriculum carefully with the help of Patricia Miller. After working through *The Celebration of Discipline, Fully Human, Fully Alive*, and an option I offered on the New Testament in July, 1986, they are working now with personal issues of spiritual formation. Quite a step forward for a group which is part and parcel of the past strengths and future hopes of Epworth.

Theology and ethics are subjects which often send twinges of terror or nods of boredom into the lives of lay people. I have tried to guide our people through these obstacles. I have both failed and succeeded in doing so. Progress slow but, I trust, is being made.

Three times each year (Fall, Winter, and Spring) I offer a six to eight week component of "Literature and Theology." Those sessions are held for an hour and a half on Sunday evenings. What an enlivening experience this has been! It is exciting to help people demythologize religious jargon in order that they might remythologize the eternal verities for their own lives. Interestingly, this effort has been an effective evangelistic arm of Epworth as persons who had forsaken the church during postadolescence have begun to find both answers to their questions and new questions for their old answers.

There is a core group of fifteen to twenty persons—physicians, elected local officials from both political parties, teachers, retirees, cultural leaders, homemakers, business people, and young adults— who will not miss a session; there are forty or so others who filter in and out depending upon the subject matter at hand.

The format for this group is somewhat Socratic in nature. We read the same bloc of material, and then I lead a question and response session which occasionally is broken by a mini-lecture, field trip, or structured debate. As in most of my classes, we also employ small groups, one-on-one dialogues, and many other techniques to open persons to the subject matter and to one another. This group has been variously a seminary classroom, a social witness cadre, a supportive community, a therapy group, and a disgruntled band of middle-class dissidents.

We have read widely and imaginatively as I have sought to help the participants see theology in art, life in theology, and ethical issues everywhere. Occasionally, our readings are organized around a theme, such as "The Problem of Evil," but usually we read several challenging authors who have spoken to me or members of the group. About one-third of the books studied have been suggested by class participants.

Included in the sessions of "Literature And Theology" have been books such as: *The Power And The Glory* (this was particulary helpful in addressing the hurt and anger at Epworth in the early years), *The Clowns of God*, *The Second Coming*, *Zorba the Greek*, *Final Payments*, *Lancelot*, *Night*, *Why We Can't Wait*, *The World Is Made of Glass*, *When Bad Things Happen To Good People*, *The Road Less Traveled*, *The People of the Lie*, *Evil: The Shadow Side of Reality*, *The Theology of Hope*, *The Crucified God*, *The Celebration of Discipline*, *Money, Sex and Power*, *Into the Whirlwind*, *The Speed of Love*, *Christ And Culture*, *Reaching Out*, *Clowning in Rome*, *The Wounded Healer*, *Journey Inward*, *Journey Outward*, *Megatrends*, *Hiroshima*, *Beyond God The Father*, *Dreams: God's Forgotten Language*, *Invisible Partners*, *Sacred Journey*, *Now And Then*, *Nature And Destiny Of Man*, Vol. I & II, *Moral Man And Immoral Society*, *The Unsettling of America*, *Agenda for a Biblical People*, *Original Blessing*, and *God, Christ,*

Church: A Practical Guide to Process Theology. These are many, but not all of the texts which have blessed us.

"Literature and Theology" sessions, coupled with all else being done at Epworth, have helped to stimulate our growing appreciation for worship and our deepened commitments to care for one another, Marion, and the needs of God's complex world.

Part of the response to adult religious education in general, this class in particular and the whole new ethos at Epworth has been the emergence of task groups. Some of these include Homebound Care for Shut-Ins, Spiritual Formation, Peace With Justice, a Weekly Soup Supper, the creating and ongoing support for a center for the unemployed, an annual commitment to provide first four and now five tons of food for the hungry in Marion, support for and involvement with the local hospice unit, and much, much more. Adult education, as part of the whole garment, is beginning to wear well.

However, I see in retrospect that, particularly in "Literature and Theology," I offered too much too soon and in the process frightened some of those who would benefit most from such exposure. Presently, sensing the fact that the heady fare of this class in a "no" for many, my colleague, Patricia Miller, administers or offers a second adult option in parallel with "Literature And Theology." This other option seeks to attract those who have expressed more conventional needs for nurture and study.

Patricia's Sunday evening options tend to be heavily experiential in style and have featured such offerings as, "Health, Healing, and Wholeness," "Fully Human, Fully Alive," "The Life and Teachings of Jesus," "The Rudiments of Prayer," "Parenting," "World Religions," and films by James Dobson and Tim Timmons, with debriefing sessions following the films.

Church history, while not addressed by my teaching as systematically as are scripture, theology, and ethics, is approached primarily through quarterly classes in United Methodism. These focus on the history of the whole church in general and The United Methodist Church in particular. In these classes a rich mixture of veteran Epworthians and newcomers receive instruction regarding the beliefs, organization, and social commitments of our denomination. It is an amazing thing to see how few veteran members are acquainted with our polity, *Book of Resolutions*, Social Principles, and organization for missional outreach. It is fulfilling to watch them grow in their appreciation of the denomination which is home to them.

Laypersons in positions of leadership share in guiding these classes in United Methodism, and we use these settings, along with personal time spent with newcomers, for the preparation of new adult members for Epworth.

Additionally, I teach a Sunday morning class each year, usually in the spring, on United Methodism's Social Principles. Given Epworth's increasingly activistic style, these sessions, along with occasional panels and social issues series led by outside resource persons, are proving invaluable to Epworth's life.

CONCLUSION

I am convinced that my two working presuppositions are correct and that the emerging health of this parish is the direct result of a well-integrated total ministry, which is drawing strength from intentional work in religious education.

Our strengths are to be found in the way we integrate worship and education, congregational care and missional outreach, physical renovation and spiritual formation, increased giving and social witness, demanding journeys inward and risky journeys outward. Our staff sees all of ministry holistically, and we work together accordingly.

My religious education work with adults is made easier due to companion programs at parallel times with children and youth. The wholeness our staff envisions and seeks to model is becoming a realistic working model for our people. Revitalization is underway at Epworth. Nevertheless, I have made some blunders along the way. Included among them are:

1) Not spending more time initially with the neo-fundamentalists who were the leaders of the parish. I became task-oriented in regard to needed surgery while not tending carefully some of those who hurt and were hurting most;

2) Offering too much, too soon, in the biblical and theological courses, thus frightening some who need and want nurture;

3) So majoring in a rational, reflection-action style, that I failed to touch the intuitive "other side," and also those who operate primarily experientially;

4) Demanding so much preparation and extensive reading that the 200-plus I touch regularly might be twice that number if I had enabled them to work at a more leisurely pace;
5) The failure to provide guidance in spiritual development early in the process for some who had grown beyond what I was offering; and
6) Not making enough use of retreats, weekends, and other intense periods of time away, especially with the many established groups.

I am seeking now to correct these flaws as I continue to labor as a pastoral educator. Now that a teaching model is in place at Epworth, I will be more intentional about beginning to work with lay teachers to equip them further to be the subversives they, too, are called to be within and without the church. I am convinced that pastors, no matter how busy, who are not teaching adults regularly are missing a very rich opportunity to proclaim and model that release to the captives which the gospel of Jesus Christ is.

EPILOGUE: MILLER AND SPRAGUE

The specific religious education programs, classes, and activities that heve been shared in this chapter are not applicable in every parish setting. But the basic understandings, approaches, and principles should guide the pastor as religious educator in any local church. Taking the time to know those with whom you work is the beginning point. Knowing their feelings, values, and daily experiences informs the pastor's religious education response. Being willing to risk, trying new approaches, and pushing the learners toward new understandings help to keep the teaching-learning exchange fresh and meaningful. But all of these ideas must begin with a genuine appreciation for the learners and a deep commitment to the religious education task. Even the greatest programatic plans will not succeed without these understandings of the role of the pastor as religious educator.

10

Case Study II: Coming Down to Earth—An Alaskan Learner's Guide to Religious Education by a Pastoral Team

JOHN PITNEY AND DEBBIE PITNEY

This note before the chapter is for the reader's presence of mind. One of our greatest challenges as a clergy team (husband and wife) is to be continually looking for ways we can best use our individual gifts while at the same time taking advantage of our strength as a team. While we have been fairly successful at working together without getting in each other's way, writing this chapter was a new challenge to our creativity. You will find our experiences are written in the first person singular, because they are close to us individually and we see them and interpret them in individual ways. We have chosen to switch back and forth from (Debbie) to (John) without stopping except to put the speaker's name in parenthesis after the first "I" reference of any particular section or story. The plurals are obvious. (Thanks, beforehand, for your attention.) In addition, the names of some of the participants have been changed in order to protect their privacy.

We begin our story on the balcony of the administration building at the Methodist Theological School in Ohio (Methesco), let us say in the spring of 1973, although the incident has proven to be quite timeless. Dean of the faculty, Van Bogard Dunn, has crawled out there through his office upstairs window. He is wearing a gray, three-piece suit and shiny black shoes. Having readied himself for some momentous activity, he now looks down toward the ground to an assemblage of twelve to fifteen children from the Methesco Early Childhood Center. The children are now quiet as the Dean, with a sly twinkling in his eye, lofts a paper airplane toward them on the ground. They run and giggle and squeal with glee. A big person, distinguished professor of New Testament and something called "homiletics" has made their day. If your desire is to be a prophet of YHWH to children in our time, write the message on a paper airplane, because children tend not to understand words written upon stone. If you want to lead, follow. If you want to teach, learn.

Actually, the paper airplane sailing down was only the finale. The kids had visited Dunn upstairs, in his office that morning. They had taken a walk down the hill from the Early Childhood Center, all decked out in hats from the dress-up corner. Even the teachers were wearing funny hats, though theirs didn't seem to slip so easily down over little ears and eyes to hide the silly smiles. By the time they all got up the stairs to the office and went to the bathroom and sat in a jumble on the Dean's floor, they were quite a crew. He, of course, did what any self-respecting would-be prophet and teacher would do . . . he came out from behind his big desk and, one at a time, tried on each child's hat. The children were quite in awe of this—he had stooped to enter their cosmos from another realm. Then, horror of horrors, after the hats were all tried, he looked at them all and said, "I want you to listen to me, children. Most of the people around here call me Dean or Dr. Dunn, but my friends call me Bogie. I want you to call me Bogie." Before they arose to go outside to the courtyard below the office, they all practiced saying his name together. In the months and years ahead, the student moms and dads would continue to call him by title while their children, taking walks on campus on a sunny day, would spy his figure down the sidewalk and shout, "Hi Bogie!" Bogie may have started out to offer teaching and empowerment to a group of two-, three-, and four-year olds that morning but, truth to tell, *they* had taught and empowered *him*. Tell me, who is making disciples out of whom? Who are the teachers and who are the learners?

When Søren Kierkegaard first told his puzzling parable about the king who fell in love with the young peasant maiden, we can only guess at what he must have been struggling with inside himself and in his world. We have assumed, through the years, that any who have consistently listened to preachers all their lives have probably heard this story told too often already. We think we have assumed wrongly. We rarely meet church people who remember it—and much less, who can readily identify with what it would call us to do—how and who it calls us to be:

The setting, of course, is in medieval times and we have to review our history to be aware of the power of this tale. In those days the lines were strictly drawn between those of nobility, living in castles, and lowly peasants living "common" lives in the countryside. Persons of distinction did not associate with common folks unless there was some official need to do so and then the relationship was strictly one-way. Anyway, as destiny would have it, the young king was riding through the land one day and spied a beautiful young peasant maiden and immediately fell in love with her.

From the very first moment he knew that she must become his bride and queen and live with him happily ever after. He had a problem, of course. He was a king and she a peasant. How could he tell her of his deep love for her? He could go directly to her and tell her of his affection, but she, being of common blood, would surely blush away, ashamed to be in his presence, let alone to hear his surprising message. He was king and he could always command her to love and marry him and be his queen and she, being an obedient peasant, would surely follow his every command and worship, honor, and obey him forever. But the young king desired great love not worship, honor, or obedience, and so he pondered on. He decided that he might disguise himself as a young peasant man and go to her village to live. Surely then, they would meet and fall in love, even be married, peasant to peasant, and *then* he could reveal his true identity and they could go live happily in the castle. But this king was not a fool and he realized (even as he planned) that this would not get him the love for which his heart yearned. Many days and sleepless nights passed, until in steadfast soul-searching, he realized that there was only one way that he could establish the mutual love-bond he desired. It would require much of him under the circumstances of his culture, but then he was a person of steadfast courage. In order to share love with this peasant woman, he must become a peasant. The king stepped down from his nobility and went out to the countryside to live the rest of his days in love with his chosen partner.[1]

Our own experience since seminary days has not been extensive when we consider the number of years, but it has given us a certain vastness of variety which few our age (in our culture) may have had.

From the confines of the Methesco Early Childhood Center and urban ministry in Columbus, Ohio (during those seminary years), we were sent out to five years in rural Idaho. From our two congregations in Idaho we went to two others on the far west coast of Alaska on the Bering Sea. In our United Methodist and Presbyterian churches, two-thirds of our parishioners were made up of Inuit and Yupik people of the Bering Straits (to most whites, the term "Eskimo" would best describe our friends there). Wherever we have been, it seems we have been faced with the same challenge—a basic challenge of Incarnation like that so clearly described by Kierkegaard in his parable. In the Methesco Early Childhood Center the challenge is made by the questions of a four-year-old to her teacher, "Will you play lion-in-jail with me? (You get to be in jail!) In Idaho, the challenge is made by a dairy farmer, who, as you pay her a visit in her milking parlor, asks, "All I want to know is: 'Do you know what to do when the cows get out (while you're here)?' " At a fish camp up the coast from Nome, Alaska, the challenge is delivered by a small friendly Inuit woman who offers you dried fish and seal oil with a smile. By some measure, the challenge question is always an invitation from a person in another world . . . an invitation for us to come on in. By some measure it is also a test. Persons test those of us who are church leaders to see how vulnerable we are willing to be . . . how tolerant of their traditions, their languages, and values. Test results will determine how much they will trust us in the future. "If we find someone who is willing to try and learn from us—we think we could learn from them . . ." is an underlying statement which might come through our encounters in the best of situations. There will be a few good substitutes for getting in jail with the four-year-old and sticking around to help the dairy woman drive in the cows (no matter what you might step in along the way!). Though humbly acknowledging your cultural differences may be a better alternative than throwing your fish and seal oil out the front door, some way of gesturing our openness to entering another's turf and common life is essential to building the trust necessary for mutual learning. The basic challenge is to find authentic ways to become a learning partner in their lives. Just as God does not come to us through some gimmick, technique, or disguise, so a conversion of our hearts is required—often a letting go of some of our deepest fears, traditions, and biases so that we can be baptized into the life of another and genuinely meet that other on common ground. The learning begins; and, when learning begins, we can teach. Teaching entails so much more than big words spoken about the presence of Christ among us. We must become *incarnate* and thus authentically believable to *real* people.

My own conversion (John) has been painfully slow. While en-route from Idaho to the Alaska Missionary Conference, we were invited to attend a worldwide gathering of United Methodist missionaries. This was to be part of our orientation to the mission work. So, I went to Howard University in Washington, D.C., for the conference. (We both could not go.) I met people who were in ministry in churches, community centers, and stations of various kinds all over the United States and from around the world. To my dismay, I found that the friendliest people I met there were those who seemed most unlike I am. I was deeply touched by quick friendships that bonded me with particular black and hispanic people who became very important to me as I faced the unknown territory of ministry with Alaska natives. My new friends gave me a message that I will always remember. They said to me very gently, and in many ways: "You don't have anything to teach us. You will have nothing to teach the Eskimo people in Alaska. Don't go to them and try to make them the way you would like them to be. You are going into *their* land. Go learn from them. After you learn, then you can teach them. Someday, maybe you can return to your own people and teach."

The last day of the week we gathered for the closing worship service in the Jeremiah Rankin Memorial Chapel. I had listened hard to my new friends that week. They had challenged me to put ministry into the context of culture, class, and lifestyle. I felt very middle-American, very male, and very white. As a missionary I would not be just myself. I would be representative of the dominant cultural class of the planet . . . a class whose people have so often oppressed, abused, and destroyed others . . . and so often in the name of Jesus. This (YHWH had planned) would be another turning point in my slow conversion. As I sat on the end of the pew, I remember I couldn't keep my eyes from the stained glass window behind the altar. It depicted Christopher Columbus with cross raised overhead, discovering the New World that I was learning he had no right to claim for his people. Worship was moving some awful things around inside of me. So, when the liturgist later opened the pulpit for any to go up and pray I knew I had to go and share my learnings. I said I was learning that I am a racist. I confessed my kinship to Christopher Columbus the Exploiter and J. R. Ewing the Jerk and all others the world over who have claimed lands and gifts of lands to the abuse of people. I publicly affirmed my conversion (to learn from the dispossessed of the land and to speak to my own kind) that the acceptable year of the Lord might come soon upon the earth. I went back to my pew, sat down, and cried uncontrollably. The appointive process of United Methodism had again been called into question—why were *they* sending *us* to Nome? I did not want to go. I certainly did not want to go and carry on a history of oppression in another gentle land. Of course, the decision had already been made and, being pretty hardheaded and a little bit dumb, we went ahead. (Our baby's crib and the Interpreter's Bibles were already loaded on the barge anyway.) If you have nothing to teach, then there's only one thing to do—go and learn.

Ministry in a culturally mixed congregation of Caucasian people and native Alaskans is challenging, to say the least. We constantly struggled with the enduring temptation to move ahead on the expectations of the white people in the congregation and community. This was true because whites generally have louder voices and more dominant and demanding ways of communication. The first Pastor-Parish Relations Committee meeting we had with the United Methodist parishioners proved a case in point. The lone Inupiaq woman was Helen Senungetuk. She sat quietly through the entire meeting without saying anything. Toward the end (of course we did not know anyone very well at the time), we asked Helen if she had anything she wanted to say. She remained quiet. And we didn't know if she was not going to speak or if she was thinking. The silence seemed longer than it probably was, but then she did talk. She said a young Eskimo woman had visited our church a few Sundays earlier and she saw how white people sat on one side of the sanctuary and Eskimos all sat together in the back on the other side. The woman did not want to come to our church if that's the way it was between whites and natives in our church. The others around the circle quickly jumped to their own defense and said it wasn't as it seemed. Helen didn't say any more at this or any other meetings. Try as we might to change patterns, the whites would always be dominant in meetings. Sometimes when natives were alone with us they would share how they felt around whites who could read and speak better English and had been to school. They were ashamed to speak. This was nobody's fault—just the way it was. It was an uneasy lesson we learned because we wanted everyone always to be all together in groupings in our church; but, segregation was necessary.

It was in closed groups with other Inuit people that the native folks could begin to share their deeper feelings, values, and commitments about life with each other. From the support of the closed group they could, then, occasionally move out to share across cultural boundaries. Our main group met for "Bible Study" on Wednesday mornings at Polly Koweluk's house. "Bible Study" was only the label. We did study but we always laughed and told stories and drank tea and ate Mary Natungok's muffins. When Mary arrived at Polly's, Helen Senungetuk would often break into a chorus of "Hello Mary Sunshine, why did you go so soon . . . ?" Mary always smiled but didn't say much. We met at Polly's because her mother, Josephine, lived there with her. When we sang, Josephine, who was a little deaf and very blind, could sing along. It made her day. We met at Polly's because it seemed right and it was always warmer there than in the back of the sanctuary. We met at Polly's because Polly loved taking care of each one of us. We met at Polly's because we *always* learned something from each other in her house with our friends. At Polly's house we learned each other's *real* names. Missionaries had picked English names for the people . . . Helen was really Alaasiaq. Esther was really Agunaat. Polly was Agupgaaq. Nancy was Sanigaq, and Virginia was really Ayona. How our faces would light up when we used real names. (I was given the name *Atqiituaq* which means "No name.") From Willie Senungetuk I learned how to say the Lord's Prayer in his language and to drink tea with evaporated milk and two sugar cubes. Polly knew I drank tea with evaporated milk. One day, in the middle of Bible study, she got up and went outdoors and took off down the street without saying a word. She came back in awhile with a can of evaporated milk. She had remembered she was out of it and knew I "couldn't" drink tea without it!

One morning we were discussing Matthew 5:5, "Blessed are the meek for they shall inherit the earth." Ayona read it aloud in English and then we talked. We talked for a long time about meek or humble people we knew. A couple of the women decided that Polly was just about the meekest one they ever saw—always thinking of others and always helping without saying much. We asked how they would translate this verse into Inupiaq (their language from the village of Wales, Alaska). We were always translating and found it very important to compare our English translations with the Eskimo way of speaking which they had learned from their elders. Anyway, they translated Matthew 5:5. They talked in Inupiaq to each other for quite a while, and we just sat and listened. When they were satisfied with their words they told us how it would be in their language. We tried to figure out what their words were saying about "meekness" and about "inheriting the earth." As nearly as we could tell, the elders had taught these women (having been taught themselves by early white missionaries) to say it something like this: "Those who are humble can be happy, because they will go to heaven when they die." "Damn those missionaries!" I often thought to myself. Surely we could see how persons who were ashamed of their names, their insufficient schooling, and their inability to find a way to speak or to be able to contribute to a domineering foreign culture wouldn't feel as though they had any claim on this earth. But, *we* felt deeply that these meek ones had already received their inheritance here. Through their humility, they laid claim to the God-given sacredness of each life, and each moment of time, each piece of ground, and each people. As teachers, though, neither could we hit them over the head with a foreign way (our way) of believing. After all, *they* were the ones who had said my name over and over again (Atqiituaq). "Here come Mr. No Name," they would say and laugh and laugh.

It was from them that we learned that we also have no claim here and if we were going to teach them to know the God that we were certain had already come within *their* lives this presence would only be taught as we continued to lay aside our distorted perceptions, trying to find ways to enter God's kingdom through *their* experience. We are convinced that there are no prescribed methods or pedagogical gimmicks which allow a would-be teacher to validate the experience of another person or another person's culture short of a change of heart and being. Not everyone can learn another language. I tried hard. I learned in a classroom setting, but I had to learn the Eskimo way to speak a language that was not written until recently. In our class, Margaret Seeganna, a woman from King Island, would walk us through motions and activities and exchanges while speaking Inupiaq. We were not allowed to speak English. I so often left class totally frustrated—with my insides about to burst with expression, but being able to say nothing. Someone had ordained that it might be important for me to experience what it is like to live in a society where I was prohibited from speaking the language of my heart. It was really Margaret Seeganna who gave me the name, Atqiituaq, partly as a loving mockery to me—that I would realize (I think) that no one can be everything to everybody. I finally became so frustrated and so bursting with phrases and feelings and words that I became confident enough to try some expressions with our Bible study friends. Typically I would arrive at Polly's and ask, "Naguu viin?" This was supposed to be, "Are you good (today)?" They would look at me blankly or burst out laughing. One day Sanigaq tells me that she thought I was saying, "Are you cross-eyed?!" Red-faced, I kept trying. No one should have to experience the humiliation of being forced into another people's way of living, speaking, or believing. However, those of us who dominate society and systems of belief and leadership must suffer voluntary humiliation, it seems, in order to understand and learn—and therefore, teach.

Out of trust we were able to encourage each other to share scriptures, prayers, and songs in the racially and culturally mixed worship service on Sunday morning. We learned the Inupiaq Doxology and began singing it and the English version one after the other in corporate worship each week. Some of the Caucasians in worship surely felt this was probably a bit too much culture to have on a regular basis, but most were openly warmed by our communal ability to share each other's lives this way. We used our Bible Study group to remember translated church songs that had been all but forgotten, and we wrote them down and printed an Inupiaq songbook. We did an original translation of "Kum Ba Yah" that became a favorite of our group. The Inupiaq "Kum Ba Yah" and the Eskimo version of the Lord's Prayer are two of the most precious gifts I have received from anyone in my life. They are in my heart with my Inupiaq name, and they define me as a teacher.

Many of us Christians who have grown up in middle-class white America have absolutely no personal understanding of living in oppression. And yet our Old Testament heritage proclaims the story of an oppressed people struggling to experience the fullness of life in the promised land. There is a part of me (Debbie) which truly questions my own ability to be a faithful witness of the gospel when my own life experiences are so out of touch with the history of oppression and God's intervention with our forefathers and foremothers in faith. I really do not know what it means to remain faithful and hopeful in the face of overwhelming persecution. I can only experience such profound faith vicariously as a learner. We mentioned Virginia before. Her real name is Ayona. Ayona has been a good teacher of such faith in my life. She was born in the village of Wales, the oldest of nine children. She moved to Nome as an adult with a family of her own. She lives in a tiny, broken-down house about two blocks from where we lived in Nome. Her husband is an alcoholic. So is her daughter. What little money they have is often spent on liquor before Ayona even sees it. She does the best she can to raise her two grandchildren who are living with her because their mother is unable to care for them when she is drinking. There are many days when Ayona does not know how she will feed her family nor pay for heating oil and necessary clothing. More than once, Ayona and her grandchildren have spent the night at the women's shelter when her husband's drinking has threatened their safety. It was following just such a night that Ayona shared with us at Bible Study. We were talking about recognizing God's presence in our lives. Now I'm used to such discussions in other settings. I must admit that I have grown accustomed to people speaking of God's presence during happy and joyful times of life as in the birth of a baby or the discovery of a new friendship. I was not expecting Ayona to share her story of recognizing that God was with her when she returned home late one cold winter night to find that her husband was drunk, had locked her out of the house, and she had no way of getting him to let her in the house. Remember that a cold winter night in Nome is twenty degrees below zero with a windchill factor that can push the temperature down to forty degrees below zero. I was shocked to hear her story. I knew that she had endured much hardship in her lifetime. But I did not know the extent of the pain and suffering that she endured on a daily basis. Ayona didn't talk much about her problem. She just lived life. Surprisingly enough, she often appeared to be happy. In speaking about that night when her husband locked her out of the house she simply said that she knew she was not alone. She knew that God was with her and kept her safe through the night. I'm not sure my faith is that deep or strong or resilient to survive such testing. I'm not sure I would even stop to think about God if I found myself in that situation. The stories of faith, shared by these people of faith who have lived through oppression and come out hopeful, have taught me much. Isaiah's words take on new meaning when I listen to those who have experienced much struggle in their own personal quest for the promised land: "They who wait for the Lord shall renew their strength, they shall mount up with wings like eagles, they shall run and not be weary, they shall walk and not faint" (Isaiah 40:31, RSV). As one who has been "sent" or "called" to proclaim the faith, I am moved to a place of sincere respect and appreciation for the Ayonas of my world. They teach what it means to be faithful and challenge me to be more faithful in my own life.

Willie Senungetuk is another teacher of the faith. He is not a seminary professor nor a noted theologian but a quiet, dedicated man also born in the village of Wales, way out on the western tip of Alaska where the North American continent comes within a few miles of the Soviet Union. He was orphaned as a young boy when his parents died in a flu epidemic that wiped out the majority of his village. What he learned about hunting and subsisting off the land was mostly self-taught. As a young man, the father of five children, hunting was important for survival. Willie was a good hunter. He had a well-trained dog team and he would go out on the sea ice in the spring, hunting for seals and walruses that would provide his family with food to eat and skins for parkas and mukluks. The sea ice in the spring is not the most secure place to be. Leads or openings in the ice come and go with the wind and tide. On one particular occasion, Willie found himself several miles from land, returning home after a successful hunt. He stopped for a short while to rest and warm himself with a cup of tea. It soon became apparent that a lead had opened up between Willie and the shore ice. He and his dog team were floating on a large piece of ice with no way to get across the open water. As he described the experience, he said that he unloaded most of the seals from the sled so the dogs would have a lighter load. He calmly talked to his lead dogs, reassuring them, and then . . . he waited. Because of his keen eyes and sense of balance, he soon realized that the large piece of ice under his feet was slowly moving—pivoting to be exact—and, at some moment, would come in contact with the shore ice. Willie was ready for that moment. As the ice moved and just a small tip of the floating island touched the secure shore ice, Willie gave his dogs the command and they pulled him to safety across the narrow strip of ice. The moment after he had his feet on solid footing, he remembers looking back and watching as the ice which had held him crumbled into a thousand pieces. At the end of this story, told to me so many times, Willie always affirmed his profound faith in God . . . God who had been by his side the entire time . . . God who had given him life and given it abundantly. Who am I to speak to him of a God who has been with him and with his people for generations—long before I was born . . . long before the missionaries came to his land? How can I as a "missionary" . . . as a "minister" . . . teach Willie anything about the faith that is so much a part of who he is? If I want to teach, I must learn.

Upon moving to Nome, we were quickly introduced to a new denominational structure (new to us, that is) as we became pastors for the Presbyterian parish there. With this pastorate came the added responsibilities of another set of denominational meetings. Soon after we arrived in Nome, I (Debbie) drew the right straw and had the opportunity to attend my first Presbytery meeting. Together with one of the elders from the Session and my daughter Erin (who was still nursing and went everywhere with Mom), I left by plane heading for Delta Junction, a small town outside of Fairbanks, Alaska. It was there that we would meet with other pastors and elders from churches throughout Alaska. I really had no idea what to expect. I had been to lots of sessions of Annual Conference in the United Methodist church. So, I knew of one denomination's idiosyncracies, but a Presbytery meeting was a new thing all together. My friend, Lucille Wongittilin, was the elder from our congregation. She was new to Presbytery as well. The agenda for the day called for "Elder's Reports" to be given in the afternoon. I stood in the back of the small sanctuary holding Erin as she slept on my shoulder. One by one, the elders went up to the pulpit to give their reports. Each report got a little longer and a little more elaborate and a little more boastful. New buildings, growing church schools, and overflowing worship services were spoken of with great pride and a little bit of a "my church is better than yours" attitude. I kept hoping that Erin would wake up and cry so I would have to leave the room. I had no idea how Lucille was going to make it through the report on the Nome parish—my parish. What would the people think when she told them that only fifteen to twenty people came to worship in Sunday evenings and that sometimes we had no prayer meeting at all when only two people showed up? What would people think of my ministry when she told them that we couldn't even pay our bills and had no program of attracting new people into the congregation? Oh, if Erin would only wake up so I could leave the room! Finally, the moderator of the Presbytery called out "Nome" and Lucille made her way up to the front—I wanted to sink into the floor or blend into the woodwork. How well I knew how to play the game of making my church, my ministry sound better and best . . . but did Lucille? Lucille is so short I could barely see her over the heads of the people sitting in front of me. She began to speak, slowly and quietly, as was her way. First she told of her joy in belonging to the Presbyterian Church because the church had a van (it really belonged to the United Methodists!). She told of being picked up for church on Sundays when folks from other churches walked through the ice and snow in order to get to worship. She told of being able to go berry picking in the church van and being able to take her friends along as well. Then she said, "Let's clap for our church van!" Everyone clapped! Lucille continued, telling the people that her church had new ministers and she pointed to me saying, "Her and her husband. Let's clap for them!" Everyone clapped! Lucille sat down. Somehow the average worship attendance and the increased pledging and the expanded parking lot were no longer the focus of our attention. Instead, she raised for us the important question—what is the church and how can the church meet the real needs of people instead of being overwhelmed by budgets and buildings, membership statistics and net growth? She taught us how to rejoice and celebrate being a part of the body of Christ. In that moment I understood why Jesus changed the water into wine when he could have been healing the blind and the lame, and why he befriended the woman with the alabaster jar who knew enough to anoint his tired body with oil. There in that tiny church, so many miles away from the hallowed halls of my seminary, I heard the gospel proclaimed anew by a grandmother from St. Lawrence Island.

We did not get off to a good start as Presbyterian pastors in Nome. It might have had something to do with our introductory experience. We visited Nome in May, when our daughter Erin was two months old. We were to move there in July. The night we arrived, the Presbyterian Executive from Seattle was also there. He met with the church elders that evening. Though we did not participate in that meeting, the pastor reported to us later that the native elders had asked continually throughout the meeting, "When are you going to give us our own building?" "When are we going to get *real* Presbyterian pastor?" This new Presbyterian congregation had been using the United Methodist building and sharing the United Methodist pastor. We, of course, felt rejected. We had not even moved there yet! Probably though, if we were to tell the truth, our biggest struggle was with the hour of worship. The regular Presbyterian service was Sunday evening at seven o'clock. No offense, but for two people who had grown up being close to family and being able to spend Sunday evenings with that family sleeping on the couch or playing games or watching the "Wonderful World of Disney" Sunday evening worship was physically and emotionally hard to lead and experience.

Ed Meyer at Methesco had taught us homiletics with a sensitive vengeance. We preach from a manuscript. Just try preaching from a manuscript on a Sunday evening in Nome, when the outdoor temperature is forty degrees below zero and the faces staring out at you from inside the wolf-skin ruffs on seal-skin parkas do not tell you anything. You don't speak Siberian Yupik and they do not understand much English. Your text for the evening is the Parable of the Prodigal Son, and you just learned that the grandson of the wisest of the elders who sit in the front pew took a rifle and blew his brains out on their back porch that afternoon. You have a translator standing beside you in the pulpit ready to try to translate sentence after sentence to the congregation after you speak in English. Sorry Ed—the manuscript has got to go and, horror of horrors, we've got to come down from behind the pulpit and get into some *real* faith talk here. Will it have to do with the parable? Probably so, but it will not come off the paper. Also, there will be some pauses for thinking of what to say next. Your heart may be beating faster than normal, and your eyes might be wet before you're through. Week to week it was the hardest thing we have ever had to do in the church. It made us say what we *felt* more than what we *thought*. There were many nights when we should only have sung, prayed, and read the Bible, because it was clear we had nothing worth preaching. Moreover, it became clear that what we ended up preaching anyway had traveled from our brains out through our mouths without consulting our hearts. In Presbyterian worship on Sunday evenings, we learned to come down from the pulpit to the level of common experience and claim what we say as our own. It is at this level that good news meets bad news in real life and finds the basic gospel moment there, free from the confusion of too many words and the intellectual polish that seems to defy feelings and obstruct possibilities for learning. We did not move down there because of any great outward show of success, indicated by responses of the people or other such rewards we look for as preachers. I guess we often stepped out because someone was jerking on a pantleg or the hem of a skirt—someone who wanted us to be more trusting or faithful or compassionate to people who could not begin to understand our language until we did so move toward them.

During our second year in Nome, I (Debbie) was invited to become a part of the culture of the St. Lawrence Island people who were the members of the Presbyterian Church. I was given the opportunity to learn how to dance. Dancing is an important part of Inuit and Yupik culture. Through dancing, the stories of life and death are told, shared, celebrated, and passed on to the next generation. It had long been Nick Wongittilin's dream to teach a group of his white friends the dances of his heart. I felt honored to be one of the group that would learn several dances and then perform at the annual gathering of elders from the villages on the Seward Peninsula. How awkward I felt standing next to Lucille, Nick's wife, as she patiently taught me how to dance. Now, I have never thought of myself as one who is blessed with any physical coordination let alone gracefulness. Yet, there I was, learning to move to the rhythmic beat of the walrus-skin drum. Over and over and over again, Lucille would show me the arm motions to "Munz Northern Airlines" and "Caribou Hunting," the two dances I was learning. I felt so self-conscious, even silly, as my long arms tried to imitate Lucille's graceful motions. We practiced week after week after week, each time we gathered, coming a little closer to understanding the stories we were sharing through dance and song. Nick and Lucille began to smile when they saw that, finally, we were catching on and dancing! Kuspuks (the native dress) were made and gamuks (the native footwear) were borrowed, and we were finally ready to share our dances with the gathered community at the Elder's Conference. Nick and Lucille hadn't told anyone that we would be dancing—it was to be a surprise. More than five hundred people were packed into the gymnasium that night to celebrate the culture of each village in song and dance. Nick and Lucille were all smiles as a motley group of white women took the stage and carefully but joyfully danced the dances of the St. Lawrence Island people. My heart was still racing as the evening came to a close and I was finding my way out through the crowd. Willie Senungetuk, my friend and a member of the United Methodist congregation stopped me as I was leaving. I didn't know what to expect. The missionaries that had come to his village had prohibited dancing, calling it pagan and the work of the devil. I didn't know how he would feel about his pastor publicly dancing the dances of a people so much like him. His words were simple. He said, "Thank you. Thank you for dancing the dances of my people." He told me that he was proud to have his pastor dance, affirming his culture and his heritage as legitimate and acceptable in the eyes of God. I have often thought of his smile and his words in the months and years that have passed. I know in my heart how important it is for me, as a pastor, to enter into the lives of the people I am called to serve.

My friendship with Lucille grew from my being her pastor and her being my teacher to just being good friends. During August, when the berries were ripening on the tundra, she would often call in the morning and ask if I could take her berry picking. I would look at my desk, usually piled high with busy work, and say, "Sure!" When I arrived at her house, she would come out smiling with buckets in hand and a whole group of her friends . . . always women and children of her neighborhood . . . and they would all pile into that old red Chevy Suburban that she had asked us to clap for at the Presbytery meeting. Lucille sat up front with me and would share with me in her own quiet way as we drove the eleven or twelve miles out toward Cape Nome where the blackberries were especially plentiful. Sometimes I would stay and pick berries too, but all too often, I would have to go back to "work" promising to come back in a few hours to pick up the berry pickers. It was on the ride home that I would learn about the real meaning of life in her culture. There, in that old red van, they would sit—faces darkened by the sun and wind that had greeted them on the Cape—hands stained by the berries that they would preserve for the coming winter—and they would share with each other and with me the fruits of their labor making sure that each person had berries to take home. I was humbled by their sharing—I had not even taken the time to pick berries. Still, they made sure that I had some to share with my family. Lucille is just that kind of person. From her I have learned the real meaning of being a part of the body of Christ, eating from the same loaf and drinking from the same cup and having plenty of berries to share.

I do remember one special evening with Lucille. I was driving her home in that same old red van after the prayer meeting at the church. It had been a particularly hard week for me. Several people in the parish were complaining again that there was not a real Presbyterian pastor to serve them. It was hard to take such complaints lightly, especially when they were spoken in a language I didn't understand. I was hurting inside. I was feeling lonely and like a stranger in this land that was my home. Lucille was the last one to be dropped off before I could go home to hide myself away from people and nurse my broken spirit. When I pulled up in front of her house in Bering View (the government housing project on the East End where so many of our congregation lived), Lucille paused for a moment before getting out of the van. She turned toward me, sensing the pain inside my heart, and said in her soft voice, "We like you just the way you are. You are doing okay." A few simple words, spoken by one who found English confusing at best, helped the healing process begin and sent me home with a sense of comfort and hope. Just who is the "pastor" anyway? At that moment all those words of Jesus about the first being last and the last being first and loving each other as God loves us made sense as Lucille touched my heart with her gentle and loving spirit.

In Nome we lived in an apartment in the United Methodist Church building where we were responsible for doing emergency

housing for anybody who needed a warm place or a safe or sober
home for a while. We were always on call, so I (John) was not
surprised to feel my stomach tighten into little knots when the
phone rang at two o'clock in the morning the day after Thanksgiving. The voice of our friend Roger Wayman came on the line. He
said, "I'm sorry to bother you, but I thought you would want to
know. I'm over here at George and Ann's. George Jr. shot himself
about thirty minutes ago." Roger was chairman of our Church
Council, a Public Health Service dentist, and volunteer EMT.
George Sr. was one of my and Roger's best friends. I woke up
quickly and walked down the street to George's yellow house on
the corner. The scene was awful. George was in the living room
pacing around. He was in between wanting a friend close by and
wanting to be alone. He told me to go upstairs to be with Ann and
the rest of the family. I went up and sat on the bedroom floor. I
dreaded having to go past George Jr.'s bedroom door. There was
already blood leaking down through the floor and through the
kitchen ceiling below. But, I went and I was quiet. I was just there.

Finally George had me come downstairs with him and we sat at
the eating table. He said he knew his family needed him, but he
didn't think they needed to see him crying—so he would cry downstairs and then collect himself and go upstairs to be "strong." Sometimes when he was ready to cry he would send me up again. He said
he hadn't cried for thirty-five years. For thirty-five years he'd been
holding it in . . . holding in the anger from being rejected by the
St. Lawrence Island village community because of things that had
happened in their early life as a family. He had been put down by
his own people for stepping out and getting educated (he's one of
the best high-school teachers I know) and put down by much of the
white community because he is not white. He said he was letting
out thirty-five years of this stuff today. Once I tried to touch him by
putting my hand on his shoulder, but he didn't want to be touched.
At his son's memorial service, George was all smiles and the perfect
host and comforter to everyone. He wasn't at all himself. He told
me later he had made himself like iron to get through the day. After
the service he was saddest about what he had deprived in himself
that day. He wanted to feel. He couldn't. His power over his emotions was beginning to scare him.

George had an awful year that year. Earlier in the fall one of his nephews had shot and killed himself on the Island (St. Lawrence Island). After George Jr. died in November, George's best friend dropped dead during a basketball game in February. In June their yellow house on the corner burned down. The following summer, fall, and winter their youngest son began a three year continuum of drug busts, detentions, and violent behavior at school that landed him in the State Youth Facility contemplating his own suicide . . . keeping his parents in constant inner turmoil.

Through this long couple of years, George got more in touch with his need to express his feelings, and in this time George and I were building one of the most mutual friendships I think I will ever have. That is, we asked a lot of each other, and we expected a lot in return. If I called to ask George for a favor I might end the conversation with an apology like, "I hope this doesn't interfere with your plans today." "Don't worry," he would always say, "I'll get you to repay me later." And he always did. He really taught me about covenantal living, if you will. We had a special kind of accountability. If he would share some scary feelings of his own with me, he would often chastise me for not being as open with him.

Finally, the following spring, I learned about the meaning of communion from George. It was Easter morning. Living right there in the church building, we were in the midst of a flurry of activities of preparation. The Easter Sunrise Service just concluded, we were getting ready for the Easter breakfast, egg hunt, Sunday school, and Easter worship services. There was a knock at the door. It was George. He was wearing his regular clothes (workshirt, dirty blue jeans), I had on my coat and tie. He said, "I knew this might be a rough day for you and I came to pray with you and Debbie this morning." This took me completely by surprise. I mean, I knew that he knew that some of his peers had called us on the phone that week and cursed at us. They had told us that we hate all Eskimos, and no wonder nobody was coming to the Presbyterian Church anymore; and so on. All this I knew George knew, but nobody prays for ministers . . . *we* are the *givers* in the church. Nobody gives *us* care (if you know what I mean). But, there was George, called by the Spirit to gently bully his way into the place where I most didn't want him. Debbie was out, busy somewhere, so George and I sat on the couch in our living room and *he* prayed for *me*. All *I* could do was cry . . . and cry . . . and cry. I had been made to come down to where common life meets common life in resurrection and death. George went on his way. What an Easter!

It was a few weeks later on a Communion Sunday that the power of God's act in George moved me outwardly. I was leading worship and it came time for communion to be served. It had become our custom in United Methodist worship to invite people to come forward a few at a time and join hands in a circle around a small table in the center aisle. From there, we would pass each other the common loaf and cup. This Sunday the people were going to come forward to the altar rail to be served and then Debbie and I would place our hands on each one's head as a blessing and say some meaningful words to send them out in mission to the world. As the time approached I didn't want to feed anyone. I really felt as though I needed to be fed. I didn't want to exist as the "feeder" any more. We did feed and bless everyone and, as the process goes, after all had been sent back to their pews, we were left alone again, unfed and hungry. This was not planned (at least by me), but I knew what I had to do, because something was moving my insides around. I stopped and told the congregation what I was feeling. I asked if someone would come up and feed *us* and touch *us* and send *us* out. I'm not sure I remember who came up, but someone did, maybe two someones, maybe Caroline and Nancy. I *do* remember being fed and touched and I remember my own wet eyes and a warming inside me. It was not lengthy or elaborate. Actually it was rather simple and it was over quickly, but it will never be over inside of me. I understand a lot more why Jesus made John baptize *him* instead of the other way around. I understand why George had to cross over the boundaries and pray for *us*. I understand better why God turns the world around before we can see straightly. We had taught each other again in personal touch and prayer and ritual. We had seen Christ in George. I find I am unable to do the sacrament of the Lord's supper the same any more—not in good faith. I do not want to go back. Sometimes I really do not have any nourishment to offer and at those times there are others who can give. They are usually close by.

Ora Gologergen lives in the village of Savoonga on St. Lawrence Island. She runs the Savoonga Hotel . . . Ora's Hotel. Well . . . it's not *really* a hotel by Southern standards. The hospitality is better. No neon signs or elevators. Just a warm house and well-made beds;

and Ora might cook you breakfast. You will have to dump your own honey bucket into the ocean if it gets full. Ora is Ora. She can laugh at you without smiling. She is an elder in the Savoonga Presbyterian Church and speaks Yupik better than English, but her humor is really her best gift no matter whose words she uses.

The first time I (Debbie) met Ora was at the first fall Presbytery meeting in Delta Junction. She had heard about John and me (the new ministers in Nome) through her brother, Clarence Irrigoo, who was an elder in the Nome Presbyterian Church. She shook my hand and told me that their minister in Savoonga would be retiring soon and that I (not both of us) should come to Savoonga to be the new pastor. I explained that this might be difficult since I was married and have two kids and really like working with John. Of course, during this whole conversation, Ora was absolutely stern faced. I didn't know quite what to think. After I finished explaining to Ora why I couldn't go to Savoonga, she looked back at me, straight into my eyes (still without any expression), and said, "Divorce!" Still she was serious, still no laugh, not even a smile. And then, finally, a crack. I was thoroughly destroyed. Everyone broke out into laughter.

We tell about Ora because she was a rare one who refused to let us take ourselves and our "serious" work too seriously. A couple of years later, we got Ora back. I (John) was asked to be part of a team who were to fly to the villages of Bambell and Savoonga to install the new Presbyterian pastors in our parishes there. Nobody reminded the church officials that Debbie and I had never been installed ourselves. That was apparently beside the point, so I went along.

To my surprise, I was chosen (two hours before the first service) to be the one to preach. When, just before worship, I learned that Ora would be my translator, I immediately knew what I would do to "warm-up" the congregation. I told the people the story of Debbie's first encounter with Ora, and *Ora* had to translate *my* words into Yupik. As I spoke line by line and she had to translate, her eyes grew wider and wider as she knew where the story was leading. Before we were done, everyone was rolling in the aisles and Ora was thoroughly embarrassed. I had scored a victory and God's laughter, once again, had created a new day.

Our responsibility for the emergency housing program in Nome brought with it many frustrations and also a few joys. Who would have thought that my (Debbie's) seminary education would prepare me to wash sheets and towels, clean floors, and make beds, provide transportation, and feed hungry people out of my own pantry and from my own kitchen table. A part of me is proud of feeding the hungry and providing shelter for the one who is without a home . . . you know, "When did I see you hungry and feed you?"

But another very real part of me complains bitterly that my talent was wasted when I did laundry or cleaned the bathroom so that the emergency housing program could continue. There is no glory in washing dirty towels. Deep within me, I realize that I still have a long way to go before I will really understand what it means to wash another person's feet and truly become a servant of all. On rare occasions, when I was willing to take the time to look into the eyes and the hearts of the people who came to stay with us, I did recognize the human face of God. One very cold winter day, a young woman came seeking a place for her mother to stay for the night. Her heating oil was all gone and she needed a warm, safe place to sleep. The old woman spoke no English and had only the clothes she was wearing and a few tea bags in her possession. One night turned into a week, and this quiet, frightened little woman stayed with us spending her hours as a stranger in a strange land. No matter how hard I tried to make her feel at home, she could do little more than respond with a weak smile. She was warm and safe and well-fed, but she would have returned to her cold home in an instant where she knew who she was and what was expected of her.

It was in the "common room" of the emergency housing section of the church that I first met Estelle. She had come to Nome from Gambell to attend a meeting and knew that the church would provide her with a safe and sober environment. Estelle was a joy. She would come to Nome several times a year and always choose to stay with us. Her friendly face and warm embrace would greet me as I walked through the common room on my way to or from the office. Her laughter would beckon me to come in to share and commune together late into the night after my kids were asleep and my work was done. We would drink tea together around the table and share stories of life in those places we called home. Estelle was a woman of great faith. She never missed worshiping with us when she was in Nome. Her presence in the worship service was always a welcome joy for me. One evening, as we asked people to share prayers of concern for people in our community and world, Estelle asked that we pray for her. The next day she would go to the jail to visit the young man from her village who, several months before, had nearly killed her son by beating him with a chain. How could I pray for a saint? How could I, who found it so hard and still find it so hard to forgive the wrongs that have been done to me, pray for one so special, one who would visit the man who had almost killed her own son? We prayed for Estelle and we prayed for the young man spending a part of his life behind bars. I realized again how unamazing it is to love those who love me and felt again the call to love my enemies and pray for those who would persecute me.

> "Woe to me, for I am lost. I am one of unclean lips and I dwell in the midst of a people of unclean lips. For my eyes have seen the Sovereign, the God of Hosts."

This is the way Isaiah blurts out his discovery of faith and no scripture has broken into my (John's) personal consciousness the way this one has. No other says to me so clearly that my problems—our problems are not our own. I have been forced to look at things culturally—nothing is private. Sins that are important enough to talk about are deeply personal but never in isolation from others. The conversion we need is the conversion of the heart of a people. I'm convinced no one can be saved alone. My Alaska experience has made me raw to this. I didn't realize how hurt I was until we left. I carry within a healthy shame which is for myself but also for my people.

After my experience in the Chapel in Washington, D.C. I had taken an intellectual position—that we would not impose *our* values on Alaskan natives. That was just head stuff. We were outsiders in a land so full of God's gifts that it became a paradigm of the Promised Land to us. It was a land where miners, traders, missionaries, and teachers had raped and stripped the land *and* the people to exploit the treasures of both. When miner's dreams died they left their machinery to waste on the tundra. They also left orphaned children to wonder why they had ever been born. Missionaries and religious educators left behind many converts, but a people lost. It was a land filled with vast gifts of nature and human community. Brace against it as I might, it brought out the worst in me, in my heart, soul, and glandular system, in my whole orientation toward life, in the way I lived.

I could walk or drive up the bed of Glacier Creek in the early fall and see tracks of a grizzly bear on the gravel bar. She was hunting the silver salmon as was I. Around the bend, I would come face to face with one of the deepest pools in the Snake River where the creek flows in. One year there were four or five hundred silvers lying in there just waiting to be caught. I caught many more than my share. I'd see them right there in front of me, and my hands would shake. I could not bait my hooks fast enough. I wanted to catch them all. Like an alcoholic saying, "I'll quit tomorrow," I would fish on—long after I told my family I would be home. I could always convince myself of some extra need in order to bargain within myself to justify catching just one more. This was me. This is us. I am lost and I dwell in the midst of a people who cannot get enough and cannot get enough fast enough. This becomes clear because I have seen another people who live another way. Through them the sovereign God is seen, and we are brought low—one at a time and all together.

In July of 1985 there was a beautiful summer Sunday that was just unbelievable. The sun shone for about twenty-two hours. There was no wind and the Bering Sea off Nome was smooth as glass. After the evening service the kids went to sleep. The sun was still bright at ten o'clock so we decided to let Lucille (our Presbyterian volunteer) sit with them and we got out of the house for awhile. We decided to take a ride down the beach on our 4-wheel all-terrain vehicle to visit some of our friends at their summer fish camp at Fort Davis. The evening was gorgeous. As we arrived we heard a commotion down at the water's edge. As we parked our Suzuki and walked on down, we saw it was a whole clan of our friends, the Koweluks, gathered around a young female walrus, which they had just brought in. Everyone was busy skinning and cutting and scraping and dividing up the meat and blubber. They were all speaking their own language, laughing and yelling and telling the story of the hunt. Uncle Ray had got this walrus. They had been out thirty or forty miles into the ocean and they had found a herd of fifty or sixty out there. Bertha had gone hunting with them for the very first time. They had wanted her to get this walrus. Everyone was so happy.

With smiles on their faces they waved at us and talked to us while they worked. Pretty soon Esther came over to us. She was busy and completely covered with blood and hair and oil, but she took a little break to talk. We were so excited by this scene and the thought of so many walruses out there that we asked what now seems like a typical dumb white person's question, "Are you going to go back out and get some more?" Esther looked up at us with her big smile (she was always gentle with us). With a light sparkle in her eye she said, "Oh no. With this one we have just enough for our family."

For the rest of our days we will thank Yahweh for Esther and her way. It was not her words that opened us up. It was the way of life of her people that peeled our hide as surely as if she had sliced us with an ulu (her knife). So, through us maybe you can see the emptiness of how we really are—exposed to the flesh. It was Israel in the wilderness who knew how to live with just enough from the desert. There was never too much and never too little. How do we reclaim this in our teaching? How does the gospel of the wilderness make sense as we now live one block away from fast-food alley in our city? It seems our words to this effect will be totally empty unless we are better taught—in a way that changes our lives and our communities. Somehow the wilderness must be created by our hands and our hearts. Recalling Kierkegaard's parable, we find that the young king does not contemplate changing his life or raising his consciousness in order to love his lover. He becomes the other. As Mary Evans, a teacher of preschool teachers used to say, "You can talk the talk, but can you walk the walk?"

We are convinced we must place ourselves and our people into contact with those who can lead us in different ways. We learn how to live differently by living differently. If we are not to be about living differently then . . . well let us go back to the Methesco Early Childhood Center for a moment. Once a quarter or so we at the Center were allowed to lead seminary chapel services. On those occasions we made every effort possible to "subject" the congregation of faculty and students to the leadership of the children in this worship. The time I remember most, we built the worship around Mark 1:20: "And immediately they left their nets and followed Jesus." We played "follow the leader" in chapel. We gave authority to the children to take us where they would—and they did. We did *not* sit them down for a children's sermon. We allowed ourselves to be put under the control of *their* experience. Again, we allowed ourselves to be changed by the lives of others. We change our ways by putting ourselves into different ways. It's really not too complex. The only complexity is so often just between our ears.

The woman who taught me (John) to speak Inupiaq was also my spiritual elder. The simple fact that she had named me "No Name" convinced me that she was wise and extremely perceptive. She had been orphaned by the 1918 flu epidemic and ended up at the Roman Catholic orphanage at Pilgrim Hot Springs. As a young woman, she had married a King Island man and had gone there to live in the village and raise her children. It was only as an older adult that she began to understand where she was from. Margaret and I attended a conference in Spokane one summer, where in five minutes one morning she explained to me the facts of life.

Before the missionaries came (she was learning) the King Island people had a traditional belief about a Great Spirit present among them. This spirit was named "Munaqsri" (Moo-knock'-shee) who was definitely the overseer of all creation, but was particularly present inside of everything. Munaqsri (the root word of which means "to care for") was present in animals and birds, rocks and trees, in sky and tundra, in sea mammals and inside of human beings. This was a presence which was close by and people would talk to this God as we would talk to a close friend. In fact, in some senses, a person's life was a continual conversation with Munaqsri. This great spirit was always available for every need.

When the Roman Catholic missionaries came, all talk of Munaqsri was forbidden and the people were introduced to Angaayun (Ahng-eye-yoon'). Angaayun was definitely transcendent. *He* was up *there.* He was definitely *not* down here. Angaayun was all powerful. The people were taught to kneel, bow, and pray up to Angaayun. This conversation was not like a talk with an understanding friend at all. This conversation was a pleading with One who was far away, cold, and threatening. People must strive their whole lives long to please this God so that someday—someday they might prove themselves worthy and go to live with him. Angaayun was surely a fearful God up above and Munaqsri a powerful but understanding God living in and among creation.

Today Margaret lives with equal reverence for Munaqsri and Angaayun, though the feeling she has for one is quite different from that which she has for the other. We cannot speak for our friend and teacher, Margaret Seeganna, nor for other indigenous people nor for anyone, but if God is to be some day known we hope She is more like Munaqsri than Angaayun. This is who we sense God to be in our experience. It may be a balance between these that we want to hear affirmed in the lives of the people from whom we learn and with whom we teach. Often our St. Lawrence Island Presbyterian friends would gather before worship for a pot-luck and Eskimo dancing in the fellowship hall outside the sanctu-ary door. Out there the mood and the action was celebration, eating, sharing, singing, dancing, and enjoying each other's com-pany. We were affirming the goodness of self in life in community. This was in seeming partnership with Munaqsri—like spirit in and among us. Then we would leave one world and enter through the doors of the sanctuary into another. Now the mood and action was changed (most of the younger people went home before *this* wor-ship). Now we bowed our heads and with agonizing faces we sat in rows and sang songs about the "sin-stains" making us "children of hell," unworthy to be called God's children. In here we did not gather around each other, listening and learning from each other and sharing our stories. In here we came to feel guilty and to listen and learn from the preacher who is "the" teacher about that God we do not understand who is out there somewhere even though He sends us Jesus to rescue us from this horrible life. We came to plead with God to forgive us. Out there the direction of our activity (it seemed to us) had been centered in the encircling community and togetherness with God in life. In here the direction was forward and upward. We looked to the preacher and to God in private solitary fashion, waiting for goodness and learning to come down to us. The contrast of worshiping actions from one setting to the other has been instructive to us as teachers who would be learning with others.

We are convinced that the ways in which we perceive God and the ways in which we choose to relate to others as teachers are dynamically interrelated. We are vulnerable enough to these experi-ences to see how a teacher's image of God changes when she squats in the middle of a preschool classroom to meet her three-year-old student face-to-face where in the past she might have tried looking *down* to meet his or her need from her level. These experiences are raw enough within us today that we believe those teachers will find a Munaqsri-God who knows what it is to let the poor, the woman, the child, the underprivileged, the undereducated, and the outcast lead and teach us. We believe this God demonstrates Her omnipotence . . . we believe this God demonstrates His real power and models how *we* ought to be by entering into our world as one of us while still maintaining a just and righteous integrity to self and creation. To us, this is the Incarnation: Those who would teach must learn; those who would lead must follow. Christ disarms and inspires us in this very way.

SUGGESTIONS FOR CHANGE

We feel sorely inadequate when it comes to transfering our learnings to others, but it seems important to summarize our discoveries in a usable form. We do not think our experiences need only apply to the "mission field." Below we list some suggestions which may help pastors as religious educators wherever they serve:

1. *Learn the language of the people.* Each community has its own languages. Here we have talked about Inuit languages, but just because an entire community speaks English does not mean that we know and understand who people are and what they mean when they say and do various things. What could pastors be doing with their people to better understand and celebrate the gifts of their culture? What has happened in their lives that has formed their values? Pastors would do well to describe the language they use to express these values. Having preached for five years with an interpreter standing beside us we wonder if English-speaking congregations could use interpreters too. If clergy always preach, is there a place in our worship for lay people to translate what is preached into "the language of the people?" We think there is.
2. *Visit people where they live and work.* Frankly, we see too little of this today among pastors and other religious educators. For all teachers, calling is essential. To enter into people's lives we go out of our territory into theirs. In all our religious education activities, we have worked with Sunday school teachers to help

them visit the home of the people in their classes. When visiting young children, the pastor-educator often has to visit with a partner so that if the parents want to monopolize the visit, the partner can talk to the adults thus freeing the pastor-educator to explore the child's room and her/his cosmos. Come to think of it, visiting with a partner is often a good idea so the children in a family do not get left out anyway. We sometimes hesitate to visit people where they work, but many people find their primary meaning and rootage in life through their labor in tundra, farm, ditch, factory, office, or vehicle. Youth leaders will want to put in their time at basketball games, 4-H fairs, rodeos, schools, and wherever "the scene" is happening. Get out and go out.

3. *Let the children lead*. Meetings of teachers of children *often* focus attention on what the children have taught us. How do children communicate the gospel to you? So many have never thought about this. To us it is primary. Truly we can set up our learning experiences to be taught by children. As religious educators, pastors can keep a log or journal of what the learners are doing and saying so that the pastor can reflect together with other teachers. Have teachers' meetings. In worship it is so easy to patronize children. Do they perform for us or lead us? When they sing, do they put on a show or do they teach us a song or a special meaning? The children's "sermon" has been trendy since the 1970s. It is amazing to find churches with no special time during the worship service for children. These times, of course, can be limited in scope. By and large, children are more spontaneous than adults. Let them move around the sanctuary and pass things out. Let them bring adults up to share. Let them be the center of communion. Let them serve it? Let their prayers be heard by having spontaneous prayer times so that they share aloud along with older persons. They have authority to teach the rest of us that the true worship is more to be *sensed* and *wiggled* and *voiced* than it is to be *thought*.

4. *Ordain lay people*. Our time in Alaska taught us that those denominations who have a legitimate way of "calling" all persons into ministry are the ones whose churches are thriving among indigenous people. Many of these have "lay deacon" training programs and orders of elders and deacons in their

local congregations who are ordained to carry on special ministries to people in their communities. In "mission territory"
where other congregations of other denominations rely heavily
on outside financial support and have difficulty finding native
people to take leadership, these denominations have self-sup-
porting churches and native pastors and bishops. In the United
Methodist Church, our way is to call people to serve on a
church committee or encourage people, who would be so motivated, to go to seminary. In between these options we miss lots
of persons who would be ordained to serve in ministry if we
had a way to do it. We have lay speaking and we have the
diaconate, but we have no official way to call common people
into local mission and ministry. Let's make some changes.

5. *Encourage laity to tell their personal stories of faith.* In Nome we
   created a narrated slide program on the people of our church.
   We got good slides of everyone's faces (close-up) and we asked
   eight different people (native and Caucasian) to tell a story of
   something that had happened to them that moved them in a
   special way, made them aware of their special purpose or place
   in God's world, or confronted them with the presence of God
   in everyday life. To us, of course, the presence of Eskimo
   stories in the midst of others made it extra-special. The personal sharing of these stories came together with overwhelming
   power. When are the times in our church life when those
   (other than clergy and lay leaders) get to share their faith in
   terms of their experience? As long as specified leaders monopolize teaching and preaching we will continue to imply that only
   a chosen few have anything worth sharing. In our main services, classes, Lenten luncheons, camps, retreats, and informal
   worship settings, let us invite many more to reflect on a scripture in terms of their life story and accept whatever comes.

6. *Come down from the pulpit to real life.* Our experience in Alaska
   did force us to cut down on needless words and to get to the
   point of our faith in preaching, or be quiet. Today, we understand that the pulpit is often in the way of our sharing feelings,
   ideas, and commitments that really move us. If clergy can come
   down from the pulpit and sometimes leave the paper behind
   they can be heard much better. Also, laity can be encouraged to
   share more easily—even when they feel as though they have no

training or credentials to do so. The physical, visible change of place is a large part of it. Let them see you struggle for words once in awhile. So much of the rest of our reality is built upon paper, perfection, and polish. Our churches die for lack of passion. Let go and come down.

7. *Travel, work, and study to make disciples.* In many ways, ministry in Alaska was a five-year "work team" experience for us. In fact, in 1985 our United Methodist congregation in Nome decided we had received enough mission support from everyone else in the world. It was time for us to reach out. So seventeen people went up to the Inuit village of Wales to paint their church building and teach Vacation Church School. The work, of course, was only the excuse. There is just no way that God's vision of a new creation can be all locked up inside of what we only know and experience in our local setting and culture. A parish that is vital has work-study teams continually going somewhere to meet a different people and experience a new way of life. Few hearts and minds are changed by hearing. Nothing will make disciples like concrete immersion in relationships with people of other cultures or subcultures. Service to *others* can be the excuse—but this is really *our* learning. Don't leave this to youth groups. Mixed groups and adult groups of just a few (less than ten) persons are best. Go and learn. In these kinds of settings we have a chance to see faith as a "people" not just as individuals. We learn that poverty is a problem for all of us, created by all, and that salvation is something we must work out and receive in partnership with others. We find that change in our way of life as a culture is needed and possible. Without these experiences it is possible for us to continue living as if we need no one else. Also, formal Volunteer-In-Mission opportunities exist through many of our denominations. Young, middle-aged, and older adults are often eager to find a way to serve and teach us.

8. *Establish Covenant groups.* Make these groups whatever seems to be needed. These are people who meet together in an attempt to share faith, hold each other mutually accountable for the way we live, and give support to one another for change and service. So much of what we suggest here calls for changes from the tradition of more solitary leadership/teaching styles

into ways which involve more sharing of faith and power. Few will be able to become new leaders without a regular bunch of folks who agree to meet regularly and push and support each other in faith.

9. *Let people laugh at you.* Nothing keeps a pastor or other religious educator down to earth better than some regular gentle humorous self-ridicule. We must confess that we have a hard time trusting those who cannot laugh at themselves and their positions. We have often gotten into trouble poking fun at ourselves and others to expose some of our most serious misgivings about ourselves. Nothing is too sacred to laugh at. In fact, we think that God snickers at all of us most of the time when God sees what we do. Sometimes this involves letting others participate in telling the story (like Ora) because *they* can laugh when sometimes *we* cannot. Churches shouldn't miss Shrove Tuesday as a chance to party together and laugh at all the ridiculous things that we do—before Lent begins. We find that God's truth may be much more like a public roast than traditional Sunday worship. Do not leave this one out.

10. *Refuse to be alone.* Do things in partnership with others. As teachers/learners we really do need each other. Sometimes the fact that no one comes to help us means that we are breaking new ground. Often though, if we are alone in what we do, it is time to share our concerns and reveal our feelings with others so that they may respond and join us with their own unique contributions.

Through the Incarnation, God chose to become like us in the person of Jesus Christ. As pastors we are called to enter into the lives of those we lead and to learn from them so that we can teach, learn, and serve together. Through such sharing we discover who God is and what God is calling us to be and do.

Notes

1. Adapted from "The King and the Maiden," *Parables of Kierkegaard*, ed. Thomas C. Oden, illustrated by Lonni Sue Johnson. (Princeton, New Jersey: Princeton University Press, 1978), pp. 40-45.

The Contributors

Robert L. Browning is Chryst Professor of Christian Education at the Methodist Theological School in Ohio. Before joining the faculty in 1959 he served as a Minister of Education in churches in Pennsylvania, New York, and Ohio. He has also been involved in interprofessional education, having served as the first Executive Director of the Commission on Interprofessional Education and Practice and as a Fellow at the Academy for Contemporary Problems. He is the author or co-author of several books, resources, and articles including most recently, *The Sacraments in Religious Education and Liturgy: An Ecumenical Model* with Roy A. Reed (1985) and "Interprofessional Continuing Education" in *Theory Into Practice* (1987). He and his wife, Jackie, have seven children and nine grandchildren in their merged family.

John Lynn Carr is Associate Professor of Church Ministries and Director of Continuing Education at Candler School of Theology, Emory University in Atlanta, Georgia. A third generation United Methodist pastor, he founded congregations in Cleveland, Ohio, and Indianapolis, Indiana, and was Teaching Theologian and later Interim Senior Minister at First Community Church in Columbus, Ohio, before coming to Candler in 1976.

With his wife, Adrienne, who is also a member of the Candler faculty, he is the co-author of three educational programs which have been used in thousands of churches throughout the U.S. and Canada: *The Experiment in Practical Christianity, The Power and Light Company,* and *The Pilgrimage Project.* Together they regularly teach and consult with groups of clergy and laity about Christian adult education.

Charles R. Foster, an ordained United Methodist minister, served on the staffs of The Riverside Church in New York City and the First United Methodist Church in Corning, New York, prior to joining the faculty of the Methodist Theological School in Ohio. From 1981 to 1988 he was Professor of Christian Education at the Scarritt Graduate School. Currently, he is Professor of Christian Education at the Candler School of Theology at Emory University. His published works include *Teaching in the Community of Faith, The Church in the Education of the Public, The Ministry of the Volunteer Teacher,* and *Ethnicity in the Education of the Church.* He and his wife Janet have two children, Anne and Scott.

Robin Maas is Assistant Professor of Christian Education at Wesley Theological Seminary in Washington, D.C. Married and the mother of three grown children, Dr. Maas has Masters' degrees in Sociology (from Makerere University in Kampala, Uganda), and in Biblical Studies (from Wesley Theological Seminary). Her Ph.D. is in Religion and Religious Education from The Catholic University of America. In addition to biblical catechesis, Dr. Maas is interested in the areas of faith development, religious identity, and spirituality. She is currently working on research related to the subject of spiritual formation in seminaries. Her publications include *Church Bible Study Handbook* (Abingdon) and *Job.*

Paul Eugene Miller is Associate Minister at Epworth United Methodist Church, Marion, Ohio. His particular professional focus has been on the religious education of children. A graduate of The Methodist Theological School in Ohio with both the Master of Divinity and the Master of Religious Education degrees, he has served as a pastor in the West Ohio Conference since 1977. He is especially interested in the spirituality of children, visual and textile arts, liturgical arts, and missions. He is a member of the national and local associations of young children, the Christian Educators Fellowship, and the Fellowship of United Methodists in Worship, Music, and other Arts. He and his wife Pat, also ordained, have two children.

Deborah and John Pitney. Debbie was born in Hawaii and lived there until she was three years old, the daughter of Methodist missionaries. She grew up in Riverside, California, and graduated from San Diego State University. John grew up on a Century Farm near Junction City, Oregon, and graduated from Oregon State University. They met on the playground of the Early Childhood Center at the Methodist Theological School in Ohio and were married a year later near the duck pond. They received Elder's ordination together in the Oregon-Idaho Annual Conference of the United Methodist Church and have served congregations in Juna and Nampa, Idaho, and Nome, Alaska, as a clergy team. They now live in Corvallis, Oregon, where Debbie serves the United Methodist congregation and John is on a sabbatical leave, studying the church and rural issues. They have two children, Joel and Erin.

William (Bud) Phillips is Vice Principal, Director of Advanced Studies, and Director of the Centre for Study of Church and Ministry at the Vancouver School of Theology. He has been a broadcaster on the Canadian Broadcasting Company and commercial radio and television for over twenty years, developing program formats which interpret religious subjects in ways that speak to nonreligious audiences. Dr. Phillips pioneered the V.S.T.'s Knowledge Network programs in British Columbia, through which courses of theological education are offered via satellite, to distant study groups linked, for discussion, over telephone networks. The model is developed in his doctoral thesis "A Systematic Approach to the Continuing Education of Clergy, Utilizing Media" which integrates adult education theory with theories of media effectiveness when applied to the particular needs of clergy. He and his wife, Kathleen, have two children, David and Deborah.

G. Temp Sparkman has been professor of religious education at Midwestern Baptist Theological Seminary since 1972, where his primary teaching areas are foundations of and issues in educational theory. He also teaches a course in educational planning. He is the author of six books, his major work being, *The Salvation and Nurture of the Child of God.* He paints, sketches, and writes poetry. His *To Live with Hope* (Judson, 1985), is the fruit of his poetic bent. He is active in ecumenical contexts. His academic degrees are from Belmont College, the Southern Baptist Theological Seminary, and the University of Kansas (Ed.D., 1980).

Grant S. Shockley is Professor of Christian Education and Director of Black Church Affairs at the Divinity School, Duke University. He brings a broad experience as a teacher, administrator, and consultant. He has taught at several universities and theological schools, has served as President of Philander Smith College and of the Interdenominational Theological Center in Atlanta, and has been a consultant to many institutions and groups. He has traveled widely in Africa, Asia, and Latin America. He is the author of *The New Generation in Africa* and *Black Pastors and Churches in Methodism.* He has been a contributor to many books, dictionaries, encyclopedias, journals, and curriculum resource materials.

Joanmarie Smith is a member of the Congregation of St. Joseph from Brentwood, New York. After a number of years teaching philosophy at Saint Joseph's College she is currently professor of Christian Education at the Methodist Theological School in Ohio where she regularly teaches a course in spirituality to future pastors. She is author, co-author, and co-editor of several books and many articles, including, *Modeling God, Religious Education for the Future,* with Gloria Durka, and *Family Ministry* with Maria Harris.

C. Joseph Sprague is the Senior Minister at the Epworth United Methodist Church, Marion, Ohio. A graduate of Ashland College and the Methodist Theological School in Ohio, he has served both of the United Methodist seminaries in Ohio by teaching in the areas of homiletics and church administration. In addition to teaching, along with customary parish duties, he has extensive experience in ecumenical, interfaith, and community issues serving often as a bridge person among divided factions. Additionally, he is an often tapped resource for peace and racial issues in the life of the church, and has been quite active as a mentor for younger clergy. He is the parent of four children. He and Diane, his spouse of twenty-eight years, enjoy the active life of their extended family which includes their first grandchild and a new, frisky Labrador puppy—both of which add zest and excitement to family gatherings.

Index